SKILLS
IN BUSINESS

To our children:

Bethany Raddon-Sung, Kate Ashton,
Dr Heidi Ashton and Wendy Ashton

SKILLS
IN BUSINESS

The role of business strategy, sectoral
skills development and skills policy

Johnny Sung & David N Ashton

SAGE

Los Angeles | London | New Delhi
Singapore | Washington DC

Los Angeles | London | New Delhi
Singapore | Washington DC

SAGE Publications Ltd
1 Oliver's Yard
55 City Road
London EC1Y 1SP

SAGE Publications Inc.
2455 Teller Road
Thousand Oaks, California 91320

SAGE Publications India Pvt Ltd
B 1/I 1 Mohan Cooperative Industrial
Area
Mathura Road
New Delhi 110 044

SAGE Publications Asia-Pacific Pte Ltd
3 Church Street
#10-04 Samsung Hub
Singapore 049483

Editor: Chris Rojek
Assistant editor: Gemma Shields
Production editor: Katherine Haw
Copyeditor: Solveig Gardner Servian
Proofreader: Camille Bramall
Marketing manager: Michael Ainsley
Cover design: Stephanie Guyaz
Typeset by: C&M Digitals (P) Ltd, Chennai, India
Printed and bound by CPI Group (UK) Ltd,
    Croydon, CR0 4YY

MIX
Paper from
responsible sources
FSC   FSC® C013604
www.fsc.org

© Johnny Sung and David Ashton 2015

First published 2015

Library of Congress Control Number: 2014938548

British Library Cataloguing in Publication data

A catalogue record for this book is available from
the British Library

ISBN 978-1-84920-109-4
ISBN 978-1-84920-110-0 (pbk)

At SAGE we take sustainability seriously. Most of our products are printed in the UK using FSC papers and boards.
When we print overseas we ensure sustainable papers are used as measured by the Egmont grading system.
We undertake an annual audit to monitor our sustainability.

CONTENTS

LIST OF FIGURES AND TABLES

Figures

Tables

ABOUT THE AUTHORS

David N Ashton is Emeritus Professor at the University of Leicester and Honorary Professor at the University of Cardiff. He established the Centre for Labour Market Studies at Leicester University in 1989 as a centre for research and teaching on skills and labour market issues. He has researched and published extensively on skill formation, human resource development, and the analysis of national systems of workforce development and training. His most recent book with Professor Brown and Lauder is *The Global Auction. The Broken Promises of Education, Jobs and Income* (2011, Oxford University Press).

He has provided consultancy services to various government departments within the UK concerned with issues of education, business and skills and most recently the United Kingdom Commission for Employment and Skills. Outside the UK he has provided consultancy services to government departments in South Africa, Singapore, the EU and to international agencies such as the International Labour Organisation and World Bank.

Johnny Sung works at the Institute for Adult Learning, Singapore Workforce Development Agency. He is Head of the Centre for Skills, Performance and Productivity, conducting three strands of national research: a) Skills utilisation and job quality in Singapore; b) The sectoral approach to skills and performance in key industry sectors; c) Adult competencies and job performance.

Prior to the appointment in Singapore, Johnny was Chair of Skills and Performance at the University of Leicester (UK). He carried out research projects for UK government agencies, research councils, professional bodies, international agencies such as the International Labour Office, the World Bank and other national governments. Professor Sung is also currently Honorary Professor at Cardiff University (UK).

ACKNOWLEDGEMENTS

The ideas in this book have had a long gestation period. Over the past decade we have been working together on a variety of projects funded by research councils and government departments and agencies in a number of countries. Most of that research has been involved in case study work with organisations both public and private, which has enabled us to test and refine our ideas. So we have numerous organisational leaders, human resource (HR) directors and industry experts to thank for their time and input into our work. In addition, we have presented the ideas to numerous participants on the postgraduate courses we have taught in the UK, Ireland and Europe, and their inputs, usually as HR professionals, have been very useful. Academically, we have had discussions with many colleagues but would like to acknowledge Phil Brown, Hugh Lauder, Ewart Keep, Francis Green, Geoff Mason and Mark Spilsbury as colleagues with whom we have had longstanding conversations on skills issues over a number of years from which we have greatly benefited.

This book has a strong policy focus that stems from our constant engagement with the policy process at both national and international levels and our conviction that the research process combined with good theory can make a substantial contribution towards more effective policy. In the UK, we would like to acknowledge staff at the UK Commission for Employment and Skills and in Singapore at the Workforce Development Agency, especially Dr Gog Soon Joo who shared with us her idea of 'institutional logics' for changing employers' competitive behavior. We would also like to acknowledge the contribution of anonymous reviewers for their helpful comments on the manuscript. At SAGE Publications, we would like to thank Ms Gemma Shields for her excellent editorial support.

Last but not least, we would like to thank our families, who have been so tolerant in allowing us time and space to write this book. In this respect, we would like to thank Dr Arwen Raddon and Maureen Ashton for their constant support and encouragement, without which this project would not have been possible.

INTRODUCTION

Skills have become the global currency of the 21st century. Without proper investment in skills, people languish on the margins of society, technological progress does not translate into economic growth, and countries can no longer compete in an increasingly knowledge-based global society. But this 'currency' depreciates as the requirements of labour markets evolve and individuals lose the skills they do not use. Skills do not automatically convert into jobs and growth.

OECD (2012a: 3)

The 2011 OECD publication *Skills Strategy* captures much of the raison d'être for this book (OECD, 2011). So what are the reasons that skills may not automatically convert into jobs and growth? One answer lies in two main strands of skills policy, education on the one hand and training on the other, being dominated by what are known as the 'supply side' considerations – the belief that if we improve the supply of skills, economic growth and enhanced competitiveness will follow. The principles that underpin this approach to skills policy are still those of market failure and human capital theory. We argue that, while these guiding principles were appropriate for economies in the 20th century, they are now becoming inadequate on their own to understand the role of skills in 21st-century economies. Nevertheless, they are still used to inform policy approaches to education and interventions to remedy 'market failures' at the lower reaches of the labour market.

The second reason for the difficulties in converting skills into jobs is our tendency to overlook factors that are influencing the productive system, the ways in which production is organised within businesses, as it is this that drives the creation of jobs as well as the type of skills demanded. Thus, while the OECD statement captures the changing nature of skills demand in the 21st century, it unfortunately tells us nothing about what is driving this demand. It is here that our book makes its major contribution. The late 20th century and early 21st century have witnessed major transformations of the economy creating new demands that conventional supply side policies cannot meet. What we provide is a theory of the business drivers of skills, enabling us to explain how and why the demand for skills is changing. At the moment our understanding of employers' demand for skills is at best fragmentary and at worst lacking in theoretical coherence. Yet, it is here with respect to employers' behaviour that new forms of government action are needed if countries are to compete effectively in the intensively competitive global markets that we all now face.

The main source of the problem is the fact that we have never defined what 'skills policy' means. We argue that the lack of proper understanding of what skills policy means leads to the confusion that skills policy, especially in the Anglo-Saxon world, is always synonymous with human capital theory, creating the view that investing in skills is what skills policy is all about. It is not. To develop an effective skills policy that is also highly skills-oriented and utilising, skills policy needs an understanding of how skills demand is derived within a productive system. Skills policy, viewed from this perspective, is about what might influence the employers' competitive behaviour and their business strategy.

In the next seven chapters of this book, we will explain the sources of our argument, and how we arrive at this conclusion. Those readers with a more detailed knowledge of the theoretical and policy issues involved are advised to start their reading at Chapter 2. The following is the structure of the book.

Chapter 1

The book starts by showing how the conventional approach to skills policy among Anglo-Saxon countries, namely to concentrate on improving the supply of skills and to leave it to market forces to ensure that these skills are used to improve economic performance, has become unfit for purpose. The approach worked for a period in the mid- to late 20th century but is now running into serious problems. Moreover, comparative analysis reveals that reliance on the market to convert this supply of skills into highly skilled jobs is now becoming a failed strategy. Other countries such as Germany and Singapore have adopted very different strategies and have had more success in delivering higher-skilled jobs with higher incomes for their citizens.

To understand these different outcomes we need to start by examining the factors that drive the demand for skills from employers. These are to be found in the business environment within which employers make their decisions about which type of product they will produce and how they will use the available technology to secure a competitive advantage in the market. These factors range from the availability of opportunities in the national and international markets, the supply of skills from the vocational education and training (VET) system, the cost of labour, how they can use those skills that are shaped by the industrial/employee relations system, the system of economic governance and others. These are all factors over which governments have some influence, and how they use that influence through their approach to skills policy plays an important part in explaining why some countries such as Singapore and Germany have succeeded in enabling companies located there to compete at the leading edge of world markets, while countries such as the UK have been less successful.

One of the most important factors shaping these approaches to skills policy is the location of the country in relation to international markets. In the UK with its long history of dominance in global and later Empire markets, the policy was to minimise state intervention and rely on the market to deliver growth. However, this policy failed to sustain a great deal of industrial production resulting in the replacement of those jobs by low-skilled, low-paid jobs in the service sector. In countries such as Germany that had to break into world markets dominated by British and American companies, the state was more active in helping establish a framework within which the social partners, employers and unions collaborated in developing a highly skilled labour force for companies competing in high-value engineering products. In Singapore, after the Second World War, the government had to establish a framework that would ensure that foreign multinational corporations (MNCs) were attracted to the country in order to help them break into world markets. Once they had a foothold in global markets, the government's policy ensured that firms moved into high value-added product markets creating highly skilled, high-paid jobs. As will be discussed in Chapters 6 and 7, these 'interventions' are key to forming the institutional logics that govern the way employers see how they compete.

This chapter is devoted to explaining how these broader government policies were instrumental in generating these different outcomes at the organisational level. It is presented in the form of a historical overview, not for the purpose of understanding the history of the countries concerned, but to show how the demand for skills is shaped by two specific factors that are usually absent from the current debate, namely the importance of the position occupied by a country in global markets in shaping the approach to skills policy and how the type of industry, or 'production system' as we call it, that dominates the domestic economy shapes the demand for skills.

Chapter 2

Rarely would any skills analysis start from what businesses actually are. However, this is the starting point of our book before building our strategic skills model. Key to this unusual starting point is to recognise that businesses are 'purposive entities'. In other words, they exist for a reason, and the reason is seldom about learning or skills – unless you are in the education and training business. But of course learning and skills are all very important to the success of a business and any organisation. So how do we get learning and skills back into the business performance equation? The answer lies in business strategy – the very element that makes a business 'purposive'.

This chapter therefore has two sections. The first identifies the inadequacy of the business strategy research that may include skills but has never formalised the role of skills in any business strategic model. The end result is a simplistic understanding of the relationship between skills and business performance, which at best means that skills are 'unproblematic' in any of the existing strategic models. Skills (higher or lower) are simply a given in a business model. Generally, skills are treated as a cost factor. And at worst, more skills and higher skills are inevitably linked to higher business performance. The assumption is that any available skills will be translated into drivers for business performance. Well, how does it work? The first section of this chapter will show us that research has never answered this question, let alone treated it seriously.

The second section of this chapter will propose a new strategic skills model. The new model makes two major contributions compared with previous efforts. The first contribution is that business strategy is the key concept influencing the level of skills utilisation. The second contribution is that business strategy consists of two components, product market strategy and competitive strategy, each of which impacts skills in very different ways. The product market strategy determines the type of product or service the company will market and the type of technology it will employ to do so, and the competitive strategy identifies how the firm will seek to achieve a competitive advantage in the market to secure its future. The product market strategy adopted in turn determines the technical relations (TRs), which shapes the level of skill demanded by the employer from its employees. The competitive strategy determines the interpersonal relations (IRs), which shapes how the firm manages and uses the skills of employees. At one extreme the skills of employees can be the most important source of its competitive advantage; at the other the firm can use its technology to reduce the skill required and seek a competitive advantage through the use of low-cost, low-skilled labour. Unlike previous attempts, our strategic skills model allows the business owner a degree of choice in selecting any combination of product market and competitive strategies. Likewise, there is no universal best-approach assumption, other than that different strategic combinations will lead to different levels of skills utilisation and different types of skills demanded.

Chapter 3

This chapter is the first of the two chapters that examine the strategic skills model in depth. In Chapter 3, we focus on how the product market strategy of the firm determines the TRs which shape the *level of skill* it demands from employees. Crucial to the TRs is the type of technology the firm uses to manufacture its products or deliver its services. The product market strategy is shaped by the business opportunities and market environment in which the firm operates, the knowledge of the entrepreneur and type of technology available at any one point in time. History is therefore crucial in determining these relationships and we therefore have to adopt a historical perspective in order to show how these relationships worked out in practice. Once established and proved effective in delivering performance these technical relationships may persist over time.

The chapter distinguishes between different types of TRs. It starts from the early industrial form of mass production, whose TRs were characterised by combining mechanised production with a high division of labour, which first occurred in the UK. This was followed by Tayloristic mass production characterised by large organisations using Taylorist forms of management and the moving assembly line that was developed in the USA. What we term the 'mature form' of mass production is characterised by the application of new information technology to mass production capable of producing smaller batches which had its origin in Japan. More recently, we have seen the emergence of knowledge-intensive forms of production, which started in the USA in Silicon Valley. Each of these forms of production makes different demands on the level of skill required from managers and white-collar employees as well as manual workers and service staff. As the mix of these systems changes through time so too do the skill demands on the VET system.

Chapter 4

In Chapter 4, we explore how the competitive strategy adopted by the employers shapes the IRs, the ways in which companies manage and *use the skill* of their employees. Employers using early industrial systems of production usually sought a competitive advantage through their mechanised technologies and an extreme form of the division of labour to create jobs that required little skill, enabling them to recruit unskilled females and young people to produce the low-cost products that delivered the employers' competitive advantage. The skills that mattered were those of the entrepreneur and a handful of managers. In our strategic skills model, this form of production had huge implications for the competitive strategy and therefore interpersonal relations of the workplace. In effect, the productive system would be focusing on 'task-focused' processes, which tended to make use of very limited ranges of worker skills. This process of 'deskilling' was best represented by the emergence of mass national markets in the USA, where employers were able to use Tayloristic forms of the division of labour together with the moving assembly line to deskill other production processes and secure their competitive advantage by lowering the cost of consumer products. However, while deskilling one large section of the productive system, these were complex technologies requiring not only professional managers but also skilled engineers and administrators. These were the staff whose skills were crucial to securing a competitive advantage in the market, and company resources were devoted to developing their skills.

With the advent of mature mass production the source of the company's competitive advantage shifted from reliance on the use of skills by managers, professionals and administrators to those of the core production or service delivery staff. Not only that, but the nature of the skills that were utilised shifted from those required to function in a command and control organisation to those required for the flatter high-performance organisation. This meant that their character changed. Management no longer relied on command and control systems of authority, but now had to acquire more participative skills in leadership, while other employees required problem solving, communication and teamworking skills. Commitment to the values of the company also started to become important for most employees. The commitment of employees to the company and the use of these 'new' skills now had to be managed through the use of competence-based systems of learning and skill formation. Therefore, the result of this development 'pushed' the competitive strategy towards the more 'people-focused' type of work processes.

With the development of knowledge-intensive forms of production for both products and services, the use of employee skills becomes even more central to securing the competitive advantage of the company. Almost all the staff are highly qualified and managers rely on the continuous application of judgement by highly skilled staff to produce the creativity and quality that are crucial to the company's advantage in the market. Here commitment to the values and goals of the company facilitates the exercise of discretionary effort that enhances the overall performance of the organisation. The management of employee commitment, learning and skill formation become central to the qualities expected of managers and team leaders.

Chapter 5

In Chapters 3 and 4, we have assumed that different types of TRs tend to be associated with different types of IRs: Taylorist mass production with the development of management and white-collar skills but low skills for manual operatives, and knowledge-intensive production with high levels of skill use by virtually all employees. This is a relatively static snapshot of what in reality is a continuous process of change, so in this chapter we shift the focus. In this chapter, we focus directly on the process of change as firms continuously seek to adapt to the market through the introduction of change in their business strategy, which in turn affects either the technical or IRs or, as sometimes happens, both dimensions at once.

The academic literature has already identified some of the problems encountered in the process of change. Here we are especially concerned with the decision making of owners and senior managers because it is they who are the powerful agents in changing strategy and, through that, the dimensions of the TRs and IRs. Yet there is evidence that this group are often resistant to changing their business strategies. At the same time, it is possible that managers and workers may lack the skills to implement the new practices associated with, say high-performance work practices (HPWPs). There is also substantial evidence that even if owners and senior managers want to change their business strategy and introduce change in either TRs (e.g. through introducing new technology) or IRs (e.g. through introducing HPWPs), that this is a very difficult process which can take considerable time with no guarantee of success. So there is a risk element as well as the knowledge that is required in effecting change in business strategy.

To explore these and similar issues in greater depth we examine the case of Glenmorangie, a company that successfully introduced change along the IRs dimension through adapting high-performance management practices to a mass production technology. Yet many companies may not be so successful, so we move on to examine in detail another company where the attempt to introduce HPWPs to a system of batch production of airframes encountered major problems. This case illustrates the wide range of contextual factors and barriers that firms encounter in their attempts to change management practices and consequently the process of skill formation in the enterprise.

Chapter 6

Having traced the mechanisms through which business strategy drives the process of skill formation in organisations and how contextual factors may hinder or prevent the process, we return in Chapter 6 to our initial focus on policy approaches. The aim is to apply the lessons we have learnt to questions of national policy. What is abundantly clear is that the crucial area where employers and senior managers make their decisions about business strategy is in the market environment of their particular industry or sector. It is here that they identify the opportunities either in the domestic or international markets and how they should respond. That response is shaped by the interactions of factors at two levels, the national and the sectoral.

At the national level these are factors such as the availability of finance and technologies, the cost and availability of labour, the supply of skills and the perceived threats to their business from competitors. At the sector level they are affected by the regulations that govern their industry and its products or services (including those that govern the use of labour), the demands from customers in the supply chain to meet industry standards, the availability of skills from the local VET system, the relations with unions and professional bodies that influence how they can use the skills of employers and so on. It is also at the sector level that these factors (what we call the 'institutional logics') interact and shape the decisions of employers about their business strategies and their use of labour. In view of this interaction, it is therefore important that action be taken at the two levels. First, a sectoral agenda has to be set at the national level, though some of the early action may have to be facilitated by the government. This means a vision of an industrial strategy that will focus on building those sectors in which the country has, or can build, a competitive advantage in world markets and actions to create an infrastructure that will support this vision.

Crucially, this will involve building institution at the second level, that of the sector or industry, which will ensure the implementation of the strategy. We use 'institution' in an environmental sense, which may include regulations and processes that govern the way competitors compete (e.g. more incentives for high value-added productive systems). This means the formation of powerful, employer-led sector bodies that have the capacity to influence the business environment. They need the capacity to shape the regulations that govern the industry or sector, to shape the institutions that supply the skills and to influence the local employee organisations such as unions that can help reduce the attraction of the low-skilled route. It has to be a body that can influence regulations embedded in the supply chain and provide assistance to employers to pursue a higher value-added, high-skills business strategy. Many of the levers to introduce such a policy approach are already in existence. In many respects it means just coordinating them within the context of a policy that places the encouragement of companies pursuing high value-added strategies and highly skilled, good-quality jobs as a national priority. In this chapter, we conclude by placing such a policy in context and discuss what we can expect from such an approach.

Chapter 7

This is the concluding chapter. Instead of providing a summary of the analysis, this chapter is used to put forward a set of important and related points that have not been formally mentioned in the previous chapters. Some of the points are crucial in the successful implementation of the strategic skills model and the sectoral approach to skills development. For example, if demand factors are so important in shaping skills demand and skills utilisation at work, what role does supply side policy play? Would our proposed model work in every sector? Are we expecting too much from skills? What is the fine balance between high utilisation of skills, high-performance working and work intensification?

Also, before the reader begins the book, it might be useful to spell out our argument in the following summary:

1. The demand for skills is primarily determined by the changes in the productive system and these demands are constantly changing through time.

2. Societies have developed different ways of responding to these demands in terms of their policy frameworks and these frameworks adapt to these changes in demand in different ways.

3. Human capital theory has provided just one way of shaping these policy frameworks. It provided a basis for a framework that 'worked' for a limited period of time in the Anglo-Saxon countries, when the modern corporations associated with Taylorist mass production were expanding in the mid-20th century, with their huge bureaucracies that required a constantly growing supply of educated personnel for the new white-collar jobs. Since then, as economies have become dominated by different types of productive system, namely mature forms of mass production and knowledge-intensive production, the demand for skills has shifted pushing issues of skill utilisation to the fore. In this context human capital theory and the notion of market failure that provides its theoretical consistency has become increasingly irrelevant, only capable of generating a skills policy that is based upon augmenting public provision for training and increases in qualifications, and nothing more.

4. What is required in the current context is a skills policy that is focused on influencing the company's productive systems towards the adoption of business strategies based on high value-added forms of production and high skills utilisation in order to provide their competitive advantage. Only then will there be the basis for the demand for high-skilled jobs.

Figure 0.1 summarises the argument by illustrating the changing meaning of skills policy. It shows on the right-hand side that human capital theory uses the concept of market failure to provide some general reasons for what is claimed to be employers' (and individuals') 'underinvestment' in training (e.g. uncertainty, lack of information, barriers to access capital funds or technology and so on). But all this can provide is policy pre-scriptions for augmenting public provision for training and increases in qualifications. It is too blunt an instrument to provide any effective policy prescription to encourage the adoption and use of mature mass produc-tion and knowledge-intensive forms of production that depend on high levels of skills utilisation. To do that the Anglo-Saxon nations have to explore how skills policy can shape the left-hand side of Figure 0.1, some-thing with which other societies have already been experimenting.

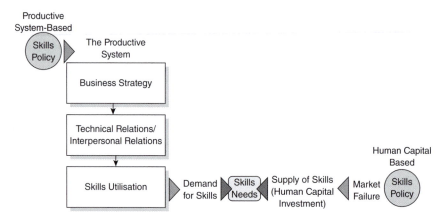

Figure 0.1   The changing nature of skills policy and skills demand

Source: authors

The left-hand side of Figure 0.1 illustrates why contemporary skills pol-icy demands an understanding of the productive system. This is because of the key role that business strategy plays in influencing skills demands. The figure shows that within any productive system, the level and extent of skills deployed are influenced by the relevant business strategy via TRs that determine the demand for skill levels, and interpersonal relations IRs that determine the ways in which skills are used. It is the interaction of these two dimensions which determines the nature of the workplace in terms of the value it adds to the output, the design of work and work processes and the way that employees and their skills are deployed. As we will show in later chapters, the specific combination of TRs and IRs directly impacts on skills utilisation and therefore skills demand.

1

THE CHALLENGES FACING SKILLS POLICY IN THE 21ST CENTURY

As a matter of fact, capitalist economy is not and cannot be stationary. Nor is it merely expanding in a steady manner. It is incessantly being revolutionized *from within* by new enterprise, i.e., by the intrusion of new commodities or new methods of production or new commercial opportunities into the industrial structure as it exists at any moment. Any existing structures and all the conditions of doing business are always in a process of change.

J.A. Schumpeter ([1942]2003: 31)

Overview

The aim of this chapter is to further our understanding of the national context within which business leaders and the leaders of large public organisations make decisions about the business strategy, which in turn shapes the skills they demand and the ways in which they use them. We highlight three major factors that shape this national context. The first is the nature of the opportunities that are available to the business or organisation leaders to pursue their objectives, which in the case of businesses is to deliver a profit. These opportunities are structured by the position of the company in national and increasingly global markets. This is also the case for political leaders as it is their remit to help business deliver economic growth and create quality jobs. This international context therefore plays an important part in influencing the type of approach that the nation adopts to skills policy.

The second is the political struggle within the country, the alignment of interest groups and political parties and the outcome of this struggle for power that shapes the dominant ideology and institutional framework through which the various components of the national approach to skills policy, including the vocational education and training (VET) system, are delivered. The third major factor is the type of productive system that dominates the economy at any one point in time. We use the term 'productive system' to refer to the types of market the company chooses to compete in and the ways in which the process of production is organised, the type of technology it uses and the ways in which it manages employees. This has a very important influence on shaping the level of skills demanded by employers in order to operate their businesses and the ways in which they use those skills.

These factors interact in a specific historical context, which itself affects the outcomes in terms of how the economy develops. To illustrate this we examine how approaches to skills policy change in three different countries that industrialised at different points in time. Each has passed through a distinct series of phases during which the interaction of these forces created distinctive challenges and produced different outcomes in terms of the skill policy that they adopted and which they have modified over time. This interaction also gives rise to different academic theories that seek to explain what is happening and what the appropriate policy solution would be. Our argument here is that the UK and other Anglo-Saxon countries developed a policy based on reliance on the market to deliver skills and informed by human capital theory that may have been appropriate at an earlier stage of economic development but is now failing to meet the demands of an economy facing increasingly competitive conditions in a global market.

What this exercise shows is that the type of policy framework adopted by the state (and the academic theories that underpin it) interacts with the productive system and influences the direction in which the economy moves. The intention of the analysis is to provide the reader with a greater understanding of the forces that shape policy and the business strategies that employers adopt. Just how these factors interact at the level of the firm and so shape the demand for different levels of skills and the ways in which employers use them is the task of the main body of the book. Once we have made headway in this task we return in the final chapters to re-examine the policy process and the potential we have for improving the effectiveness of policy.

Introduction

The above quote from Schumpeter reinforces the main message of this chapter, namely that economies are constantly in the process of change. Yet at any one point in time they are characterised by specific types of productive systems, be they early industrial mass production, Taylorist mass production, where a detailed division of labour was combined with assembly line technology, mature mass production where high-performance working practices were combined with modern mass production technology, or knowledge-intensive production. From our perspective each of these creates specific types of skill demands. In response to these, politicians create policy frameworks to deliver what they perceive to be the skills required. Our argument here is that the most recent change from Taylorist mass production to globalised forms of mature mass production and knowledge-intensive production has shifted the point of political intervention from the supply side to the demand side. (This is illustrated in Figure 0.1, where the intervention shifts from the right-hand side of the diagram to the left-hand side.) While other countries have sought to adapt their frameworks to these changing demands, especially the most recent industrial countries such as the Asian Tigers, the UK and some other Anglo-Saxon countries have failed to adapt their policy frameworks in an appropriate manner.

In order to show empirically how these relationships change through time we have identified a series of stages that symbolise major changes in the systems of production. Economies and societies are never self-contained systems, so we start by briefly examining the international context which shapes the ways in which these relationships play out at the national level. Then in each stage at the national level we outline the dominant type of productive system that generated a particular type of skills demand. Next, we examine the theoretical ideas and policy framework through which politicians respond to these skill demands. Finally, we explore the effectiveness of these policy responses.

While the processes we are examining are universal, the precise form taken by policy responses and, to a limited extent, the demand for skills generated by the productive system are also shaped by the values and institutional structures of each society. Here we are talking not just about the VET systems but also the broader institutions that structure relations between the state, employer and union organisations and the broader legal framework within which they are embedded. These not only affect the policy response of governments to changes in skill demand, they also have an impact on the business strategies that are crucial in shaping those changes in demand, a reciprocal influence.

So in terms of Figure 0.1, what we witness over a time is that changes in economic, political and cultural institutions result in changes in business strategies, which in turn trigger changes in the productive system. These create new demands on employees in terms of the level of skill required to operate within the business and the ways in which those skills are used. During the 1950s and 1960s a policy response that just acted on the right-hand side of Figure 0.1 and increased the supply of skills was appropriate to meet the demands of the productive system, but over time, as the business strategies of employers have changed the need has arisen for an approach that tackles skills policy from the left-hand side. As we shall see, other countries have already moved much further in this direction.

The countries we use to illustrate this are the UK to represent the Anglo-Saxon countries, Germany for the Germanic countries that use the dual system and Singapore for the developmental states of South-East Asia. All of these countries are responding to the same changes in the global economy, but the way in which employers have responded (namely the productive system) is influenced by the policy environment within their political boundary. In a short treatment of the issues such as this we cannot go into detail about all of the three models, but we can use them to illustrate the ways in which these global changes impact on the productive system and the associated demand for skills in different institutional contexts.

Three contrasting approaches to skills policy

To place these divergent approaches in context we provide a brief description of the historical evolution of these approaches to skills policy. The UK being the first industrial nation in world markets never developed a coherent policy approach to employee training. The early industrial training was governed by legislation concerning the master–servant relationship with its origins in the guild system. Abuses of this by early industrial employers led to legal regulation of the conditions of child and female labour, but in general employers and unions were left to agree among themselves on the regulation of training and where unions were ineffective employers were left to control the process of training. For the professions, these were regulated during the late 19th century by their professional bodies. It was not until the early 20th century that, with increasing competition from the USA and Germany, the government started to initiate moves towards some form of regulation of industrial training. These culminated in the tri-partite system of industrial training boards after the Second World War but they were largely dismantled and an attempt at government direct regulation ended in the 1980s. Following that the UK relied on the 'free market' to deliver training and skills. This does not mean that these activities were not regulated at all, only that the regulations and legal framework meant that employers were left to determine the levels and types of training offered subject to the restrictions laid down in employment law and to any conditions that unions or professional bodies were able to impose.

Germany industrialised after the UK and USA but did so very rapidly and by the early 20th century was a major contender in world markets and a serious political threat to the UK. However, because the process of industrialisation took place within the framework of the old guild system, the apprenticeship remained as a strong institution that shaped the training of those entering craft work. At the national level the unions developed a strong base. This system was rebuilt after the Second World War when there was an urgent need to regenerate German industry and help the country regain its position in world markets. To this end the government, unions and employers agreed on a strong institutional framework to govern the apprenticeship, which was to embrace not just narrow vocational training but also more a broadly based system of schooling for citizenship. This ensured that young people had a thorough training comprising both off-the-job college education in theory and practical on-the-job training under the direction of a 'Meister', a qualified person responsible for overseeing their training in the workplace. The system was overseen by the Federal Institute for Vocational Training (BIBB) responsible for research and development and for ensuring that the system was constantly modified to accommodate changes in the industrial and occupational structures.

In Singapore the situation was very different. From its birth after the Second World War as a small trading nation with high levels of poverty and no natural resources it faced a difficult task to break into world markets and stimulate the process of industrialisation. From the start the government took an active role in attracting foreign capital and providing the infrastructure that would encourage employers to grow their businesses. Initially this was to take advantage of the low-cost labour but as the economy developed the government actively steered the economy into the production of higher value-added goods and services. To achieve this it provided higher levels of education and training and delivered higher standards of living until today it has one of the highest standards of living for its citizens in the world.

Changes in our understanding of national business and skills policy frameworks

Even such a cursory examination of these different approaches to skills or workforce development highlights three major sources of change that shape national approaches. These are the international context in which the policies are formed, the outcomes of the national political struggles and the type of productive system that characterises the economy. The international context is important because, as we will show, it shapes the country's competitive position in world markets and provides the context in which skills policy is to deliver its outcomes. All too often the study of VET systems fails to take this into account and these systems are treated as if the only factor that affects their development is the national political context. While the national context is important, it cannot explain why some countries have developed highly coordinated systems. These are crucial if the country has to break into existing markets. For politically powerful countries such as the UK in the 19th century they were not necessary as they could forcibly impose their goods on the countries they dominated.

The national political context is important because that provides the resources and ideological guidance for policy makers. The characteristics of the productive system are crucial because this determines the type of skills required by employers. The major changes that characterise the various phases in the development of the productive systems and the policy responses are summarised in Table 1.1. It illustrates in summary form how these various factors change through time and also how our theoretical understanding changes in accordance with them.

Phase 1: 1950s, 1960s

International context

We pick up the story in the post-Second World War period, which contains the origins of the present problems in the Anglo-Saxon world. This was the time when the USA dominated world markets and trade was governed by international institutions such as the World Bank (WB), the International Monetary Fund (IMF) and the General Agreement on Tariffs and Trade (GATT). The objective was to stabilise and consolidate world markets in the pursuit of free trade. In ideological terms the USA was firmly wedded to free-market principles precisely because it was in their interest to remove barriers to trade as it enabled their national companies to grow, exploiting the advantages of mass production in manufacturing companies competing at the leading edge of national markets.

Internationally, the UK was also committed to the free market, competing across a wide range of markets, both at the high end and the low end, but this was in the context of its Empire which it was in the process of losing, thereby exposing UK companies to the full weight of global competition.

Changes in the productive system and skill demands

Within the Western countries during this period the economies were increasingly dominated by large corporations, able to exploit systems

Table 1.1 The impact of changes in productive systems on skills policy

Phase	International context	Changes in productive system	Theoretical understanding	Anglo-Saxon (UK) policy	Germanic (German) policy	Asian Tigers (Singapore) policy
1950–60s	International markets dominated by US and UK MNCs.	Growth of large bureaucracies using Taylorist mass production.	Birth of human capital theory.	Initial attempts to influence demand and supply side.	Building the dual system.	Demand side attract foreign capital, supply side establish education and training system.
1970–80s	Germany and Japan enter markets. Relocation of low value-added production.	Challenge of mature mass production. Growth of Taylorist mass production in services.	Dominance of human capital theory.	Eradicate most demand side measures. Reliance on supply side investment in education. Free market approach.	Start amending the dual system to meet changes in productive system.	Demand side measures to move up value-chain, supply side measures coordinated to ensure skills available.
1990–2000s	Tigers and later BRICs enter global markets, intensify competition for high value-added production.	Growth of knowledge-intensive production. TNCs fragment production process across countries.	Inadequacies of human capital theory revealed as demand side issues become more pressing. Importance of skill utilisation recognised.	Supply side, free market policy continues but demand side issues fragment overall policy.	Dual system starts to struggle to adapt to changes in productive system.	Demand side policy to foster knowledge-intensive industries. Supply side to increase knowledge workers.

MNC = multinational corporation; BRIC = economics of Brazil, Russia, India and China;

TNC = transnational corporation.

of Taylorist mass production to service the growing national markets in the USA and Europe for consumer goods. Where they spread abroad, as many of the large American corporations did, this growth took the form of transplanting the whole production process, sourcing the materials and parts and assembling and marketing the finished product, all within the boundaries of national markets. The result was the growth of large corporate bureaucracies, offering careers for the emergent middle class, from office clerks to administrators, professionals and managers. In addition, in the public sector there was the significant growth of public administration and health care provisions in the UK and in the USA, what Galbraith (1967) referred to as the 'military-industrial complex'. This rapid growth of white-collar jobs increased the proportion of middle level jobs and created what appeared to be ever expanding opportunities for social mobility, enabling children of the working class, through successful school performance, to enter middle-class careers.

In order to exploit the advantages of the Taylorist system of mass production, new skills in the management of large bureaucratic organisations had to be developed, new systems of accounting introduced and, in addition, new professions such as those of marketing had to be established in order to persuade customers of the value of the products on offer. These created new demands on the education system for highly educated recruits. Further down the hierarchy the burgeoning clerical and administrative jobs in both private and public bureaucracies required relatively high levels of literacy and basic problem-solving skills. The spread of mass production also created a growing demand for the intermediate level skills of maintenance workers and engineers. However, at the base of the hierarchy, the assembly line techniques required large groups of semi-skilled and unskilled operatives. For them the only skills required at the point of entry to the firm were low-level literacy skills, sufficient to understand the rules and regulations of the firm, with other elementary manual skills being acquired on the job. Overall, the introduction of this productive system was making major new demands on the systems of education and training but only from the level of intermediate skills and above.

Theoretical thinking during this period

There was relatively little theoretical thinking to inform skills policy following the Second World War. At that time the countries that had industrialised in the first phase, such as the UK and USA, had reached what was seen as industrial maturity, Germany and Japan were rebuilding their economies, while the third phase countries such as the Asian

Tigers had only just initiated the process. Yet there were sufficient cases of industrialisation for academics to provide an understanding of the regularities in the process of economic growth, what Rostow (1960) termed the 'Stages of Economic Growth'. Other labour economists (Kerr et al., 1960) looked to explain this in terms of a 'logic of industrialism', referring to the forces that were driving societies through these stages of growth. One of the most important of these was the imperative of technological change that was seen to require a constant increase in the skills level of the labour force. In responding to the imperatives of technological change and the political demands of modern democracies, investment in education and technical skills was seen as essential.

It was this context within which human capital theory was born. It was a time when opportunities in education and in the labour market were opening up after the Second World War. Becker's theory captured this dramatically. Prior to the war he had shown how returns to college and high-school education declined from 1900–1940 (Becker, 1964: 8). However, this all changed after 1940, even though the relative number of college and high-school graduates grew. Becker acknowledged that the returns to individuals were linked to the effect of their family background and also to the rapid growth of expenditure on research and development (R&D), military technology and the expansion of the service sector (1964: 9) in the post-war period, but understandably the theory focuses on the returns to education. The policy implications were clear: invest in education as this was a win–win scenario promising both economic growth for the country and future increases in income for individuals. By the end of this phase academia was sending out a clear message to policy makers to invest in education as a contribution to meeting the country's skill needs.

Policy frameworks

The UK

The policy framework in the UK, following the experience of mass deprivation caused by the war, was shaped by the rise of the Labour Party. They attempted to improve economic performance (what we now refer to as the 'demand side', the left-hand side of Figure 0.1) by nationalising key industries such as coal, steel and telecommunications, all industries serving a largely national market. On the supply side (the right-hand side of Figure 0.1) they introduced a national system of industrial training boards on a tripartite basis (state, unions and employers) organised on a sectoral basis in 1965. In the face of employer opposition all but two of these were removed by 1983, with the Manpower Services Commission (MSC) having overall responsibility for them after it was established in 1973. The MSC provided oversight of national training issues and delivered programmes for those at risk in the labour market, but effectively the responsibility for training was now in the hands of employers.

The new mass production techniques were introduced after they had first been developed in the USA, but unlike the USA where business schools soon emerged to provide the managerial and professional staff required by the large corporations, in the UK there was a delay in introducing business schools because of the older aristocratic values that permeated higher education and resisted giving academic credence to these 'new' vocational subjects.

There was less of a challenge in delivering institutions to provide the intermediate-level literacy and problem-solving skills. The skills required by the modern corporation for administrative and clerical work could be delivered through a good level of literacy and numeracy provided by a solid secondary education. The additional skills in typing required for the new clerical jobs filled by women could be delivered either through the public education system or through specialised private training prior to entry into work. The policy response in the UK was for the government to authorise and pay for the expansion of secondary education, initially in the form of grammar and secondary modern schools.

For those at operative level, entry to the semi-skilled and unskilled jobs required by the Taylorist mass production system required only basic literacy, no academic qualifications and just the positive attributes of a willingness to accept factory discipline and attend regularly.[1] During this phase in the Anglo-Saxon societies there was a relatively good fit between the skill demands of the economy and the output of the educational system as the education system was also delivering large numbers of unqualified, unskilled workers supporting those employers wishing to pursue a low value-added cost, low-skills strategy.

Germany

In Germany the situation was different as the system evolved to meet the challenge of these changes in skill demand. The dual system, a combination of college learning and work-based training, underpinned by strong employer and union institutions, was introduced to provide three years of apprentice training for most school leavers. This was based on a consensus between employers and unions on the need for a national system of training. In addition, the introduction of works councils in larger enterprises, together with strong unions, ensured that the employees' voice was heard with regard to the implementation of business strategy. These factors together with the availability of long-term finance functioned to close off the low-cost, low-skilled option for employers in terms of their business strategy, encouraging them to exploit their higher skills base and adopt higher value-added strategies (Bosch and Weinkopf, 2008). While ensuring a constant supply of highly trained workers (operating on the right-hand side of Figure 0.1), the system functioned to make it difficult for employers to adopt the low-skills strategy typical of many employers in the UK and USA (thereby operating on the left-hand side of Figure 0.1).

Singapore

By contrast the Tiger economies were seeking to break into world markets. Their comparative advantage was their low-cost labour and to exploit that they either had to attract new industries or create them from their resources. From the start of the industrialisation process they had to operate on the left-hand side of Figure 0.1. For this they required pro-active government institutions. In addition they had also to act on the supply side (on the right-hand side of Figure 0.1). This meant providing basic education and programmes to create and improve literacy for workers together with basic training. This involved creating the institutional foundations for an educational and training system that could deliver low-level worker skills as well as the skills for lower-level management. Not only that, the systems had to be very responsive to the demands of new industries, many of which countries such as Singapore had no previous experience of. From the outset of industrialisation these countries had to operate on both sides of Figure 0.1.

Phase 2: 1970s, 1980s

International context

At the international level, USA companies continued to dominate world markets. However, while American multinational corporations continued to expand their systems of Taylorist mass production in national markets, they were increasingly challenged by German manufacturers in the markets for advanced engineering and by the Japanese. UK manufacturers continued their retreat from Empire markets and lost out in many markets to American, German and Japanese companies. During this phase the capital for labour-intensive manufacturing was increasingly being relocated to what was euphemistically termed the 'third world', a process that had a particularly profound impact in the UK, which had significant textile and footwear sectors. Here we start to see a major shift in the global division of labour. The Tiger economies were the recipients of much of this relocated capital, and this, together with the new capital which their initial success was generating, provided the basis for their success in making inroads into world markets, especially for low value-added manufactured goods.

Changes in the productive system and skill demands

Continued economic growth in the West provided the basis for the expansion of mass markets in car manufacturing, white goods and electrical appliances, as well as banking and financial services and health and personal services. This provided the basis for the continued growth of the demand for professional, technical, managerial, administrative and scientific workers and the white-collar workers that supported them. However, the relocation of capital for the more labour-intensive forms of Taylorist mass production to countries with lower labour costs was reducing opportunities for skilled, semi-skilled and unskilled manual workers in these industries, especially in the UK. In addition, new more efficient and productive systems of mature mass production were being introduced, initially by the multinational Japanese manufacturers and later by some American companies.

Changes in political power led to a political drive in both the UK and USA to re-introduce the discipline of the market in a more forceful manner. Under the Thatcher and Reagan administrations the state sought to deregulate the market across a range of industries. In the UK state-owned industries were privatised, and in both countries markets for financial services were deregulated. Although not described as a industrial policy, this did create new business opportunities in industries ranging from air and land transport to financial services. These were policies operating on the left-hand side of Figure 0.1. In the USA, Silicon Valley, in part a consequence of government funding for R&D for the defence industry (Mazzucato, 2013), emerged as the centre of innovation for the new information and communications technology (ICT) industry that would provide a major spurt for the growth of more knowledge-intensive forms of production.

The other major change that was occurring during this phase was the expansion of Taylorist mass production techniques in the service sector. The increase in discretionary spending associated with the growth in living standards in the West stimulated the demand for goods and services in retail, hotels, personal service and finance industries. The result was a major shift in skill demands. While these were still largely low-skilled jobs they made very different demands on recruits, requiring what sociologists referred to as 'emotional labour' – the ability to control the emotions and to provide a constant smile and pleasant experience for the customer, sometimes referred to as 'customer service skills'. While the decline of manufacturing and the growth of Taylorist service industries did not threaten the traditional middle-class career which provided the incremental increase in income that human capital theory predicted, they did destroy many working-class communities, creating a demand for a very different type of lower-skilled worker.

Theoretical underpinning and skills debate

The continued growth of bureaucracies designed to coordinate Taylorist forms of mass production created an increase in the demand for education. This meant that for those who possessed such credentials there was little difficulty in accessing a 'career' in either these large corporations or in government and in accessing the increasing economic returns that provided over a lifetime. This was fertile ground for Becker's theory, which was enthusiastically received. Moreover, a substantial body of research confirmed his empirical findings, not just in the USA but for other industrial societies and also for the new developing societies (Psacharopoulos and Patrinos, 2002). This justified increased public and private investment in education and training.

Given the weight of evidence the theory 'took off' in policy terms. Policy makers started to see the investment in education and skills as 'the' driver of economic growth; moreover, in the Anglo-Saxon countries this was one that the government could directly influence without 'distorting' the operation of the market. As international competition started to increase with the recovery of Germany and Japan, there was a good fit between the messages from human capital theory and political need to foster economic growth and improve national competitiveness. As a result, supply side economics came to dominate the policy discourse of workforce development, and indeed such dominance continued to grow with the rise of monetarism in the fight against inflation in the 1980s.

As new professional jobs were being created in the emergent ICT industry more and more manual jobs were lost in manufacturing; the response of the politicians was to place even greater stress on education and skills. Authorities such as Robert Reich (1991) in the USA responded by arguing that the West must now focus on raising education and skill levels even higher, as these were their source of competitive advantage, because they could no longer compete with the emergent economies in the production of mass-produced standardised goods. Human capital theory became detached from its economic and social context yet appeared to have universal validity. Investment in education was crucial to ensuring continued economic growth and in lifting the poor out of poverty.

The other important impact of human capital theory on national training policy was the establishment of a belief that national economic adjustment is hindered by inflexibility at the workers/skills level. It was seen that individuals were either reluctant or unable to prepare themselves for the rapid economic changes to come. As such, the high unemployment that was witnessed in the late 1970s and early 1980s was seen to be caused not by the failure to create jobs but by the inability of individuals to prepare and re-skill themselves. This paved the way for the increasingly popular notion of 'lifelong learning' within the context of employability to come in the next decade. From a theoretical perspective, the source of blame is firmly seen as a supply side issue – the lack of skills on the part of the workers.

The skills debate in this connection is quite subtle. On the one hand, there was never any 'measurement' that said that the unemployed or the poor had inadequate skills. This would have been difficult to measure because there was nothing to compare with. The adequacy of skills was simply derived from the fact of whether a worker was employed or not. Thus, for those who were in employment, clearly their skills were needed. If they were unemployed, the assumption was that their skills were no longer required. The same logic went further: if job seekers were unemployed for long period of time, the assumption was that they lacked generic skills and basic knowledge of job seeking. Labour market conditions became rather irrelevant to the explanation of unemployment. Thus investment in education and training, action on the right-hand side of Figure 0.1 provided 'the' solution to economic difficulties, the problem lay with the supply of labour not with the operation of markets or the behaviour of employers.

Policy frameworks

The UK

The privatisation of the nationalised industries represented the final elimination of attempts to influence the demand side, apart that is from the deregulation of financial services, which stimulated rapid growth there. The result was the further intensification of competition, which led to many British manufacturing companies collapsing. Those that survived were world class but there was also a very long tail of poorly performing companies. However, high value-added business and financial services companies were expanding, as were lower value-added services such as retail and hotels.

On the supply side, with the triumph of neoliberalism, the MSC represented something of an anachronism as the last vestige of state intervention. However, the government was faced with a dilemma as the growth of youth unemployment required some form of policy mechanism to deal with it, so the MSC was retained and charged with this task. There was also another problem: while the continued growth in the demand for professional, managerial and technical workers could be met through an expansion of the education system, the growth of mass service delivery in sectors such as retail and restaurants was making demands for certification that the traditional academic education provided by schools and colleges could not meet. The new jobs required certification of practical customer service skills that were required for effective performance in the workplace. The government responded by introducing a new system of competence-based qualifications, the National Vocational Qualifications (NVQs). For some of those with low-level educational achievement the new competence-based qualifications provided a form of certification, but there was limited uptake by employers. Such changes gave further impetus to the 'relevance' of human capital theory. By continuing to operate on the right-hand side of Figure 0.1 the policy was sustaining the use of a strategy of low value-added production by employers in the service sector. The government was now funding certification for such low-skilled work. Skills were now delivered through the 'free market', a policy which continued to support the low-skills option.

Germany

In Germany the response to these changes in skill demand took a very different form. The prior existence of the dual system meant that all that was required was a modification to its structure. New professions were recognised and incorporated into the system. For the new lower-level soft skills, these new competences were incorporated into a broader curriculum framework that provided knowledge of the trade as a whole as well as preparation for citizenship. This provided certification of such skills but within the framework that extended the provision of highly skilled labour to the service sector. There were complaints that the system was slow to respond to these changes, but the process was one of progressive adaptation not radical change. The lack of an extensive supply of unqualified and unskilled labour continued to make the high value-added strategy preferable for German employers.

Singapore

In the Tiger economies such as Singapore the process of adaptation was more comprehensive as it involved more direct changes to both the demand and the supply side. The aim of government policy during this phase was to move up the value chain towards industries that would create high-skilled and higher-paid jobs. On the left-hand side of Figure 0.1 steps were taken to identify those industries higher up the value chain where it was felt the country could compete. Policies were introduced to attract and support such industries. Then, with knowledge of which skills this would require, derived from the experience of Japan and the West, steps were taken to modify and extend the existing education and training system to meet that demand. Educational provision was extended, technical education expanded and programmes introduced to upskill existing workers. At the heart of this process of adaptation were government mechanisms designed to coordinate changes on the demand side with those on the supply side. Thus as the demand for higher level and industry specific skills grew, the education and training systems expanded to meet the challenge. This way there no bottlenecks in the supply of skilled labour to hold back the process of growth.

Phase 3: 1990s–2000s

International context

By the end of the 20th century the international context had changed significantly. On the economic front world trade had increased 22 times between 1950 and 2000 (WTO, 2014) a change that was symbolised by the transformation of GATT into the World Trade Organization (WTO) in 1995 with its remit to ensure that global trade flows freely. The second-wave industrialisers such as Japan had established themselves in international markets, followed by the Asian Tigers and then China, India and Brazil. In this rapidly changing international arena, the second- and third-wave industrialisers had almost all sought to break into global markets through the use of industrial policies, operating on the left-hand side of Figure 0.1, in spite of the opposition to such a strategy by the world powers and the international agencies they dominated such as the IMF, World Bank and the WTO. In addition, governments in countries such as China had state-supported industries where the major players were rapidly becoming proficient in the latest production technologies. The competition for high-skilled jobs at the international level was intensifying. It was no longer just a competition between the older industrial countries seeking to pursue a 'high-skills route'.

The spread of the World Wide Web and other information and computer technologies had transformed the process of production by modularising it (Berger, 2006). This was a profound change with major implications for the global division of labour. Modularisation enabled companies to break down the production process into various components, each of which could be located in different countries across the globe to exploit differences in skill provision and the price of labour. Production for many goods and services was no longer contained within the geographical boundaries of the nation-state. This in turn freed the skill formation system from the confines of national boundaries, enabling the emergent transnational corporations (TNCs) to extend their control over the skill formation process. The older industrial countries and the Tiger economies now found themselves in a competition to attract the high value-added components of these global corporations. In this situation the UK became only a small player in the international stage, while the dominance of the USA was increasingly challenged by the new industrial countries, especially China.

The other major change that took place concerns the global supply of educated labour. The very success of skills policies based on human capital theory was starting to create problems. As governments increased their investments in education, this resulted in a dramatic increase in the supply of educated and skilled workers in the older industrial societies. While Western governments were increasing their investment in education so too were the new industrial countries. In China with a population of over a billion, participation in higher education rose from 3 per cent in 1990 to 22 per cent in 2006 (Brown et al., 2011: 33). For large multinational employers the change over the four decades was almost unimaginable, from being faced with a very small number of graduates in the mid- to late 20th century, they were now faced with a huge pool of highly educated labour (Brown et al., 2008).

Changes in the productive system and skill demands

During the past two decades we have witnessed major changes in the productive system. The success of Japanese companies in capturing larger shares of world markets stimulated the spread of mature forms of mass production, or 'lean production' as it is sometimes termed. Consequently, many companies moved away from the traditional command and control systems of authority of the past to more participative forms of organisations, demanding new skills in leadership, teamworking, communication and problem solving among employees at all levels.

Within the firm these changes involved stripping out the layers of management thereby undermining the foundations of many middle-class careers.

Perhaps the most significant change has been the growth of knowledge-intensive forms of production where continuous innovation is the norm, for example in ICT, telecommunications, finance, biotechnology and aerospace. The spread of such innovations in information and telecommunication is also starting to have a significant impact on other industries such as distribution and parts of the retail sector. This increasing dependence on knowledge-intensive industries provides a continuing impetus to the demand for higher level intellectual skills, while the need for constant innovation increases the demand for creativity.

These companies are more likely to engage in the highly competitive international markets and be a part of TNCs or MNCs where they are more exposed to new management (high performance) practices (Bloom et al., 2011). This combination of a demand for high-level skills and the use of high-performance work practices (HPWPs) means that the development and utilisation of employee skills are crucial for the competitive success of these companies. The utilisation of employee skills therefore becomes a much more important priority both within the company and nationally.

With the spread of mature forms of mass production and knowledge-intensive production, new forms of controlling the behaviour of managers and senior staff had to be developed. These took the form of company competences, shaped by the core values and capabilities of the organisation and against which the behaviour of all members of the organisation could be judged. These were far more profound in their implications for behaviour than the competences required of retail staff in customer service. This is because they affected the values and orientation of staff and shape the process of learning within the organisation. All this meant that the process of skill formation was becoming increasingly detached from national systems of education and training and becoming more and more focused on processes within the organisation – on-the-job learning and training was becoming far more important.

In the service sector Taylorist systems of mass delivery were increasingly used by retail and restaurants as well as banks and financial services. This involved the extensive use of new technology to routinise business processes. This reduced skill levels and enabled employers to make more use of new groups of workers such as students and housewives, as well as facilitating the outsourcing of many jobs through the use of call centres abroad.

While we have been primarily focusing on the new forms of productive system, it is important to point out that many companies remained wedded to older types of productive systems, using Taylorist systems of mass production in the service sector and parts of manufacturing such as food processing. Even within companies that adopted some of the new systems such as HPWPs they would only use them in parts of the organisation, for example with regard to their R&D, while other parts of the same organisation would still use traditional forms of mass production with their associated command and control systems. A business strategy based on the use of low-cost, low-skilled labour remains attractive for many UK employers. It means that as unskilled and semi-skilled jobs in manufacturing have been relocated, these continue to be replaced by low-skilled, low-paid jobs in the service sector. In the UK there still remained almost one in five of the jobs (19.3 per cent) that require a learning time of less than one month (Felstead et al., 2007). However, this does mean that in these areas of low-skilled employment the demand for skills has remained unchanged. As the use of ICT becomes virtually ubiquitous, basic information technology (IT) skills are demanded by employers. In addition, the growing intensity of competition in sectors such as hotels, restaurants and retail, and the growing sophistication of customers, mean that higher levels of service are demanded. Even in retail companies that effectively operated systems of mass service delivery, staff are expected to deliver high levels of service, making further demands on their emotional and presentational skills.

Theoretical underpinnings and skills debate

The changes in the productive system and the associated demand for skills that have taken place over the previous two decades are now creating serious problems for our understanding of skills issues. Initially, the introduction of a national competence-based training system meant that more jobs than ever required some form of educational or training credential for entry. For example, in the UK by 2012, 77 per cent of jobs required educational qualifications (Felstead et al., 2013). In addition, the stirrings of the new knowledge-intensive industries was starting to introduce talk about the future 'knowledge-based' economy (Powell and Snellman, 2004) where higher levels of education were seen to be essential.

Yet against this background there was a growing sense that perhaps the supply side approach inspired by human capital theory had reached its limits. Changes were taking place on the demand side that human capital theory could not explain. The rapid spread of competences being used by companies suggested that there was more to skill formation than just an investment in education or training courses. To understand these new skills required inputs from occupational psychologists, educationalists, management scientists and sociologists as well as economists – the understanding of skills was now an inter-disciplinary task, with Prime Minister Blair bringing together an interdisciplinary team to advise on the development of the Workforce Development Policy in the UK (Cabinet Office, 2001). In addition, there was also a growing awareness among academics that merely con-tinuing to increase the supply of educated workers would not on its own guarantee increases in productivity and performance. Research, in large part instigated by the National Institute for Economic and Social Research in the UK, was demonstrating that national institutional fac-tors such as training arrangements and provision were important in determining the demand for skills as well as the business strategies of the firms themselves.

Partly in response to this, Finegold and Soskice (1988) developed their skills equilibrium model that did emphasise the importance of policy acting on the left-hand side of Figure 0.1. They used the concept of a 'low skills equilibrium' to illustrate how low levels of skill demand from employers in the UK reinforced the low skills output of the educational system, suggesting that the way out was for employers to raise their level of demand. In the following decade the argument was made more strongly that if skill levels were to be raised, it would mean raising the demand from employers as well as individuals. To ensure against the continuance of the low skilled equilibrium, government policy should pursue a skills strategy that would create the conditions for the achieve-ment of a high skills equilibrium (Ashton and Green, 1996; Brown et al., 2002). However, apart from using the equivalent of the German dual system to close off the low-skills route, there were few suggestions as to how to change employer's business strategies and there was little research that was successful in identifying any levers that governments in the Anglo-Saxon world could use to raise employers' skill demand (Keep, 2013).

Academically, human capital theory was not without its critics. Following Becker's pioneering work, further research in the USA started to reveal that human capital investments in formal education could not account for more than a fraction of variation in wages (Osterman and Shulman, 2011: 42). What was happening in this phase was that the increased supply of highly educated people was outstripping the growth in demand. In effect it meant that the increased supply of graduates and the slow growth of the knowledge-intensive forms of production meant that there were no longer sufficient high-paid jobs to deliver the returns to education that had been the case in the past (Green, 2013; Felstead et al., 2013).[2] It was now becoming clear that the increased supply of highly educated people was not in itself leading to an increase in highly skilled, highly paid jobs. Indeed, in the OECD Programme for the

International Assessment of Adult Competencies (PIAAC) (2013: 168, 1771) study of 22 countries, the UK recorded the second highest proportion of jobs for which only a primary education or less was required (over 20 per cent) and the second highest incidence of over-qualification (30 per cent) of workers whose highest qualification was higher than the qualification necessary to get the job. The five decades of investment in education and training had not eradicated the low-level jobs and had provided an oversupply of highly educated people for the other jobs.

The other problem with human capital theory as a source of inspiration for policy was that the investments in the employability skills of those at risk in the labour market, the unemployed and the marginal groups, have only been partially successful in ensuring continued employment. In the USA it helped some young and older people into jobs but usually only at a low level, and rarely did it enable them to move into higher skilled and higher paying jobs, merely recycling them through low-skilled, low-paid jobs (Grubb and Ryan, 1999). In the UK, programmes such as the Youth Training Scheme and the subsequent Apprenticeship Scheme as well as those for low-skilled adult workers suffered from high levels of deadweight while employers had to be 'incentivised' to participate in them. Even those who obtained low-level qualifications through their training did not always receive a premium in the labour market (Dickerson and Vignoles, 2007), and neither did those who were delivered on-the-job training in low-skilled jobs (Wolf et al., 2010).

Meanwhile research was revealing other issues on the demand side to the left-hand side of Figure 0.1 that human capital theory could not address. Work on the success of Japanese management practices and 'lean' production techniques (Womack et al., 1990) and high-performance management practices had revealed that these were important in raising business performance. Skills were now increasingly seen as a derived demand, one that stemmed from the business practices of employers. The growing awareness of innovation as a source of business growth raised the importance of exploring sources of innovation and public policies designed to support it. What both these strands of research indicate was the importance of skill utilisation in the workplace (Ramstad, 2009). As Keep (2013) notes, this led to a realisation that innovation, work organisation, job design, systems of employee relations and the demand for skills utilisation in the workplace are all interrelated, stimulating an interest in the development of public policy that can support it.

While there has been some development at a theoretical level on the theory of high-skills ecosystems in furthering our understanding of the institutional conditions that supported high levels of skill utilisation, our knowledge of the underlying drivers of business practices, the drivers of learning in the workplace, remains thin (Anderson and Warhurst, 2012). As a result the academic debate shifted to emphasise workplace learning (Felstead et al., 2009) or the establishment of a 'skills culture' (Campbell, 2012). Yet there was no clear indication of how this increase in learning at work or the creation of a skills culture could be achieved.

Intellectually the debate reached an impasse, on the one hand human capital theory had been shown to be inadequate to meet the challenges of skills policy in the 21st century and research had indicated that the major issue was now on the demand side, but on the other hand there was no guidance as to how employers' behaviour could be influenced. It appeared that their business strategies were the key, but there were no intellectual tools to enable academics to understand how these strategies were formulated or how the state may be able to influence them.

Policy frameworks

The UK

While academics were arguing for policy to address the demand side on the left-hand side of Figure 0.1, policy makers still remained wedded to the supply side, 'free market' approach. In the UK the continued expansion of education systems reinforced the message that individuals were responsible for their future success in the labour market through increasing their investment in education and training. Greater reliance was placed on the market to deliver the restructuring of the economy, with 'market failure' providing the acid test for government intervention.

Under the influence of the neoliberal ideology, in the UK the Thatcher government swept away the last vestiges of any pretence of a national training strategy. The Training Agency was replaced by a series of locally based Training and Enterprise Councils (TECs). Based explicitly on the US Private Industry Councils (PICS) programme, the belief was that this would place employers firmly in control of the emergent training market through their control of the administration of government programmes as well as their hoped for participation in the formation of the new competence-based qualifications. A similar strategy was pursued by the UK Labour government, with the main thrust of policy continuing to be on the supply side to the right-hand side of Figure 0.1, with its inspiration in human capital theory. The core of the approach was to be found in the LEITCH Review (2006: 2) statement that 'skills is the most important lever within our control to create wealth and to reduce social deprivation'. The form of policy remained the same, the government providing subsidies for training that met their objectives in the form of qualifications. These would be delivered through the Further Education Colleges and Training and Enterprise Councils. The main tool remained a supply-led approach based on a form of human capital theory that used government subsidies to deliver training through colleges and to 'incentivise' employers.[3] The Coalition Government retained the core of this market-led approach but pulled back from the centralised, top-down approach with targets that were characteristic of the Labour government's approach and instead sought to establish a more thorough-going market-led approach where employers and individuals would drive the system forward (Payne and Keep, 2011).

The significance of the demand side was acknowledged in different ways by all governments. At the national level it was increasingly acknowledged that the UK could no longer compete across the full range of industrial sectors as the relocation of capital and the loss of manufacturing had left the country with only a limited range of industries or sectors within which it could compete at the leading edge of world markets. By default this has created pressure to adopt demand side policies to operate on the left-hand side of Figure 0.1. Whether it is called 'industrial activism' or 'a strategy of re-balancing the economy', governments were being pushed in the direct direction of being selective in the type of industries they wished to attract and grow.

What was particularly distinctive about government policy in this phase were the attempts to focus on the ways in which skills were deployed and utilised within the productive process inside organisations, in order to nurture the industrial basis for a high-skills economy. This was acknowledged in the development of the Investors in People (IiP) standard in the UK. Similar in some ways to the Malcolm Baldridge award in the USA, the IiP standard provided a means of establishing whether employers were using the most effective human resource development (HRD) practices in developing their employees. The introduction of Sector Skills Councils and the establishment of the United Kingdom Commission for Employment and Skills (UKCES) was a partial acknowledgement of the importance of the demand side. This was manifest in their advocacy of HPWPs as a means for employers to increase skill utilisation and enhance performance. In Scotland there was a more explicit attempt to encourage greater skills utilisation among employers (Keep, 2013).

It was becoming clear that attention had now to be paid to the demand side, but policy was still firmly embedded in a supply side approach and so new policy initiatives to tackle the demand side were ad hoc and unrelated. The framework for skills policy had become fragmented and more importantly did not appear to be having a significant impact in shaping the direction in which the economy was moving. Its voluntaristic ethos and unwillingness to 'interfere' with employers was seen as useful in attracting foreign investment from TNCs. However, the general direction in which the economy was moving, led by a small knowledge-intensive high-skilled sector and with a large tail of low-skilled, low-paid sectors does not appear to have been impacted by these policies to any great extent. By default policy continued to support employers choosing the low-skilled option.

Germany

The German dual system faced a number of challenges during this period. The reunification of Germany imposed strains on West Germany. The forces of deregulation in the EU, while not as extensive as the deregulation that took place in the Anglo-Saxon countries, saw the end of state monopolies in areas such as transport, telecommunication and health. In addition, financial restructuring at the national level saw the introduction of more short-term finance. All these imposed new constraints and opportunities for companies' business strategies. However, the basic features of the policy framework remained the same. German industry continued to compete at the top end of world markets for manufactured goods, supported by a strong supply of highly skilled labour. The supply of university graduates remained limited, with the main supply of highly skilled labour continuing to be delivered through the dual system. Nevertheless, strains were starting to appear in the dual system. The proportion of employers offering places declined, while those who remained within it demanded higher-level entry qualifications from new entrants. It appeared that the system was moving to support the higher-end jobs, a process that would bring it into conflict with the extension of university education.

However, there was no attempt to deregulate training. The Federal Institute for Vocational Education and Training (BIBB), which embodied the collaboration between the employees, unions and state, consolidated training for the declining occupations and instituted new ones to capture the shifts taking place in the occupational structure. Between 1996 and 2006, 68 new occupations were introduced, mostly in the service sector, with 8 new ones in IT and media occupations (Bosch and Weinkopf, 2008: 75). New forms of training were introduced to meet the demands of employers for a greater breadth of skills, and in the service sector the acquisition of competences in customer relations and teamworking were introduced while retaining the depth of knowledge about the company, business systems and citizenship associated with the traditional system. However, problems and tensions still remain, with the transnational employers demanding that they should only take those modules that were immediately relevant for the requirements of their productive system, thereby threatening the coherence of the system.

In general, it appears that the dual system is continuing to provide effective support for the high-end German manufacturing industry competing in world markets through the provision of a highly skilled and efficient labour force. However, the cost of this was the further deregulation of parts of the economy and the extension of low-wage work, much of which was outside the scope of the dual system. Fewer young people were entering the dual system and more were obtaining low-level qualifications in the further education sector, thereby offering more employers in the service sector the option of the low-cost route (Bosch and Weinkopf, 2008).

Singapore

Similarly in Singapore the system continued to be modified. In the 1990s, the rise of China and other low-cost countries meant that industrial policy in Singapore has been focused on developing higher value-added industries, thereby influencing the right-hand side of Figure 0.1. For example, one new industry was the aerospace industry. The state-led initiative in the 1990s resulted in Singapore Technologies Aerospace (ST Aerospace) becoming the world's largest third-party maintenance, repair and overhaul (MRO) provider. This also spurred on the emergence of significant research and development activities at local universities working with private companies. This enabled Singapore to break into the original equipment manufacturing (OEM) market, establishing a niche in the international supply chain, growing at an average of 14 per cent compound annual growth in the 2000s (Ng et al., 2012). Ninety per cent of the 19,900 workers in this 'new' sector are highly skilled workers, which reputedly was one of the reasons for Rolls-Royce to move its Trent 900 engines to Singapore in 2012.

To support all these developments, on the supply side the Singapore Workforce Development Agency introduced a variety of new competency qualifications for those in the middle and lower levels of the labour market, to ensure that the new soft skills were embedded in the labour force. These were delivered through a sector skills system charged with ensuring that the training responded to the changing demands of employers. To meet the demand for higher-level skills, new courses were introduced in polytechnics and universities.

When Singapore was still catching up with the advanced economies it could rely on knowledge of their industrial trajectories to identify the skills it would need in the next stage of development in Singapore. Now that they are also members of the advanced industrial societies, competing at the high end of knowledge-intensive industries this is no longer possible. Consequently, they have to rely on their own intelligence about the next set of skills the economy will require and therefore the coordination of the demand and supply of skills becomes more problematic but is still done at the highest level though government committees which periodically review the process of economic change.

Like all systems the Singaporean one faces new challenges, not least that of its reliance on foreign workers for economic growth and the internal political tensions this generates, but the system continues to succeed in keeping the country competing at the top end of world markets, now delivering one of the highest standards of living in the world.

Conclusions

We have seen dramatic changes in the international context within which politicians formulate their policy frameworks. With the rise of new industrial nations the UK has inevitably declined from a major world player in a range of industries to a lower-ranking industrial power trying to rebalance its economy after the financial sector-led growth collapsed. Germany has retained its place as a powerful industrial producer of high-end engineering and manufactured goods. During this period Singapore has successfully moved from being a producer of low-end manufactured goods to a producer of high engineering and financial services at the leading edge of world markets.

What is clearly evident from the three countries we have used as examples is that there is no one universal policy framework. Different policy frameworks work in different international and national contexts. Germany has been successful in continually adapting the system to meet the challenges of new productive systems and new global conditions, although it is now under considerable strain. Singapore has been successful in breaking into world markets and moving from low-skilled, low-value production to high-skilled, high value-added production, and in coordinating the tremendous shifts in demand with a constant supply of appropriately trained labour.

By contrast the UK has seen a decline in its share of world markets across a range of industries, lost a large part of its manufacturing industries, although still retaining leadership in a narrow range of industries such as aerospace and pharmaceuticals, restored the competitiveness of its car manufacturing industry under foreign ownership, but also supported the growth of an overblown financial services sector and is now trying to rebalance the economy. Ideologically, politicians have refrained from actively supporting an explicit industrial strategy arguing that the market knows best, although they did play a significant part in supporting the growth of the financial services.

Given the magnitude of the changes that we have documented in the productive system's demand for skills, what is surprising is that the UK's skills policy has changed so little. The policy framework has been to rely on the market to deliver the skills with the assumption that if this is sorted out, everything else will be looked after and 'prosperity' will come. The heavy investment in human capital has rapidly increased the supply of highly educated labour. While this has undoubtedly helped provide the base for knowledge-intensive production and higher-level work, it has now run into problems with the supply of highly skilled labour outstripping the ability of the national economy to generate high-skilled jobs. Indeed, the growth of the low-skilled service jobs merely serves to aggravate the problems.

As a way out of this dilemma the government have committed themselves to helping ensure that the economy competes at the high-skilled end of the continuum. Yet given the belief in the efficiency of the market in delivering solutions, there is little that government agencies could do to improve skill use by employers, apart from exhorting them to 'value' training and make more effective use of their employees. Even the most recent demand side policy proposals to provide support for HPWPs to encourage skill use and innovation are unlikely to work because they fail to address the basic drivers of skill use, namely business strategy. It is changes in business strategy that have created massive changes in the process of skill formation during the last two decades. This has a number of important consequences for skills policy.

The first is that skills will be the basis for the current and future competitive advantage in these industries. If these are the basis for a high-skills economy, then ways must be found to nourish and enhance the development of these industries as it is their business strategies that are driving the growth. The second is that a skills policy which is supply driven has not and will not deliver the support required for these industries to grow and prosper across a range of markets. It means challenging the conventional economists' view of the firm that is very much like a black box, that employer decision making is likely to be the most appropriate (optimal) response to market signals, leaving the policy maker as a mere spectator on the side-lines, cheering on those firms that are seen to adopt the 'correct' high-skills strategy.

What is required is a better understanding of the decision making processes in firms with regard to skill issues embedded in a view of the firm as an active agent in the process of competition. This means challenging the philosophy that government must not interfere with questions of job quality and job design as these are the exclusive province of the employers. Once the relationship between business strategy and skills utilisation is understood, it is clear that this is an area where there is a great deal that governments can do to support and enhance the performance of business while developing the skills of employees. We take this as our central task in the following chapters. Once this is achieved we can think of reconstructing a skills policy that will take the enhancement of skills as a central component of future prosperity.

Notes

1 There is an extensive literature in the UK and USA that examined this 'fit' between the outputs of the education system and the demands of the economy (see, for example, Ashton and Field, 1976; Willis, 1977; Bowles and Gintis, 1976).
2 Green (2013) provides an extensive discussion of the whole issue of skills matching (Ch. 8) and over-education (Ch. 11).
3 For a detailed critique of UK policy based around these issues, see Keep (2009), Keep and Mayhew (2010), Keep (2011) .

2

THE LONG WAIT IS OVER: LINKING BUSINESS STRATEGY TO SKILLS

What business strategy is all about; what distinguishes it from all other kinds of business planning – is, in a word, *competitive* advantage. Without competitors there would be no need for strategy, for the sole purpose of strategic planning is to enable the company to gain, as effectively as possible, a sustainable edge over its competitors.

Keniche Ohmae (1982: 36)

Many times in my life I have seen how one individual can make a big difference, particularly when working in a great team. The quality of our people and of our teams is our most valuable resource, particularly in today's changing world where knowledge flows round the globe with lightning speed and is easily available.

Klaus Kleinfeld, Chief Executive Officer of Siemens[1]

Ryanair's objective is to firmly establish itself as Europe's leading low-fares scheduled passenger airline through continued improvements and expanded offerings of its low-fares service. Ryanair aims to offer low fares that generate increased passenger traffic while maintaining a continuous focus on cost-containment and operating efficiencies.

Introduction to Ryanair's strategy document[2]

Overview

The focus of Chapter 2, which looks at business strategy, can be described as a little 'unusual' compared with many publications on skills. Yet, it is so central to many of our arguments in this book. Chapter 2 looks at the causal link between business strategy and its direct impact on skills utilisation. It starts by reminding us that nearly all organisations are purposive entities. They are in existence for a reason. The most crucial thing about the purposiveness of an organisation is that they have a 'game plan' to get from A to B, or to achieve some specific goals, though admittedly, this game plan may vary enormously in sophistication.

To study business strategy is generally problematic because we can approach the topic in a number of ways, some of which may by-pass any reference to skills while others may include the role of skills implicitly within the analysis. In this chapter, we will demonstrate that many of the previous attempts to link business strategy to skills utilisation have ultimately failed. They failed not because they were not analytically useful. They failed because they had allowed other foci to become the primary drivers of the analysis, e.g. business growth is the key concern of business strategy while skills are automatically implied by the strategy adopted. In this sense, we argue that the role of skills vis-à-vis business strategy has never received a proper analytical treatment. Our strategic skills model in this book is therefore one of the rare attempts, if not the only attempt, to link business strategy explicitly to skills utilisation.

Upon examining previous efforts, one may find that not only did they treat skills as unproblematic, there were also no distinctions made between skills acquisition and skills utilisation. These two concepts are hugely consequential on the performance of an organisation. Thus, the human capital approach assumes these two concepts are the same, which is clearly a big assumption to be made, and it is one that is often at odds with reality. A proper analytical treatment of skills and business strategy, as advocated in this book, will have to address how business strategy is linked to these two concepts in order to provide an analytical insight into the role of skills and how skills impact on business performance. Chapter 2 therefore forms the beginning of our current effort.

Introduction

At a discussion with a government official, an interesting question was put to us: 'Is there any evidence that employers are prevented from taking on more innovative, productive strategies or work organisations because of a lack of skills in their workforce?' This question is very clear and seems reasonable, but given the argument put forward in this book, it is the wrong question, laden with inappropriate assumptions. Whatever answer is given, it is unlikely to enhance the effectiveness of policies.

This is a typical question based on the assumptions of 'supply side' economics. It assumes that it is a natural decision for employers to adopt the latest, the most effective and innovative work practices, and the only constraints on such decisions are the availability of higher skills. Implicitly, other factors, if they matter, may play only a small part. The old axiom 'supply creates its own demand' is the crux of this question. It totally overlooks the crucial role played by business strategy. Here, we need to recognise that business organisations are purposive entities that are driven by a set of structures, environment (market and socio-political), the available technology and even personal business philosophy.

The statements at the beginning of the chapter suggest that the relationships between business strategy, competitiveness and skills are often acknowledged as closely related and interdependent. In everyday discussions we accept that skills are an important part of competitiveness. We may also accept that business strategy acts as a crucial link between competitiveness and skills. However, how it all works often turns out to be a little like a 'black box'. This is because depending on who you ask, you will get a different explanation of what business strategy is. Worse, as we will see in the following discussion, with almost 70 years of strategy research behind us, skills hardly enter business strategy research in any explicit form. If we look hard enough, we may see skills as a component of competitiveness, dancing around the corner of the different business strategy models, but it just misses the entrance to the centre stage, every time.

Who or what is to blame? There is certainly no shortage of intellectual capability or rigour. After all, we have the almost unanimous acceptance of the importance of skills from all key stakeholders and frequent acknowledgement of how central the concept of skills is to business or organisational success. The origin of the problem turns out to be the consequences of a combination of historical events. While most of these events might have led to an acknowledgement of the role of skills, the obsession of academics and consultants with cost control and investment planning models meant that at every turn the role of skills failed to be incorporated into the strategy research model as an explicit element. This obsession can be found in the two broad components of strategy research: one deals with the so-called 'corporate' strategy, while the other examines strategy at the 'business level'. Also, while the former tries to answer questions concerning what, where and how companies gain competitive advantage, the latter mostly focuses on how to gain a competitive advantage.

What we argue is that the omission of skills from the analysis was mostly due to the predominant focus of the analysis being on aspects of the market environment, while other factors regarded as internal to the organisation (which include skills capability) were treated as generally unproblematic. We demonstrate this by tracing the historical development of these major research eras. This shows how the strategy models in the post-Second World War era were driven by the needs of big businesses, the commercial concerns of the dominant consulting firms and the needs of academics to identify models to explain business strategy within the 'neo-market' framework. We build on Pankaj Ghemawat's (2002) excellent analysis of the historical development of strategy research in the USA, where much of the business research was carried out. We augment Ghemawat's analysis by examining the reasons why skills were omitted from high-profile strategy research and show how subsequent research is opening up new possibilities for skills to be integrated back into the analysis.

Time for re-examining market forces again: strategy attempts to shape the market

For a long time in the 19th century, the central position of market, free trade and laissez-faire capitalism reigned supreme. However, the irony was that as capitalism developed there was a tendency for firms to reduce in number and grow in size. Eventually this led to huge 'corporations' operating in many markets, both nationally and internationally, selling a wide range of products and services. The size of such large corporations became a threat to competition and reduced the ability of markets to function for the benefit of the consumers. However, academics such as Chandler (1962) argued that this growth in the size of firms was an inevitable consequence of capitalism associated with improved transportation (e.g. railroads in the USA), new technology, rising prosperity and consumption.

With these developments a new form of organisation – the so-called 'M-form' or multi-divisional corporations – began to appear in the USA. For Chandler, the most important ingredient to support this new form of organisations with their growing complexity and operational needs was the emergence of a new workforce, the 'professional managers'. In a later book, *The Visible Hand*, Chandler (1977) proclaimed that Adam Smith's 'invisible hand' had been replaced by 'managerial capitalism' with the emergence of M-form organisations. Chandler argued that the emergence of professional managers meant that firms were now in control of decisions that would ultimately shape the present and future trajectory of their business. Firms had no reason to remain as passive participants in the markets in which they operated. These developments had major implications for the strategy–skills–competitiveness black box that we want to tackle. The first implication concerned the increasing attention and emphasis on business strategy that occurred in these M-form organisations. The second was the increasing importance of American business schools and consulting firms in developing these strategic models because there was a huge demand for them.

As businesses became more complex, business strategy was seen as a 'scientific' way of tackling the problems of running large businesses. But of course, as we will see later, this concept of strategy, in the form that became widespread in the USA, was about 'identifying' and 'taking advantage' of market imperfections in order to create sources of competitive advantage. Over time, some M-form organisations were even able to change their competitive environment. Peter Drucker argued that

> [managing] implies responsibility for attempting to shape the economic environment, for planning, initiating and carrying through changes in that economic environment, for constantly pushing back the limitations of economic circumstances on the enterprise's freedom of action. (Drucker, 1954: 11)

Drucker's argument implied that the crucial role of the manager was determining strategic planning, which could alter a business's competitiveness position. As such, professional managers at the turn of the 19th century began to look for some 'new toys' in order to enhance the future competitiveness of M-form organisations. This led to the formal development of strategic tools by business schools and consulting firms in the USA. The early attempts at designing strategic models for managers unsurprisingly focused mostly on providing tools to distinguish profitable decisions from 'less profitable' ones, as managers tried to manage different market and product portfolios. This form of strategic tool and the research that went with it had no skills elements incorporated into the model when it came to competitiveness, because of its focus on financial and investment outcomes. However, it had significant consequences for skills in operational terms: that is, the relevant content of skills in ensuring the profitability of the product markets that the firm entered.

However, before we examine this particular development, it is important to point out that academic research in business strategy could have provided an opportunity for incorporating skills into their models, but this opportunity was lost due to other events. For example, the orthodoxy of free-market principles led to an exclusive focus on identifying conditions for avoiding 'abnormal profits' (monopoly power) in the pre-war strategy research in academia. Whilst skills were implicit in the model, it was more important to identify the future (product) positions for the firm that were deemed to be competitive. Other reasons might include the assumption that if skills were required for the operation of the business, employers would simply train the workers. So it was not a concern, at least in principle. In other words, what was 'needed' would be included as part of the cost of a viable business. This might provide an explanation for the frequent omission of skills in the business strategy models that we observed.

Business strategy via 'distinctive competence': understanding your company's strengths

The Harvard Business School was established in 1908 at a time when the M-form of organisation was making rapid progress. The School was known for pushing students to think about the relationship between their knowledge of the industry in which they were located and the competitive factors they faced. This method was later formalised by a professor of manufacturing, John MacLean, who employed the use of 'industry notes' and 'company cases' in order to identify competitive environments and the effect of business strategies (Ghemawat, 2002). The exercise was to identify an organisation's 'distinctive competence', which would act as the basis for competitiveness. This was essentially a case study method. It is not clear whether skills always formed part of the focus of this approach, which concentrated on 'competence'. While this was a very useful approach for managers to provide greater clarity in their strategic thinking, the methodology also suffered from difficulties in defining distinctive competence. This could be in anything, from financial, technological and marketing, to skills.

By the 1960s, this method of teaching within the Harvard Business School, especially under the 'Business Policy' course rubric, focused mainly on matching a company's 'strengths' and 'weaknesses' with its 'opportunities' and 'threats' – a method that became known as the 'SWOT' analysis. The former two elements, strengths and weaknesses, were meant to underpin what the 'distinctive competence' might be, while the latter two, opportunities and threats, attempted to identify and manage risks.

SWOT did not entirely resolve the definition problems of 'distinctive competence' because competence is very broadly defined here, but it turned out to be quite remarkable in its popularity amongst managers and business consultants. This popularity came from the fact that SWOT provided managers with a tool to visualise their competitive environment and what might be the possibilities for strategic/operational action. This is of course the reason why the tool is still used by many people today. Within the SWOT framework, there were clearly opportunities for strategy research to incorporate the role of skills. However, in reality, SWOT was frequently used as an investment tool that tried to distinguish relative risks between investment portfolios. As such, SWOT became a popular tool for strategic decisions at the 'corporate' level, determining which markets and products an M-form company should go into.

The 1960s were also a time of corporate diversification and technological change. Large American corporations were spending more than ever through long-term investment. The demand for more sophisticated strategic tools rose. Igor Ansoff (1965), who is often credited as being the 'father of strategic management', responded with a refined version of SWOT. He used the same logic as SWOT and constructed a series of concrete product market questions for managers who were evaluating their future strategic positions. The answers to these questions would form a competitive position within a grid that was also known as the 'product-mission' (or growth component) matrix.

Figure 2.1 shows the 'product-mission' matrix, which reflects Ansoff's (1965) assumption that current activities have a strategic bearing on the future direction of expansion in terms of potential risks. In this sense, Ansoff was advocating 'sticking to the knitting', but what he really tried to get at was the connection between current 'core capability' – a concept that was later taken up by Prahalad and Hamel (1990) under a slightly different label, 'core competence' – and future portfolios. In other words, knowing your core capability would minimise risks.

Combining SWOT with the 'product-mission' matrix, Ansoff argued that knowing your 'core capability' is a good start, but managers would need to systematically anticipate future environmental challenges, and to draw up appropriate strategic plans in relation to their own strengths while exploring new ground. Notice that under the SWOT approach, skills might have been included as a strategic consideration, if that turned out to be a part of the 'distinctive competence'. However,

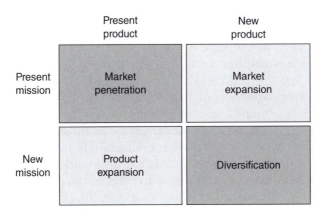

Figure 2.1   Ansoff's product-mission matrix

Source: authors

in Ansoff's new formulation, the model became preoccupied with the product and market (e.g. product markets in relation to diversification and expansion). As a result, there was little room for skills to be incorporated, even though Ansoff acknowledged the need to examine new skills, techniques and resources as part of the exercise. Thus in practice Ansoff's model was used largely to examine the future and current product market 'fit'. The omission of skills in strategy research would indeed get much worse with the ascendance of strategy consultants.

The era of strategy growth: tools to deliver financial results and steer the company through the market

The strength of 'distinctive competence' (and its later replacement, SWOT) was the ability to account for the unique characteristics of every business organisation, building on their capabilities while exploring new ground without undue risks. Ironically, this was also the Achilles' heel of the approach, because the analysis required strategies to be identified case by case (i.e. scenarios), with a huge amount of variation in their deliberations. It was complicated for many organisations. The appetite for some form of systematic methodology was growing amongst M-form organisations with many of them setting up their own 'planning' department for strategy purposes (Ghemawat, 2002).

In 1963, the Boston Consulting Group (BCG) was formed to provide a quantitative approach to solving 'corporate strategy' for M-form organisations. Bruce Henderson, BCG's founder, believed that the previous approaches were too reliant on intuition and industry-specific experience, which was fine with steady growth. However, in a rapidly changing environment with new technology appearing at a much faster rate than before, Henderson argued that a new approach was needed.

In 1965, BCG developed the 'experience curve'. The experience curve was a more sophisticated version of the 'learning curve'. The learning curve was developed in the 1920s by the military who were keen on improving the productivity of aircraft manufacturing. They noticed that the direct (labour) unit cost of production tended to decrease by a constant rate – as much as 20 to 30 per cent – as the quantity of aircraft doubled. The reason for this constant reduction in unit cost was due to a combination of economies of scale and technology improvement as well as various organisational and individual learning effects. While the learning curve only looked at labour unit cost, the experience curve factored in all relevant costs (e.g. capital, administration, marketing, R&D). In reality, the learning curve and the experience curve only differed in detail, but not in principle.

The implication of the experience curve was that if a firm were able to gain market share over its competitors, it would gain a cost advantage. On evaluating various business options (markets or products), an M-form organisation could model its pricing, marketing and production scenarios to justify a particular (long-term) investment option. This meant comparing the different experience curves of the different product markets.

It is not difficult to see that the experience curve worked on a set of static assumptions. For example, the model made no allowance for the behaviour of the competitors. What if they all pursued very similar strategies? In fact, the more rivals that pursued the same strategy, the more costly it would be to gain market shares for all rival, which would also lead to a lower rate of return to investment. Likewise, the experience curve model relied to a great extent on the advance of technology. Once an investment in a particular form of technology was committed to, it would be difficult to 'switch' within the short term, as loan capital had to be paid back and the cost of switching might be prohibitive. New entrants to the same segment of the market would benefit from the new technology, and this would make all the previous calculations irrelevant.

From the skills perspective, the experience curve had little in the way of a specific contribution to offer. Like distinctive competence before it, the experience curve could have incorporated an explicit component of skills as part of the learning effects. But in practice, consultants with financial and marketing backgrounds sold the experience curve to M-form organisations as a form of corporate investment planning tool. Everything was expressed in terms of costs of entry, prices and units produced. Skills (and for that matter, work processes and work practices) were not an explicit element that explained competitive behaviour and outcome, but they were part of a group of (unknown) learning effects that brought about the constant reduction of costs. In fact, the experience curve was a vast simplification of a complex competitive environment, created mainly for quantification and investment planning needs. Arguably, the learning curve was not necessarily about the strategic use of all resources and capabilities. Indeed, Bruce Henderson of BCG once described the experience curve as 'the business of selling powerful oversimplifications' (Henderson, 1979: 6).

On analysing the structure of the experience curve, Day and Montgomery, concluded:

> While [the experience curve's] appeal as an organizing framework remains high, there is a realization that the experience curve effect is itself a product of underlying scale, technology and learning effects. Whether the experience curve is strategically relevant depends initially on whether these three effects are influential features of the strategic environment. (1983: 56)

Despite these fundamental issues, the impact of BCG's experience curve was significant. It triggered off an unprecedented growth in business strategy focusing on cost–market share–profit modelling, and with it the arrival of McKinsey, one of the most influential consulting firms.

The dominance of financial planning as the basis for business strategy evolved further with the arrival of 'portfolio analysis' in the 1970s. Some would argue that the 'powerful oversimplification' was about to get worse (Ghemawat, 2002: 46). Portfolio analysis was essentially a two-by-two 'growth share' matrix, differentiating markets in terms of their potential for growth against the company's potential market share (see Figure 2.2). The tool worked at the level of business units within a large organisation. BCG's consultancy practice would identify the experience curves for every business unit within an M-form organisation. Then the consultant would compare their relevant potential by plotting them on the growth–share matrix.

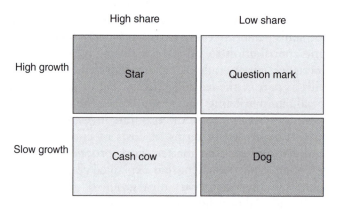

Figure 2.2   The Boston Consulting Group's growth–share matrix

Source: authors

Within the growth–share matrix it is not difficult to see that any 'sensible' business strategy would leave the 'dog' business and instead put resources behind the 'cash cow' and 'star activities'. Once they had enough 'star' and 'cash cow' businesses, then the company would feel safe to gamble with the 'question mark' ventures.

Before long, McKinsey, which had adopted a similar consulting approach to that of BCG, came up with a nine-block growth–share matrix because many companies felt that the four-state matrix was not sufficient to describe the possibilities of some of the business units. The principle of the nine-block design was the same as the BCG four-state design, but there were more in-between states on the grid. By the end of the 1970s, virtually every consulting firm had some form of growth–share model. The widespread use of the growth–share model to complement the experience curve also meant that business strategy was more-or-less cemented into the cost–market share–profit model with little attention paid to skills, or for that matter human resources (HR) in general, within the organisation.

One may ask why this was the case. After all, more skilled workers must matter to the market share of the business. The problem is the methodology. Supporters of the experience curve and growth–share models would argue that skills would be part of the cost component – as we pointed out earlier – the higher the skills involved, the higher would be the cost (in principle), or the bigger the HR department. So the assumption was that skills were already 'factored in'. However, the model was also implicitly saying that it would be important to minimise cost in order to have a greater competitive advantage over your rivals. But ultimately, we cannot escape the fact that the basis for the popularity of the experience curve and the growth–share matrix was the need to distinguish different investment opportunities for M-form organisations. Hence, up to this point, business strategy research had little formal treatment for skills, although skills were recognised as important. Instead, skills were identified as costs. Moreover, these were firms that were still using Taylorist forms of mass production in which the skills of manual workers were treated as costs. In this sense the popularity of these tools and the lack of attention to incorporating skills into the strategic tools reflected the reality of the prevailing type of productive system.

The rise of consultancy-driven strategy research also meant that business strategy had a 'universalist' orientation: that is, the existence of a 'superior' business growth strategy. However, in 1978, Raymond Miles and Charles Snow published *Organizational Strategy, Structure, and Process*, which followed a very different approach to understanding business strategy. This book turned out to be far more significant than previous attempts. The Miles and Snow model moved the universal nature of business strategy to 'strategic equifinality'. The concept of strategic equifinality means that there are more ways than one to build a competitive strategy as they are also capable of changing over time. But more importantly and unlike previous attempts, the four strategic types under the Miles and Snow model come very close to creating a theoretical link between business (or in their context, competitive) strategy and skills utilisation.

At the heart of the Miles and Snow model, the four competitive strategy types describe all competitive behaviours at the firm level. These four types are:

1. *Defender* – prospering through stability, strengthening what you know best, efficiency and reliability.

2. *Prospector* – prospering through finding and securing new market opportunities.

3. *Analyser* – prospering through being a defender but taking on risks like a prospector in a cautious manner.

4. *Reactor* – failing to prosper because of the inability to establish one of the three strategies above.

What is most interesting in the Miles and Snow model is that it postulates that all businesses will have to deal with critical decisions on three operational problems in order to attain one of the first three strategic types. These decisions are known to form the 'adaptive cycles' that shape business strategy. Thus, all businesses have to deal with:

- the *entrepreneurial* problem (choosing and adjusting the product market domain, or what the business is about);

- the *engineering* problem (producing and delivering the product, or how the product is produced, e.g. technology, division of labour etc.); and

- the *administrative* problem (designing roles, systems, relationships and work processes; or how we work together in the workplace).

Businesses have to continually work through those problems in order to pursue their chosen strategy (e.g. being 'defender'), tweaking their systems as they go through each adaptive cycle. The successful businesses are the ones that manage to align their systems and resources to resolve those problems. Those who fail to do so become the 'reactors'. These latter organisations struggle to prosper until they manage to resolve those problems or they will cease to exist in due course.

At the theoretical level, the skills implications are interesting in the Miles and Snow framework for organisational competitive behaviour. The defender is expected to have a strong internal structure to support training because they want to strengthen a system and values that have proved to be working. The prospector is expected to explore new markets and new ideas. They may not always have the ready skills to do that, so a lot of their skills may have to be brought in from outside. The analyser has a mixture of the two. However, other than the reactor, skills utilisation is expected to be high in all other cases.

The adaptive cycle suggests that the structure of a business is therefore linked to its work processes and business strategy. While there is a clear recognition that business strategy, structure and process will influence HR matters, the Miles and Snow model does not explore how business strategy impacts on skills requirements, acquisition, utilisation and retention. The Miles and Snow model came very close to establishing the theoretical link between skills and business strategy but ultimately failed to do so explicitly. Instead, the model inspired a series of other forms of competitive strategy research. The 'generic strategy' (cost leadership, differentiation and focus) by Michael Porter was one of the most prominent to come.

Strategy for competitive advantage: creating barriers to entry

Although much of the strategic research comes from management science, economists – especially those who were interested in competitiveness – have also made attempts to get a handle on business strategy. Competitive strategy is not generally an area where economists feel at home. This is because competitive strategy may suggest finding means of restricting entry and perpetuating a state of 'advantage' that leads to higher than 'normal' return. A perfectly competitive market would predict a normal profit for all in the long run. In other words, finding a sustainable competitive advantage might go against the fundamental principle of free-market economics where perfect competition should ideally be the state of play. But this did not stop some economists from venturing into the realm of strategy. For example, in the 1950s, economists such as Joe Bain, at Harvard University, identified some persistent reasons (e.g. economies of scale, product differentiation, legal patent and high research and development costs) so that 'established sellers can persistently raise their prices above competitive levels without attracting new firms to enter the industry' (1956: 3). Bain and others such as Edward Mason and Edward Chamberlin popularised a new strand of economic research – also known as 'industrial organisation' (IO) – which examined the consequences of 'real-world frictions' that impeded the appearance of perfectly competitive markets.[3]

Despite disagreement over what constituted 'real barriers' to entry (e.g. Stigler (1968) argued that economies of scale are not a true barrier) hundreds of research articles appeared in the 1970s to identify cases of entry barriers as a form of competitive advantage. Thus, the general results seemed to confirm that some industries were persistently profitable and entries were rare, though there were still debates about which structural variables were the most important in bringing about barriers to entry (Goldschmid et al., 1974).

The original IO research, especially under the Business Policy Group at Harvard, was meant to be a course for policy makers to understand how frictions in the market occurred. The intention was for policy makers to use this knowledge to minimise excessive profits in order to maintain a competitive market environment. This meant that IO research had very little impact on business strategy research because business strategy is about above-normal profits brought about by some form of structural competitive advantage, just the opposite to what IO research wanted to do.

All that was to change when Michael Porter published *Competitive Strategy* in 1980. It was like a touch of genius; Porter turned IO research on its head. Porter realised that IO research could identify structural forces that impeded competition, but companies could equally use these forces as a form of competitive advantage. Thus in Figure 2.3, if a company could control some of the five forces, it might be able to create some persistent competitive advantage and maintain an abnormal level of profit for a significant period of time without fear of others entering.

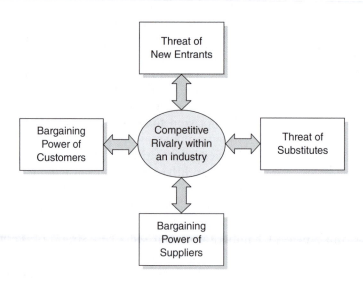

Figure 2.3   Porter's (1980) five forces of competitiveness

Source: authors

The five-force model was often used as a qualitative assessment on various dimensions of competitive conditions. Like the experience curve before it, the five-force model is determined by the conditions of the product market, though the four forces (outside the circle) in Figure 2.3 are extended concepts, compared with its predecessor (e.g. suppliers, substitutes etc.). The circle contains market share, rate of growth and a few more additional items, such as the degree of concentration and mode of competition. Market share and rate of growth were of course the main components of the experience curve and the portfolio analysis.

In the case of M-form organisations, Porter insists that the first fundamental issue in corporate strategy is the selection of lines of business in which the company should compete. Thus, each business unit has its own, industry-specific five-forces analysis. While the model gives an extensive analysis of the industry competitive conditions, it has no element incorporating the capability (e.g. skills base or other forms of competitive assets) of the organisation concerned because that is actually outside the focus of the model. Instead, the five-force model is about creating value through structural change that leads to barriers to entry.

But the five-force model is also one of those interesting ideas with surprises. In managerial terms, the model contains a sub-analysis, which focuses on 'value chain creation'. So the generic value chain that most companies face is one that contains supply logistics, operations, distribution logistics, marketing and after-sales service. The idea is that once these activities are identified in a real context, we can see if there is a performance (often denoted by cost) link that exists between any two activities. Porter sees this as the opportunity to identify 'firm-specific' activities that can be 'optimised'. Optimisation, in Porter's definition, may lead to process re-engineering or outsourcing. 'Value' is then created via a firm-specific cost advantage, quality improvement or differentiation. It is here that for the first time along the long line of strategy research that we come very close to examining skills in the strategic context. Both quality improvement and differentiation – two important elements in the strategic skills model in this book – may have significant skills implications and often form part of the competitive advantage. However, in practice, Porter's model on strategy is still primarily about unpacking the 'attractiveness' of an industry in the first instance, and then creating special competitive advantage through 'tweaking' the competitive environment around the firm. To some extent, this echoes Edward Mason's (another Harvard IO academic) research 40 years before Porter in which he argued that the competitive structure of an industry is closely related to the conduct of the buyers and sellers (Mason, 1939, cited in Ghemawat, 2002).

By the 1970s and 1980s, the cumulative effects of the BCG's experience curve and Harvard's IO analysis gave rise to a variety of refinements to Porter's original five forces. For example, the cost analysis became ever more sophisticated, involving cross-functional economies, and not just within a single line of business. Customer analysis was to reconsider the alternative indicators other than costs. By the end of the 1980s, Porter's framework of competitive strategy, involving cost leadership, quality enhancement or differentiation, was widely accepted as the standard way of thinking about strategy. Much of this model remains influential amongst many large organisations today.

So far, two things are quite clear. First, much of the theoretical development from the business schools and consultancy firms failed to incorporate the effects of skills, though the importance of skills was implicitly acknowledged. Second, not all their work was in vain, as there were glimpses of opportunities dotted around each stage of further development concerning business strategy. Early studies actually laid some important groundwork for the management schools to build on. We can see that skills became a more explicit component of business strategy from the 1980s onward as mature forms of mass production became more widespread and knowledge-intensive production started to become significant.

The resource-based view of the firm: the entrance for skills

Instead of looking at the product market when developing strategic tools, one could examine the capability of the organisation and examine strategic possibilities. The 1980s was a time when HR management began to attract attention. The publication of *In Search of Excellence* by another group of McKinsey consultants, Robert Waterman and Thomas Peters in 1982 captured a large following of academics and managers alike. Waterman and Peters came from the 'structure' consultancy division in McKinsey, which had always played a secondary and supporting role to the main 'strategy' division. *In Search of Excellence* talked about the seven 'S's: structure, systems, style, staff, skills, strategy and shared values. Suddenly, internal elements in organisations were seen to be important in driving competitiveness.

Were human resources, or internal resources in general, new to the business strategy research? From our previous discussion, it is clear that 'human resource' management as a complementary part of business strategy was not new at all. While previous attempts were often constructed around product market factors, the resource factors were always embedded in the analysis (e.g. in SWOT), though not explicitly formalised. They were certainly not treated as the driving forces in business strategy.

Birger Wernerfelt, who is often credited as the pioneer of the resources-based view (RBV), argued that product market factors and internal resources were essentially 'two sides of the same coin' (1984: 171). After Wernerfelt there were a number of variants of RBVs, but they all argued that superior product market position was derived from tangible and intangible firm-specific assets (Connor, 2002). Under a slightly different name, 'core competence', Prahalad and Hamel (1990) criticised previous approaches (e.g. under the 'growth–share' models) for focusing too much on strategic business units (SBUs) and product markets while ignoring underlying core competencies. This led to many instances (in their case studies) of under-utilisation of resources, under-investment in core activities and 'bounded innovation' – a problem of the 'tyranny of the SBU' (Prahalad and Hamel, 1990: 86). They asked 'How strange that SBU managers should be made to compete for corporate cash but never for key people?' (1990: 87). The 'core competence' concept was insightful, as Prahalad and Hamel had demonstrated systematic under-utilisation of internal resources under the SBU approach (for cost and investment planning).

If core competence succeeded in identifying HR as being important in competitive strategy, then another subsequent variant of RBV, 'dynamic capabilities', built on this emphasis. Teece and Pisano (1994) and Teece et al. (1997) argue that internal competitive capabilities should not be treated as 'given'. They ought to be developed over time:

> If control over scarce resources is the source of economic profits, then it follows that such issues as skill acquisition, the management of knowledge and know-how ... and learning become fundamental strategic issues. It is in this second dimension, encompassing skill acquisition, learning, and accumulation of organizational and intangible or 'invisible' assets ... that we believe lies the greatest potential for contributions to strategy. (Teece et al., 1997: 514)

RBV brought people and skills to the forefront of the discussion of competitive strategy. But did the discussion lead to a formalisation of skills in business strategy? Oddly, no. While RBV was insightful and directly relevant to linking business strategy to skills, in practice it proved to be very difficult to form a coherent methodology for managers to implement.

The appeal of the RBV approach quickly fell away once managers realised that this was not that different from the previous Harvard 'distinctive competence' approach developed around the 1950s. RBV relied on identifying intrinsic and inimitable resources (assets) that were both valuable (i.e. sought-after) and unique. These resources were generally classified into 'tangible' and 'intangible'. In practice, the intangible resources could be almost anything, ranging from tacit knowledge, institutional culture, metaphysical insights to complementarity or the 'people'! Many of these resources were highly generalised and qualitative in nature. Not only did managers fail to find guidance to create strategic assets, the very key items such as skills and learning simply fell through the gaps created by abstract concepts. The concept of RBV seems to raise more questions than answers: What determines strategic assets? How do we recognise a strategic asset? And how do we develop intangible strategic assets? (Connor, 2002: 313). The irony is that this time round, we are not even talking about cost-planning and market-share driven models. We are dealing with an HR model of some sort, but skills still failed to make an explicit analytical entrance.

It is no coincidence that the concern with HR as a component of competitive strategy should appear at this stage. It was during this period that new forms of productive system were being introduced with the spread of Japanese management practices and new forms of employee involvement in which the behaviour and skills of manual workers were becoming more crucial for the company's performance, but just how skills entered the equation remained unclear.

More recent attempts: understanding the role of skills

The skills debate and research have intensified in the last 15 years. The result is that there is now a greater recognition of the importance of the 'demand' for skills in the workplace. For example, we are now increasingly dissatisfied with using educational qualifications as a proxy for skills, because qualifications are what employees come with but not necessarily the skills that they use. Indeed, whether a workplace is organised in such a way to enable their employees to utilise their skills to the full is now seen as a key element for business performance and competitiveness. Not surprisingly, some researchers have begun to look at the impact of business strategy on skills utilisation.

Mason's (2004) early research in this area found that there was a high correlation between skills requirements and product market strategy (PMS) adopted at the sector and firm levels. Mason's initial approach was to investigate whether countries have different skills equilibria. However, his results seemed to suggest that it would be more appropriate to talk about skills acquisition as an outcome rather than an equilibrium. For the same reason Wilson and Hogarth (2003) preferred the term 'skill trajectories'. Mason went on to argue that:

> Enterprises' efforts to upgrade product strategies would do well to make use of concepts such as path-dependence which are emphasised in the evolutionary economics literature. This approach would do justice to the empirical reality of enterprises searching for profitable product strategies and progressively learning over time what complementary investments (e.g. in skills formation) are needed to make a success of particular strategies. (2004: 46)

The corollary of Mason's argument was that it would be important to recognise the extent to which there is a low demand for skills. He argued that public policy would do well if it were able to 'encourage more companies to move into higher value-added skill-intensive product or service areas' (2004: 46). Here it is important to notice that Mason's research moves the skills policy mantra from market failure as a criterion for intervention to one of influencing business strategy in order to create high value-added economic activities. This is an area of crucial importance to the future direction of skills policies. We will return to this discussion in Chapters 5 and 6 of this book.

Using the National Employer Skills Survey for England and a refined methodology, Mason (2011) reported a similar result, namely that product market strategy and skills were highly correlated for the period between 2009 and 2011. His data provided greater detail than the previous study. For example, establishments with an upper quartile PMS measure would have a mean skills demand level between NVQ3 and NVQ4 (UK national qualifications system) and this compared with a mean skills demand of NVQ3 for establishments with a PMS measure below the upper quartile. High-level PMS scores are also associated with a greater incidence of skill upgrading, less incidence of skill gaps and a higher level of training provision.

The realisation of the importance of business strategy is also apparent in the recent workplace learning literature. Felstead et al. (2009) focus on the significance of the 'business context' in the nature of learning within the workplace. They propose the 'Working as Learning' Framework (WALF). WALF consists of three elements that can affect learning at work:

1. the productive system

2. task discretion

3. the 'expansive/restrictive' characteristics of the learning environment.

These three elements are not new. They are all derived from previous research. However, this latest large-scale research on workplace learning makes an explicit link between the nature of productive systems, task discretion and workplace learning. Whilst the concept of business strategy was never formalised in the study, the concepts of productive systems and task discretion can be identified as the consequences of a particular business strategy. These contributions are important as they improve our understanding of what is determining the level of skills utilisation in the workplace and how workplace performance is obtained.

Again, it is no coincidence that the shift in focus to one of skill utilisation should occur during this most recent phase in the development of the economy as new forms of productive system associated with knowledge-intensive forms of production become one of the drivers of economic growth. In this context it is the business strategy that is determining the level of skills utilisation and what training the organisation needs to provide. This is the reason why so much of the business strategy research simply treats, rightly or wrongly, the skills development aspect of organisations as 'unproblematic'; the firm simply delivers the training its business strategy requires in order to get the ball rolling, as it were. Within the framework of business strategy, there is no assumption that employers are training less than they need. What there is, is a need to understand how business strategy underpins the demand for and utilisation of skills. That is the topic of the next section of this chapter.

In search for a new analytical model that links business strategy to skills utilisation

The strategic skills model (Ashton and Sung, 2006; Sung et al., 2009a, 2009b) provides a framework for taking forward our understanding of the relationship between business strategy and the demand for and utilisation of skills. In the process, it reconciles what at present appear to be contradictory findings in the research literature. The model starts with the firm's business strategy, which in turn shapes two other dimensions or relationships within the firm, what we refer to as the 'technical relations' (TRs) and 'interpersonal relations' (IRs) of production. At the beginning of this chapter we cited quotes from Siemens and Ryanair to highlight the contradictions in the literature, namely that some companies such as Siemens genuinely see their employees as key to their competitive advantage in the market, and others such as Ryanair see their competitive advantage as their ability to reduce costs. Workers in this business approach are simply costs, and the skills of the workers do not feature in the calculations. Why the difference? Is it that Ryanair is making a sub-optimal investment in their staff? Is Siemens over-investing in its staff or is it that Ryanair's values are different from those of Siemens? All these questions miss the point, which is that the business strategies of the two companies emphasise different ways of securing an advantage in the market and it is this that drives their demand for and use of skills.

Business strategy is seen as being constantly negotiated in a changing market environment, shaped by competitive pressures from other firms as well as a regulatory framework determined by government and its agencies (where it applies). Where our model differs from the approaches discussed previously is that the business strategy has two components. The first is the product market strategy, which determines what type of market the company seeks to compete in: for example, high value-added as opposed to low-valued added, and through the use of differentiated as opposed to standard products. The second is the competitive strategy, which spells out how the company will seek to gain a competitive advantage in the type of market it has chosen to compete in. We illustrate this in Figure 2.4.

Figure 2.4   The components of business strategy

Source: authors

Product market strategy

In defining the type of market the company seeks to compete in, the product market strategy shapes the production process: for example, whether this is a process that delivers a service to customers, as in hotels, or the provision of apps for a phone or computer, or whether it is a product such as bottled whiskey or cars. This requires substantial capital investment in the purchase of the appropriate plant and technology and once chosen most firms then remain locked into their original strategy for a number of years. This does not mean that product strategies remain static, just that they may change within the segment of the market within which they originally chose to compete. Thus Dench et al. (2000: 17) found that in the food and drinks industry the companies they interviewed were constantly adjusting their product market strategies within the segments they chose to compete in, rather than seeking to move between markets or segments of markets. Similarly, Mason (2005) in pioneering research into product market strategies also found that most firms were reluctant to change their product market strategy and only attempt to move between market segments within their own industry.

The product market strategy in turn determines two other components of the production process, namely the knowledge intensity of the production process and the type of technology the company uses to structure the workflow. If you are producing whiskey then you require staff with a knowledge of the production and distribution process, and in terms of technology a distillery for the production of the liquid and a bottling plant to prepare the product for sale. These two components, knowledge intensity and technology, we refer to collectively as the TRs of production.

With regard to knowledge intensity, firms using IT to produce highly differentiated products or services, such as one-off communication and information management solutions for customers in the military or aerospace companies, are very knowledge intensive, creating new knowledge during the process of production and registering patents to secure the commercial rights to such knowledge. On the other hand, those using established technologies to produce standardised products such as food snacks have lower levels of knowledge intensity. However, while knowledge intensity and technology are linked, they do not have a deterministic relationship with each other. In other words, it is not necessarily the case that high knowledge-intensity work will always involve highly sophisticated and expensive technology. A good example here is the creative sector. Much of the work is 'brain work' and innovation – the level of technology is not necessarily 'high' by any standard. Other examples may include legal firms, higher education in certain subjects or personal banking.

With regard to the technology, this is used to structure the workflow. Where the company is producing differentiated one-off products, then the production process usually takes on the character of craft production, with the employees using their knowledge to manipulate the tools at their disposal (whether these are machine tools as in precision engineering or computers as in the infocomm sector) to create a unique product or service. At the other extreme is the situation where the employee has little or minimal control over the production process to produce standardised products, here the workflow is tightly controlled by the technology, whether that is the speed of the assembly line or the control exerted by computer programmes in call centres. In this way technology also has an impact on the division of labour.

Through these relationships the product market strategy has a direct impact on the level of skill required for the company to function efficiently (Mason, 2004, 2011). For example, in the distillery the production process requires a small number of staff with knowledge of chemistry and distilling. But for the majority of staff employed in the bottling of the product, the skill levels are not so high. They require basic literacy and numeracy and work discipline in order to service the line. We can contrast this with a company producing one-off solutions for ICT problems encountered by large organisations, where the vast majority of new entrants require the high-level problem-solving skills and IT knowledge that graduates possess. It is this that explains the huge differences in the skill levels, as measured by the qualifications of staff, that we observe between industries. For example, in the Scottish food and drink industry, 59 per cent of the workforce have level 2 qualifications or less, while in financial services only 24 per cent have level 2 or less and the vast majority have level 3 or above (Sung et al., 2009b: 8). In the United Kingdom as a whole, Figure 2.5 shows the wider picture in terms of the minimum qualification required for jobs. The requirement for a degree varies hugely across the industries. While more than half (53 per cent) of the jobs in the information and communication services sector require a degree, only 3 per cent of the jobs in the accommodation (e.g. hotels) and food sector need a degree to perform their jobs.

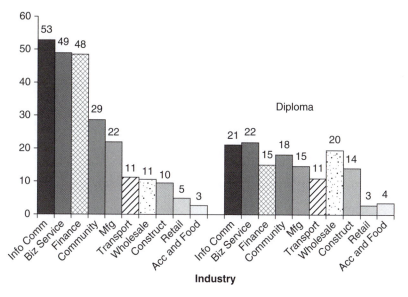

Figure 2.5 Percentages of jobs requiring degree/diploma by industry in Great Britain

Source: UK Skills and Employment survey 2012

Competitive strategy

Competitive strategies are shaped by a number of factors; these include changes in product market conditions, the degree of competition from both domestic and foreign companies, legal and contractual constraints, regulatory conditions and standards such as ISO 9000 that private firms have to meet in order to participate in the supply chain, as well as pressures from within the company and customers. However, within any one market there are a number of ways in which a firm can choose to compete. Some firms choose to secure a competitive advantage on the basis of criteria that have limited implications for their use of skills, as in the example of NIKE where value is added through clever marketing (or branding). Here, while marketing itself may be knowledge intensive, the process of mass production involved in manufacturing sportswear is predominantly not. Where skills are important is when a competitive advantage is sought through developing a unique product or service in which the quality of the product or service is crucial to its success in the market. In these circumstances the ways in which employees use their skills to secure quality in the creation of the product or the delivery of the service is crucial for success. One well-known example is that of Toyota, a company that built its reputation on the quality and reliability of its cars, which in turn depended on high levels of commitment and application of skills by its employees. In this case considerable attention was paid by the company to developing the skills of the labour force.[4]

On the other hand, competitive advantage can be sought and achieved through successfully deskilling the production process, as was the famous case of Ford in the production of its Model T. There the use of craft forms of production was replaced by the use of standardised components and the assembly line that enabled the company to reduce any reliance on employee skills and to simplify the job to enable it to use lower-skilled labour. The same process is at work today where across a number of industries the knowledge that traditionally lay in the heads of many white-collar and professional workers is being replaced by computer programmes that enable jobs in financial services, government administration and retail to be routinised or codified, and the task is to be performed by less-skilled and lower-paid labour. In the case of Ryanair, competitiveness was achieved through stripping out costs rather than deskilling.

The ways in which firms choose to make use of the skills of their employees in their competitive strategy we refer to as the 'interpersonal relations' (IRs).[5] The IRs determine how the employees are mobilised to operate the technology and function within the authority system of the enterprise. At one end of the spectrum, these relationships are what we refer to as 'people-focused'. They are used to create people-oriented skills, such as problem solving, innovation and communication skills. These are used to create products and service of the highest quality, on which the reputation of the firm and its advantage in the market rely. The human relations practices used to generate these are what are generally referred to as 'high-performance working practices' (HPWPs) or 'high-involvement practices'

(HIPs). Working practices that generate people-oriented skills usually develop skills beyond the immediate requirements implied by the TRs. At the other end of the spectrum, management practices may be geared towards the creation and use of what we refer to as 'task-oriented' skills (e.g. the simple repetitive skills associated with assembly lines or call centres). In between these extremes there are a range of other positions at which skills contribute more or less to the firm's competitive advantage.

The strategic skills model

Figure 2.6 illustrates how the strategic skills model works. It shows how business strategy, through the product market strategy and the competitive strategy, is linked to the demand for skills in two ways: through the product market strategy to the TRs; and through the competitive strategy to the IRs dimension.

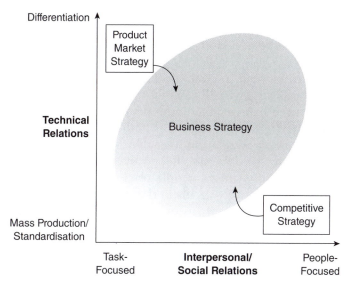

Figure 2.6 The strategic skills model

In terms of the product market strategy, if the firm chooses to market a product or service using mass or standardised production the TRs require low skill levels for the majority of the labour force. If it chooses to produce a more differentiated product or service, and it moves up the TRs dimension, then the level of skill demanded by the productive system increases. In the case of mass production, most of its recruits will be less-qualified workers, or perhaps those with minimal qualifications.

In contrast, in the case of differentiated production most of the recruits will be graduates. In general, the more differentiated the product the higher the level of skill demanded in order that the production process can operate efficiently.

In terms of the competitive strategy, if the firm adopts one of competing on costs then there are pressures on wage costs, especially those with labour-intensive technologies, to simplify or deskill the productive process. For these companies IRs are task-focused. They require the exercise of a very limited number of skills, just sufficient to perform elementary or narrowly defined tasks. Workers' behaviour in this context is tightly controlled, either through direct supervision or in the case of assembly line technology by the speed of the line. Workers have minimal discretion and there is no concern on the part of management with anything other than their performance of a limited number of tasks. At the other end of the interpersonal dimension, where the firm is competing on quality, the worker is entrusted with control and discretion over the exercise of work tasks. The worker is involved with the production process as a whole, or his or her section of it, and collaborates with colleagues on solving problems in the production process and engages in continuous learning in the workplace. Here skills are central to the firm's competitive strategy.

In general, firms tend to combine TRs characterised by mass production with task-oriented IRs, while more differentiated forms of production tend to be associated with people-oriented IRs. However, this is not an inevitable association, as both sets of relationships have a degree of autonomy in relation to each other. For example, you can have a firm where the TRs are shaped by a mass production technology but which adopt more people-oriented IRs in order to make more use of their employees' skills in their business strategy and help deliver a competitive advantage in the market. This is the dimension that the literature on high-performance working is focused on. One such example is the Glenmorangie company, which we discuss in detail in Chapter 5.

On the other hand you can have firms whose TRs are characterised by differentiated forms of production but whose IRs are characterised by a task orientation. Barrett (2005) provides examples of a series of firms in the IT industry producing differentiated products, where highly educated graduates are recruited and employed as professionals but subject to strict forms of control at work, with little support for personal or professional development. It is this relative autonomy of the two sets of relations that enables individual firms to secure an additional market advantage by moving their IRs in the direction of a people orientation. The further the movement to the right-hand side of Figure 0.1, the greater the part played by skills in the competitive strategy.

What this also means is that skills utilisation is a relative concept, as the extent of any change in skill use depends on the relationship between the TRs and IRs. Thus, as we show in Chapter 5, in the case of Glenmorangie, a company using a mass production technology, the utilisation of some HPWPs undoubtedly increased the skills of the labour force in terms of their technical knowledge of the production process and their team-working and problem-solving skills, but they still remained machine operatives because there was no major change in the TRs that would have transformed them into highly educated knowledge workers.

Technical relations

The TRs specify the basic parameters, as specified by the legal system and the use of capital (technology), which organise work. The legal system specifies contractual obligations which underscore the ways in which employers and employees relate to one another, the range of authority that the employer exercises and the obligations of both parties. These can determine the minimum pay that labour can be bought for, the conditions under which the relationship can be terminated and the sanctions the employer and employee can use during the course of that relationship. In contemporary societies these underscore a major imbalance of power between the two but they do not specify how that power can be used. Through their control of capital, employers largely determine the level of knowledge intensity of the production process and how the division of labour is structured. Take, for example, the hotel industry in Anglo-Saxon countries. This is characterised by low levels of knowledge intensity and innovation, managers require a knowledge of the industry and perhaps a management specialism such as HR or accounting, but the majority of staff such as housekeepers and waiters and waitresses require relatively low levels of knowledge. There is a limited use of new technology and conventional distinctions are used to organise the division of labour and workflow necessary to deliver the customer experience. In general, this involves a distinction between those preparing food and those providing the labour to service the rooms. This contrasts with the semi-conductor industry, for example, where the process of production is much more knowledge intensive and dependent on the skills of R&D engineers to generate new technological innovations and operatives to handle very expensive machines and products to produce high value products. For the R&D engineers, their work is usually organised in terms of project teams and structured to make the maximum use of their skills. For the operatives, the mass production of components requires knowledge of the machines and tremendous care and attention to detail to avoid what can be very expensive mistakes. In this way TRs link human activities in a pre-determined manner through the division of labour within the enterprise to produce a given product or service.

TRs are socially structured too. This means that they are designed by those with control over the relevant resources. In the case of manufacturing, the high capital costs involved in the creation of these technologies means that once they have been designed there is relatively little scope for individual workers to change the relationships involved (at least in the short run). Action by employees, either individually or collectively, will not transform mass production technologies into batch production or process production or knowledge-intensive production. Given that the technology mediates relationships between humans, there is always scope for individual employees to introduce change and modify the interaction in the course of their use. For example, through collective negotiation with the owner/managers over staffing levels or individual manipulation of the technology to adjust the speed at which the machinery runs, but in general there is relatively little scope for individual employees to introduce change in the basic structure of the technologies of the manufacturing. Where there is more scope for employees to influence change is in the case of those firms where the employees are empowered by management to modify the operation of technologies, such as the assembly line in Toyota, through the standardisation of work practices and problem solving.

The fact that in general there is little scope for individual employees to modify their use of these technologies gives the impression that they are somehow 'external' to the individual and determine their behaviour.[6] This sense of a technological imperative is reinforced by the fact that the technology which mediates the relationships does have an impact on structuring relationships between the groups involved. In the classic study of the impact of technology in the form of mass, batch and process production in the manufacturing sector of the UK, Woodward (1958) found relationships between these technologies and span of control, levels of authority, labour costs and characteristics of human relations. Later studies such as those by the Aston Group established other similar relationships (Hinings et al., 1974). Almost 50 years later, Dench et al. (2000) found a similar relationship between the technology and work organisation within firms in the food and drinks industry.

We stress the fact that these relationships appear 'external' because it is clear that in reality it is employers who are responsible for the design of the technology who largely determines the division of labour. They can use any given technology to upskill or deskill, it is not the technology which in itself is responsible for the division of labour within the workplace, all the technology does is mediate the relationships involved in the division of labour. This in turn means that the technologies are also shaped by the historical processes within which they are located. In those parts of the economy where the techniques of production are limited to hand tools and small machinery that individual employees control, then the technology does not generate these 'external' constraints because the individual employee is in control, but in these firms it is the division of labour, largely determined directly by the employer, which is more prominent as the TRs.

ICT is the most recent and radical technology, but the relationships of which it is a part are similar to those of the older technologies. In those firms producing one-off IT solutions for clients, where the staff are involved in directly creating programmes, their use of the technology is similar to the traditional craft worker as they control the use of the tools. However, where firms have created programmes designed to perform routines tasks, for example to route telephone calls and provide standard answers in a call centre, then IT functions to control the activities of the employee in the same way as the traditional assembly line, and in these circumstances the technology can appear as an 'external' constraining force, as observed by Orlikowski (1992) and no doubt will mediate similar relationships within the organisation to those observed by Woodward and others in the older manufacturing firms.

While at any one point in time these technologies appear to be relatively stable, in reality they are constantly subject to change over time. Indeed, such change represents one of the most important means for raising human productivity. Such processes of change in TRs are endemic in capitalist systems. They are sometimes introduced in a radical manner, creating what Schumpeter called 'waves of creative destruction', but are more often introduced in a more incremental manner, as when a firm introduces improvements to its computerised systems, but over time these represent a major process of change in TRs and thereby in the organisation of work.[7]

These TRs also provide the parameters which shape day-to-day activities within the workplace, and once the workers become integrated into these everyday activities they tend to become part of the background, their taken-for-granted world. Aspects of the TRs can be occasionally changed through the legal system or through the outcome of collective action, when unions may renegotiate elements of the labour contract. However, during day-to-day activities, managers and workers are not always conscious of them. They become conscious of them during periods when the potential tensions they can generate become the focus of conflict, as when an employee's behaviour breaks the contract, for example through the refusal to follow orders, or through the use of violence by employers, or more frequently when the introduction of new technology disrupts existing technical relationships.[8]

Very small firms (those employing less that 30) share the same legal relations with larger firms, which provide the basis for authority relations within the firm, although authority is exercised on a more personal basis. However, the TRs differ in some respects because very small firms in the manufacturing sector usually do not have the same capital investment in technology. This means that employees often have greater control over the use of machines and other tools, but the division of labour remains under the control of the owner. In small firms employees are therefore less likely to perceive the technology as 'external' and controlling, as is the case for many in larger mass production firms. The exception is in the case of firms using IT in the service sector where in small establishments using pre-existing programmes, as for example in the retail trade, and increasingly in medical practices, the technology can appear as external and constraining.

TRs vary not only between firms but also within firms – what some refer to as 'segmented relations' (Danford et al., 2005). Indeed, within most firms relationships in this sense will be segmented. For example, in manufacturing, a company may use a system of batch production on the shop floor to produce food products, but within parts of the office and managerial functions, computers will be used to generate one-off or customised solutions, as for example in R&D or sales. They may also be segmented in the sense that the firm may employ batch production in one unit and customised production in another. For example, a finance business may be using batch production to process sales of savings products to the general public but customised products for their wealthy clients.

TRs are also embedded in the contractual relationships between companies; these can be manifest either in the contractor specifying the type of technology employed by the sub-contractor, or indirectly by the contractors to place pressure on the supplier to produce a standardised product at ever lower prices. On the other hand, contractual relationships which structure the supply chain can lead to pressure on suppliers to change the TRs and improve the technical capabilities of suppliers. (How these impact on skill levels is explored in Chapters 3 and 5.) All this serves to remind us that TRs are continually subject to change.

While standardised systems of mass production tend to be found in industries where skills are low, it would be wrong to equate standardised and routinised production with low-cost, labour-intensive industries as they can also be found in industries where the TRs demand a higher level of education from the labour force. With developments in IT and programming, standardised production is also now being developed and used in financial services for the back office functions as well as for call centres in the service industries generally. Originally developed to deal with routine enquiries for call centres, the programming technology, in line with the growing computing power, is enabling experts to develop programmes to handle more complex problems traditionally associated with the professions. For example, many aspects of project management have now been routinised and are dealt with by less highly educated staff (Holmes, 2008). In financial services, the same processes have been reported in transnational companies (Brown et al., 2011). There the TRs require a high level of prior learning in the form of graduate literacy, numeracy and analytic skills. Here the application of these programmes requires educated staff but no longer those with a lengthy learning experience on the job. The routinisation of work is continually expanding as firms seek to codify knowledge and thereby reduce the costs of producing and applying it, but here the TRs required to produce the service require higher levels of basic skills.

Interpersonal relations

IRs, as their name implies, are embedded in the day-to-day interaction that take place within organisations and their relationships with suppliers, collaborators and so on. They are shaped by the type of authority system characteristic of the organisation. The function of IRs is to shape the ways in which work is executed within the organisation, the way in which motivation is produced, how employee capabilities are constrained or developed and how employees relate to each other and the organisation as a whole. Within the firm they define precisely where each individual employee is located in the division of labour, the nature of the tasks required to be performed and how they are performed, their position within the system of authority and the degree of discretion exercised. They determine where a person works, what the range of interactions is that is available to them (e.g. the supervisor, colleagues, how they relate to each other and what the range of skills is that is demanded of the person). In the short term these relations being part of the system of authority are non-negotiable.

The type of authority system used by employers structures the management practices such as promotion procedures, their expectations of employee behaviour, and the sanctions and rewards use to control employee behaviour, the style of leadership and the culture of the organisation; for example, whether the company is run in terms of a strict line of command with the extensive use of sanctions such as fines, threats and dismissals, or by the use of rewards, mutual respect, extensive feedback, trust and encouragement. Informally, they are observed in the attempts by employees to impose their control over aspects of work organisation and behaviour. This can take the form of junior management resisting attempts to introduce change in their working practices, to workers, either formally or informally, using their collective action to counter the impact of management practices and exert their own control. They are all a manifestation of the underlying power relationships of the organisation. In modern organisations some of these relationships are formally structured and handled by HR departments.

Where the authority system is of the command and control type, IRs are generally task-oriented. The managers, supervisors and workers are focused on the immediate tasks to be performed. The organisations are characterised by extremely unequal power balances where managers are not interested in other aspects of behaviour apart from the ability of the worker to attend regularly and accept 'work' discipline in an unquestioned manner. Hence the importance they attach to basic skills in manual dexterity, literacy and numeracy in manufacturing and keyboard skills and numeracy and literacy in the service sector. Skill utilisation is not an issue. Rewards are usually geared to the immediate output from the job and training limited to the mastery of the basic tasks required to perform it. Supervision is often close to ensure consistency in performance.

At the other end of the spectrum, in organisations characterised by a less unequal balance of power, where control is exercised more through a collective attachment and sharing of values rather than through fear of sanctions, IRs take on a more all-pervasive form. Here workers are expected to monitor their own behaviour; managers take the form of leaders who lead by example and whose function is to facilitate the learning required to function effectively in the organisation. The senior management is interested not just in the performance of the immediate task but also in broader aspects of the workers' behaviour, in their values and their commitment to the objectives of the organisation, as this is the major source of motivation and the exercise of discretionary effort on behalf of the organisation. In this context skills are 'people-focused': the skills of relating to others, of teamworking, of emotional control, of commitment, problem solving and continuous learning within the constraints of the organisation's objectives. Skill utilisation is crucial to company performance and has to be managed. Monetary rewards are linked to overall performance and collective effort. As in command and control organisations conflict is an inherent feature of IRs, but given the less unequal balance of power this usually takes the form of individual resistance rather than a collective effort to assert control.

While employees in general have little control over the TRs, they can under certain circumstances exercise considerable control over the IRs. Where there is considerable mistrust between management and workers in the workplace, then this provides fertile grounds for employees to seek to use the IRs to further their own immediate interests. This in turn will reduce the efficiency of the organisation as a whole in that it contains at least two major factions seeking to pursue different agendas. However,

IRs can also be characterised by trust and mutual gains and under these conditions can generate mutual commitment to agreed objectives and goals and be used to stimulate collective efficiency and performance.

Institutional conditions

So far we have presented the model in an abstract manner, although we are conscious of the fact that most of the examples we have used have been from countries with an Anglo-Saxon approach to markets. There is therefore a danger that we tend to think of the TRs and IRs as they appear in these countries. This means that while we may acknowledge the centrality of business strategy in driving change along the TRs and IRs dimensions, we may fail to acknowledge the importance of cultural and institutional factors in influencing both business strategy and the form taken by TRs and IRs. Theoretically this is important in establishing the usefulness of the model in non-Anglo-Saxon contexts and in highlighting the possibilities for political action that we discuss in Chapter 6.

The importance of societal factors in structuring business systems has been well established in the 'varieties of capitalism' (Hall and Soskice, 2001) and 'societal approach' (Maurice et al., 1986) literature. This has identified a wide range of factors that influence business strategy and structure, including the characteristics of national financial systems, industrial relations systems and education and training systems. To this we must also add the process of globalisation. These conditions shape the decision making process by creating different opportunities and time constraints on managers' freedom of action. What we are concerned with here is how these impact on business strategy at any one point in time and how they shape the room for manoeuvre available to managers over time and especially in terms of how it affects the relationships between the various components of the strategic skills model.

Different national cultural and institutional conditions have a major impact on business strategies. Perhaps the most well documented example is that of Germany. There the political, institutional and cultural conditions have had a powerful impact on shaping the business strategies of many of the leading export companies. Bosch and Weinkopf (2008) highlight a number of interlocking factors that have shaped the business strategies of German companies. These ranged from the relationships between the family-owned businesses and banks that provided long-term 'patient' capital, to the availability of highly skilled workers, trained through a comprehensive apprenticeship system of on-the-job and off-the-job college-based training delivered through collaboration between the state, employers and unions. These encouraged employers to invest in R&D and created high levels of cooperation between the highly skilled workers and the engineers. All this was underpinned by a system of industry-wide agreements between the employers and unions and a system of legally enforced co-determination through which workers were represented on some of the decision making bodies of employers. This reduced the opportunities for pursuing a low value-added, low-cost strategy and encouraged the employers to move into the production of high-quality engineering products, creating what Streeck (1991) referred to as a form of 'diversified quality production'. Not all German employers followed this route, especially in parts of the service sector where many of these institutional conditions were absent (Bosch and Weinkopf, 2008), and over time some of the conditions that supported diversified quality production have changed, but it has generated a business strategy that is still pursued by many of the leading German manufacturing companies.

If we contrast this with the UK, there many employers in the service sector have traditionally had a greater range of discretion available to them in formulating their business strategy in that they were not constrained either by collective agreements with strong unions or legal responsibilities for co-determination. However, they were constrained by the organisation of capital markets, which exert pressures for short-term financial benefits. This creates downward pressures on costs and with the widespread availability of low-skilled labour this led them to find ways of routinising the production process so that they could employ less skilled, often part-time, low-cost labour and adopt a business strategy based on the delivery of low-quality, low-cost services.

While these examples demonstrate the importance of these broader societal factors in creating sustained pressure over time in shaping employers' decisions about their business strategies, these pressures can also have a differential impact on the components of business strategy, namely the competitive and product market strategies. If we take the competitive strategy component of business strategy, in early forms of mass production this was firmly under the control of the owners and managers. However, as workers organised and their unions became stronger in the West during the period of Taylorist mass production, this imposed constraints on management's ability to modify their competitive strategy. Thus when faced with better quality products being marketed by Japanese producers, some owners and managers in the UK sought to respond in kind and attempted to compete by innovating on quality, but could not shift to the right along the IRs dimension because of opposition from the unions to the changes in working practices that were deemed necessary. The conditions under which to implement these 'new' ideas could not have come until there was a change in the political situation, which did not arrive until the mid-1980s when the Thatcher government reduced the power of unions. Since then the unions' influence over employers' competitive strategy has been vastly reduced. Hence it can be argued that managers regained some of the control over competitive strategy they once had. However, not all managers have used this 'freedom' to compete in terms of quality and share their gains with other employees; as we shall see in Chapter 5, some have used it merely to intensify work. Neither are unions always a negative influence in constraining management's options, especially when management are willing to share the benefits of productivity gains, or as in the case of the German apprenticeship system, which tends to push management towards the right of the IRs dimension.

The other point about the impact of these broader factors is that they change over time and one of the most important, if not the most important factor in the current context, is the impact of globalisation. During the greater part of the 20th century when the production process was largely contained within the national economy, the process of change took on what appeared to be fairly universal characteristics that occurred within societies; what the economist Rostow (1960) referred as the 'five stages of growth' from the traditional society to the age of mass consumption. Other labour economists such as Kerr et al. (1960) identified a similar process of change associated with the development of modern technology creating a demand for higher levels of education. However, the change that took place in the process of globalisation towards the end of the 20th century changed this. The growth of global as opposed to national markets provided MNCs with new business opportunities and scope for new business strategies. They had access to capital and technology and could therefore relocate some of the technology of production to economies where economic development was low and where labour was cheap, thereby reducing labour costs. In terms of their business strategy they now had more options with regard to their product market strategy, which could now be located in regions where they could evade the costs and restrictions on the use of labour found in the older industrial countries and shift the TRs to the right (Brown et al., 2011).

Initially this strategy was confined to low value-added products, such as textiles, footwear and plastics, but with the advances made in ICT these companies developed the capabilities of modularising their TRs and were then able to locate different aspects of the production process in different countries. This meant that they could now relocate not just the production of components but also the assembly process and aspects of R&D. This change, together with the increasing control that advances in HR management provided them with over the process of skill formation, meant that both high value-added as well as low value-added components of the production process could be located in the new industrial economies. The options facing managers in terms of both IT and IRs were greatly enhanced.

There have been a number of profound consequences of these changes. In the older industrial economies, the ability of the MNCs to shift production has weakened the position of trade unions in those sectors competing in global markets. This has provided management with greater 'freedom' to choose where along the IRs dimension they locate their production. In both the older industrial countries as well as the newer ones it has enabled management to strengthen practices that are to the left-hand side of the IRs dimension, reducing worker discretion. However, the explosion of higher education in the new industrial countries has also provided the MNCs with the opportunity to locate knowledge-intensive forms of production there and to move their HR practices to the right of the IRs dimension. We explore these choices in more detail in later chapters. Meanwhile, we merely acknowledge their theoretical possibility.

From the perspective of the newly industrialising societies the consequences are equally profound. Their economies no longer have to go through a linear process or the stages of development that the previous industrial societies did. They can now leapfrog some of the stages as India has done with the development of an advanced ICT sector in a 'developing' economy, or compress the process of development much as China has done by developing the higher value-added forms of production alongside low value-added forms.

While there is no doubt that these changes in global markets are the most profound in terms of their impact on companies' business strategies, and many of their ramifications may be yet to come, we must still remember that the majority of companies and organisations operate within the context of national markets. This means that they continue to operate within the political, economic, institutional and cultural constraints we mentioned above. Yet these constraints and the relationships of which they are part are not static or fixed in an equilibrium, although that is how they might appear at any one point in time. Rather these relationships are dynamic and constantly changing, providing not just new opportunities and threats for business leaders but also for political intervention, a topic we address in Chapter 6.

Notes

1 See http://businesscasestudies.co.uk/siemens/creating-a-high-performance-culture/creating-a-high-performance-culture.html#ixzz2nHe0Ki8t (accessed 7 April 2014).

2 See www.ryanair.com/doc/investor/Strategy.pdf (accessed 7 April 2014).

3 Game theory was another area in which economists made huge inroads into theoretical analysis of strategy, though this is not entirely about business strategy. As our focus is on skills, we will not pursue this discussion here.

4 Just how Japanese companies achieved this has been well documented in Koike and Inoki (1990).

5 The distinction between technical and interpersonal relations is derived from the work of Wilkinson (1983, 2002), who used the Marxist distinction between technical and social relations. We prefer the term 'interpersonal relations' because it is more precise in that we regard technical relations to be social in character, being a product of human activity. More recently Buchanan et al. (2010) have also made use of a similar distinction but this is not linked to business strategy.

6 Orlikowski (1992) refers to this as the 'duality of technology', namely that it is a result of purposive human activities but in turn assumes structural properties and once institutionalised can shape further activity. However, the author also recognises that humans interact with the technology during use and can thereby influence and further shape that technology. This is the position we adopted.

7 There is an extensive debate in the literature on the distinction between radical and incremental innovation; see Tidd et al. (2005), who identify two dynamic capabilities, namely steady state or 'doing what we do but better' and beyond boundaries or 'doing differently', which drives radical innovation. In practice these distinctions can be difficult to identify. For a review of the literature, see Smith et al. (2011).

8 These relationships have been difficult to research and therefore ignored precisely because we cannot observe them directly through typical questionnaire or ethnographic methodologies.

3

TECHNICAL RELATIONS AND SKILL LEVELS

We will not close the rank gap with our competitors *unless employers and individuals place a high value on skills*. Skills are vital to both employment and productivity. They increase the likelihood of individuals being in employment and the wages they can earn. They increase the chance of business survival and contribute to business growth and productivity. They are a critical driver of economic growth and development. In short a strong skills base is pivotal to jobs, to productivity, to our national prosperity and to recovering inequality.

UK Commission for Employment and Skills
(2009: 6, our emphasis)

Skills were once a key lever for prosperity and fairness. Skills are now increasingly the key lever.

LEITCH Review of Skills (2006: 3)

Overview

We now move on to explore the relationship between the firm's product market strategy and the TRs, which in turn determine the level of skill and types of skills required for the production system to operate effectively. We trace the way in which changes in markets create new business opportunities which are then exploited by entrepreneurs who either innovate or adapt technologies to reorganise the production process, creating a demand for new types of jobs and the skills associated with them. Here again the nature of the business opportunities and the types of technology are shaped by social and economic conditions at any one point in time and therefore it is essential that if we are to understand them we adopt a historical perspective. Moreover, once established these ways of organising production – the TRs – can persist after the historical conditions that gave rise to them have changed. However, as market conditions and our knowledge of the production process change so too do the TRs within the firm.

We identify four types of productive system: the early industrial production, the Taylorist mass production, mature mass production and knowledge-intensive production. Each was developed to respond to new market opportunities across the world and usually in different countries. Once developed each made new demands on the skill levels of different sections of the firm's labour force, which then had implications for the demands made on the national vocational education and training systems. While these forms of industrial production were first developed in the context of markets for physical goods, they have more recently been adopted to exploit market opportunities in the growing service sector. We therefore explore how Taylorist mass production, mature mass production and knowledge-intensive production systems have been adapted for use in service sector industries in the second part of the chapter as these now represent the largest source of jobs and demands on the VET system.

Introduction

Although the quotes at the start of the chapter come from the UK, the sentiment they express is global. Increasingly governments are identifying skills as a main driver of growth, and what is seen as crucial is the value that employers and individuals place on skills. But this is only part of the story and so to understand what drives the demand for skills and especially the part played by TRs we must first make a distinction between skill levels and skill use (Ashton and Sung, 2006). 'Skill level' refers to the level of knowledge and skill employers require of the employees. At the point of entry to the firm this is usually measured in terms of the educational qualifications they require. 'Skill use' refers to the ways in which employers use and develop those skills.[1]

At the moment there is little empirical research into the relationship between skill levels and types of productive system. Yet a cursory glance at the average skill levels of employees in different sectors suggests that they are linked to the type of industry (see Figure 2.5). While certain types of productive system tend to dominate in each industry, as we shall see, it is also possible for different types of productive system to co-exist in each industry, so we have to be careful in inferring any direct causal link through these observations. However, thanks to the work of Mason on the National Employer Skills Survey in England, there is stronger evidence of a link between product market strategies and the level of skill in an establishment, which he found to be 'strongly positively correlated': 'This means that those with high product market strategy scores are also likely to register higher levels of workforce skill, whereas those with lower product market strategy scores are more likely to register lower workforce skill scores' (Mason, 2011: ii). Product market strategy is only one component of the business strategy which is the focus of our analysis but the results of this pioneering work are significant.

What our theory suggests is that the level of skill employers require at the societal level is determined by the dominant product market strategies of employers, which in turn shape the TRs of production within a specific productive process (e.g. craft, mass production, mature mass and knowledge-intensive production). It follows that the availability of skills in the market at any one time is only a secondary consideration when it comes to our understanding of what determines the employer's demand for skill at the point of entry to the firm.[2] As new productive systems develop within the economy, we witness major changes in the demand for skills from employers.

In Anglo-Saxon countries changes in demand from employers are conceived of as market changes in response to which politicians make adjustments in the education system, thereby adjusting the supply of skills to meet that demand.[3] However, in those countries with social partnership models the situation is very different as the stronger collaboration between the state, employers and workers' unions leads to the establishment of more extensive and effective systems of training that produce more highly skilled workers. In addition the unions in these countries have also been effective, to varying degrees, in blocking off low-wage, low-skills strategies among employers. As we saw in the last chapter, in Germany this has created new possibilities for employers in formulating their business and especially their product market strategies. Similarly in the Asian 'Tigers', as we saw in Chapter 1, because governments had prior knowledge of the direction of economic development from their observation of the industrial history of the West, they were able to use their political power to shape business strategies[4] and use the education and training systems to anticipate changes in demand and thereby avoid the skill shortages that occur when reliance is placed on the market to signal the change (Ashton et al., 1999).

Manufacturing

Technical relations in early industrial manufacturing production

The introduction of the new TRs associated with modern forms of industrial production first took place in the UK. The growth of national and imperial markets in the 18th century created new opportunities for entrepreneurs. The end of legal regulations, the decline of the guilds and the growth of larger markets spelt the end of craft and domestic production in many industries as entrepreneurs sought to exploit these new business opportunities by experimenting with new ways of organising business activities. Substantial wealth could be created if entrepreneurs could develop new ways of mass producing products, reducing costs and increasing productivity.

One strategy that employers adopted to respond to these opportunities was to continue to use human labour power but rationalise the production process by bringing the workers together under one roof and introduce a new, more specialised, division of labour. Thanks to the work of Adam Smith, some of the best known of these new manufacturers were the pin makers. Smith observed how, by introducing specialisation in the performance of tasks, the entrepreneur could make significant gains in productivity. He estimated that under the old system one person performing all the tasks necessary to produce a pin could produce perhaps between 200 and 300 pins per day, but by combining them together in one workplace and dividing the tasks into 18 separate tasks, then one man could produce the equivalent of 2,300 pins per day (Smith, 1776 [1970]: 113).

Another strategy that proved far more effective in the long run was to harness new power sources to mechanise forms of production. In textile manufacture, and later in other industries such as engineering and pottery, this strategy reduced the unit cost of production and enabled entrepreneurs to exploit mass markets. A third strategy pioneered by Boulton and Watt in industries such as engineering was to combine some elements of craft skills with specialisation and standardised procedures to create forms of batch production.

In textiles the new entrepreneurs such as Arkwright responded to these new opportunities by developing machinery that enabled them to deskill the entire process of production. The skills that were crucial in starting this process were those of the entrepreneur and especially his knowledge of the TRs. This is reflected in the fact that the patents or intellectual property rights were jealously guarded.

Arkwright introduced the use of water power and new machinery in the form of the spinning jenny and carding machines to centralise production in single buildings to initiate 'modern' factory production and create huge increases in productivity and profits.[5] The whole manufacturing process was now under the owner's control and the organisation of work was totally separated from family relationships. Although the units of production were initially relatively small, employing less than 1000 workers, they were still large in comparison to other contemporary units of production (Fitton, 1989). In the pottery industry entrepreneurs such as Wedgewood pioneered new ways of adding value to their products through developing marketing techniques, in his case obtaining royal approval that attracted the middle classes to his products.

For the workers what was new was their subordination to the operation of machines while performing low-skilled tasks. These TRs meant that the cheaper labour of children and women could be employed, providing a labour force that was more easily conditioned to the discipline of factory work, involving as it did 24-hour operations.[6] As late as 1838 it was estimated that only 23 per cent of workers in textiles were adult males (Hobsbawn, 1968: 68), while less than 5 per cent of all workers were over 40 years of age.[7]

The impact of these new business strategies on improving productivity was huge. At the time it was estimated by Robert Owen, another early entrepreneur, that in Arkwright's mills a 'a tiny superintendent, boy or girl, took the place of a multitude of adult workpeople', resulting in each child producing at any given time as much as 200 cottage spinners.[8]

These early forms of industrial production contained within them the seeds of many later developments, but even the use of these examples illustrates the variety of skill demands that the new processes made. Yet there was no national system of education or training provision. The supply side sources were the private schools that provided education for those who could afford to pay for it. These delivered the basic skills for those entering the management of these new establishments but their industrial skills were obtained through a subsequent apprenticeship to skilled craftsmen (Pollard, 1968: 129). Various day schools provided the basic literacy and numeracy skills for the children of the 'wealthier' section of the labouring poor or emergent working class who subsequently entered the better (more highly skilled) type of apprenticeships leading to craft occupations such as masons, carpenters, wheelwrights and engineers (Campbell, [1747]1969). Such apprenticeships provided the framework within which both theoretical and practical industrial skills were acquired. Here the only role of the state was to provide for the enforcement of the conditions of the apprenticeship.

For the new group of factory 'hands' the skills employers demanded of them were minimal. In cotton production the new spinning and carding machines reduced the skill required of young manual workers to those of tending the machines. Not even basic literacy and numeracy were required as these were still relatively small workforces by modern standards and commands and instructions could be readily conveyed by word of mouth. Indeed there is some evidence that as the new system of factory production was established on a widespread basis, literacy levels in some of the regions actually fell (Krahn, 1997). In the UK, the demand for a national system of primary education to provide universal literacy had to wait until well into the next century and came from sources other than employers.

This brief foray into the early forms of industrial production serves to remind us that at each phase in the development of the economy TRs were never uniform across the economy. Earlier forms of production co-existed with the newer forms, meaning that TRs associated with craft production co-existed with those associated with the new system of mass production. As we have seen, even within the emergent mass production system TRs differed between sectors, for example between the engineering and cotton sectors. It shows how the demand for workers with different skill levels is always a mixture of pressures from different types of TRs. Finally, it highlights how, while the new system of production involved the creation of new skills for entrepreneurs, managers and engineers, it also involved the deskilling of other occupations such as spinners and the creation of a relatively unskilled group of labourers, processes of change that continue today.

Technical relations in Taylorist assembly line mass production

The next major innovations in TRs came in the USA. This was in response to the creation of what was then the world's largest internal market, which triggered major changes in the business strategy of entrepreneurs. In the USA the growing wealth of the middle classes created a mass market for new consumer products. The sheer size of this national market was much greater than anything in the UK or other countries in Western Europe. Companies responded with business strategies designed to exploit such opportunities through developments in marketing, which helped create the new consumer demand and through the manufacture of standardised products to satisfy them.

Elements of these new TRs were to be found in earlier systems of production; as we have seen the extreme division of labour was a characteristic of the 18th-century pin manufacturers, while Bolton and Watt had appropriated part of the knowledge required for machine manufacture and introduced elementary cost-control techniques and other entrepreneurs had introduced powered factory production.

What happened in the USA was that the larger size of the market and advances in technical knowledge enabled entrepreneurs to make further advances in the area of TRs. As in earlier forms of mass production the skills that were crucial were those of the entrepreneurs, but unlike the earlier system the skill levels of professional engineers, marketing and managerial workers were now also important in securing a competitive advantage in the market, while the functioning of the bureaucracy required literate clerical workers.

Perhaps the most famous of the innovators in this phase was Ford, who created a new product market strategy aimed at reducing the cost of cars through developing a system of mass production. His techniques, centred around the use of the assembly line – which came to be known as 'Fordism' – enabled management to create long runs and generate the economies of scale required to make the new forms of production viable, again creating huge increases in productivity, thereby reducing substantially the cost of cars.

Prior to Ford's innovations, the market for cars had been very restricted as they had been assembled by small teams of highly skilled workers who crafted the component parts and where necessary modified them to fit the car. Ford brought the idea of creating interchangeable parts together with the assembly line to revolutionise the production process. The standardisation of parts made it possible to break down the assembly process into a series of relatively simple steps. Tasks were divided into their most elementary components and performed by low-skilled workers. Different components were fed into a central assembly line, with the speed of operation determined by management and workers achieving high levels of dexterity in these specific tasks, but having to work at the speed of the line. This system also placed pressure on each of the departments supplying the components to build stocks in order to ensure that the line never stopped for want of such components. By 1914 Ford's system required 13,000 workers to make 260,000 cars compared with the traditional system where over five times as many workers were required to produce the same output.[9] This enabled the company to reduce the cost of the labour component even though they paid wages that were above the average for unskilled work.

A further innovation was the introduction of bureaucratic systems to coordinate and control the process of production. In the production of cars, electrical products and chemical-based products, these new business strategies involved the creation of the large modern corporation (Chandler, 1962: 77). This resulted in tremendous growth in the size of companies with many of the decision previously made through the market mechanism now being made through the management of the company: what Chandler termed the 'visible hand of management'. While in the

UK in the early 19th century there were only ten mills employing over 600 people (Pollard, 1968: 113), by the 20th century in the USA modern corporations were employing over 20,000 (Chandler, 1990: 20).[10]

To manage such huge numbers required new forms of coordination that could only be achieved at this stage through systems of centralised bureaucratic control. To administer these new forms of organisation and support managers in their regulatory function, there emerged a large group of administrators and clerical workers. Bendix (1963: 214) provides a measure of the impact of these changes on the wider society. Using the number of administrative workers as percentage of production workers he developed an index of bureaucratisation, the A/P ratio (1963: 214). In the USA this increased from 7.7 per cent in 1899 to 21.6 per cent in 1947, while in the UK the corresponding increase was from 8.6 per cent in 1907 to 20.0 per cent in 1948. The result was the creation of a huge demand for more highly educated clerical and white-collar staff to administer the process of production.

Knowledge of the production process was no longer held by skilled craftsmen but was monopolised by managers and professional engineers and scientists, a group that was set to grow in size as the companies matured into the 'modern corporation'. In addition to the engineers responsible for designing and developing the products, new management specialisms emerged, such as accounting to control costs, marketing to ensure the maintenance of demand and personnel to organise the recruitment, training and payment of workers.

These new TRs had a profound impact on the demand for different skill levels, not so much at the lower levels but at the intermediate and higher levels. Like early forms of mass production pioneered by the early entrepreneurs in the UK, the TRs under Taylorist Fordism demanded no technical knowledge for the operatives. They had no control over the output they produced and had to work to the pace of the assembly line. They were not required to have any knowledge of the broader production process or the wider market relationships within which their companies were located. They came to epitomise the modern unskilled worker, being totally dependent on the employment relationship for their subsistence.[11]

As late as the mid-20th century, workers in the UK car industry could still 'learn' their jobs within minutes: one of the most important skills to be acquired was learning to cope with the boredom and monotony of working on the line (Benyon, 1973). In the 1960s, apart from an expectation of basic literacy, these remained the same characteristics that employers in the textile and footwear industries demanded of their employees (Ashton and Maguire, 1980). Even in the early 21st century employers in the Danish food processing industry were still only demanding basic primary school education from their employees (Westergaard-Nielson, 2008).

Where the Taylorist Fordist system was generating a more radical change was in the demand for more highly educated engineers, professional managers, accountants and other management specialism. Here was a new demand for highly educated staff with high levels of abstract theoretical knowledge and the ability to apply it to the problems of management in these new bureaucracies. This was a role that was readily filled in the USA by the universities and their new business schools. At the intermediate level it generated an increased demand for skilled craftsmen to maintain the machinery required for the production process and a need for literate and numerate people to perform the clerical and administrative work – the new white-collar labour force. By the middle of the 20th century one in five of the workforce required secondary education to deliver the literacy, numeracy and practical skills required to operate in such bureaucracies (Bendix, 1963). This was a demand that the expanding community schools and colleges readily met in the USA and the grammar schools and later secondary modern and comprehensive schools met in the UK.

In short, this new system of production provided the underlying demand for a substantial increase in the part played by formal education in meeting skill needs. However, the largest single group of employees was still the assembly line and production operatives. Thus while national education systems were increasingly important in providing the credentials for entry into the upper and middle levels of the labour force, this was not the case for those entering the lower levels where only literacy and numeracy were required.[12]

What we have witnessed with the development of mass production as a productive system when it comes to the development of skills are two contradictory trends. On the one hand the growth of managerial, professional, technical and clerical level jobs that require secondary and higher education at the point of entry and which make significant intellectual demands on those who enter them, creating a form of 'upskilling'. On the other hand, 'deskilling' in the form of an increase in unskilled operative-level jobs which can have a negative impact on the intellectual development of those who enter them (Kohn and Schooler, 1983[13]). The existence of such contradictory trends remains a constant feature of contemporary labour markets, as we shall see later when we explore the area of knowledge production.

Technical relations in mature forms of mass production

The next major innovation in TRs came in the late 20th century in response to new market conditions. When Ford was marketing his

Model T the famous slogan was that customers could have any colour they liked providing it was black. His achievement was to deliver a car for a mass national market. Since then markets have become global, we have seen the growth of a large middle class not only in America but also in Europe and now in Asia. This created yet further opportunities for business. These customers now had the resources, in terms of purchasing power, to demand goods and services that were more highly customised to their own requirements. With regard to cars, demand has shifted from people requiring a basic form of transport to one that is more closely tailored to their personal needs, embodying customer preferences in terms of the quality of the product, the colour, type of wheels, type and number of seats, type of audio system, power of engine and so on. And what has happened with cars has happened across the market for all consumer goods. To meet this demand for more differentiated products required another transformation of the production system.

This time it was the Japanese who pioneered the changes in the consumer goods market. In Japan a new set of factors were operating. The consumer goods market following the Second World War did not offer the same potential for large runs of standardised mass produced goods that the American market offered for American companies. In Japan, there was clearly a demand for mass produced goods but the market was more differentiated. For example, in the car manufacturing industry they used the same basic mass production techniques pioneered by the Americans but instead of producing a limited range of standard products, the constraints of their domestic market meant that they had to produce a range of models and differentiate their products (Liker, 2004). In meeting this demand they also learnt from what they saw as the mistakes of the Americans. They wanted to overcome the quality problems associated with long production runs, as faults created early in the line were compounded by later additions. In addition, the American companies were characterised by a poor use of capital tied up in stockpiles of components (buffer stocks) built up to ensure the continuity of the line, as well as restrictions on productivity caused by frequent stoppages of the line.

In order to be more responsive to customers they re-engineered the whole production process to ensure that the system was driven by the 'pull' of the consumers' requirements. Buffer stocks were removed, which meant that employees in one section become increasingly dependent on the faultless performance of employees in other parts of the system to ensure that work flowed efficiently through the factory. If workers or their equipment were producing faulty outputs, this immediately affected workers who were performing the next part of the process of production.

In re-engineering the production process the Japanese introduced what came to be known as 'lean production' (Womack et al., 1990), epitomised by the 'Toyota system' (Liker, 2004). As part of this process they introduced what are now well-known management techniques and practices such as business process re-engineering (BPR), continuous improvement (Kaizan), just-in-time production (JIT), cellular manufacturing and total quality management (TQM). We discuss the specific management techniques that comprised this system in more detail in Chapter 4 as they also had an important impact on the structure of IRs, but it is important to note here that by reconfiguring the work process these processes helped restructure the TRs in Japanese companies, eradicating whole layers of management.

This process of change took place in the context of severe labour shortages and this also impacted on the outcome. Following the Second World War there was a bitter struggle with the unions after which there was a shortage of labour as the economy recovered. Companies responded by offering what was a virtual guarantee of lifetime employment and a form of career progression within the company to their male operatives. Even if subsequently such a guarantee became difficult to sustain, the companies always sought to put the long-term interests of employee before short-term profit considerations. It was in the interests of the companies to invest in their workforce and incorporate the workers into the everyday functioning of the firm.

The result was a significant increase in the interdependencies between the two groups. Underpinning this was the fact that a failure on the part of any one group to perform their tasks correctly would have immediate ramifications throughout the organisation. This greatly increased interdependence permeated all relationships within the organisation, and in some case with their suppliers as well. In doing so it also reduced the power differentials between employers and workers.[14] One outward manifestation of this was in the lessening of status differentials in terms of facilities at work and to a lesser degree employment conditions between white-collar and manual employees. Indeed, where the new system worked effectively, as we shall see in Chapter 5, this occasioned a higher degree of trust between managers and workers and could increase income for employees as they received a share of the productivity gains in terms of higher income or increased job security.

As workers were now taking over responsibility for more of the production process, employers and managers became more dependent on their commitment to the job for the effective operation of the overall process. In terms of job design it now meant that employees worked in teams rather than in separate job stations. A very different situation to that of the lone operative on the Fordist assembly line. In addition, employees were increasingly involved in making operational decisions.

All employees were now focused on the production of differentiated quality products, enabling the company to implement a business strategy based on the constant reduction of costs while still improving quality.

The impact of the new way of organising production on performance and productivity was impressive. Companies such as Ford using traditional forms of command and control management and mass production found it difficult to compete. For example, while the unit of manpower required to produce a Ford Transit van in the UK in 1980 was 12.5, the equivalent figure for the comparable Toyota Hi-Ace was 2.4.[15] Koike and Inoki (1990), in their comparative study of productivity in the car manufacturing industry in Japan and Thailand, found that the Japanese plants were three times as productive as the newer equivalent plants in Thailand, using more traditional forms of work organisation.

This new system of production required fewer administrators and managers (lowering labour costs) but more highly skilled engineers, marketing and personnel staff, and these had to be trained in team-working and collaborative, cross-functional working. For the operatives, it did not put an end to the 'tyranny' of the assembly line but it did mean that employees could, through the development of what Koike and Inoki (1990) call their 'intellectual skills and the devolution of authority', achieve some degree of control over its operation. In some cases the assembly line was replaced by cellular forms of manufacturing where workers would work as a group or cell, producing the product for a specific customer; in other instances, trained workers would be given authority to stop the line, time would be provided for group meetings to identify ways of improving quality and productivity, to learn maintenance skills and to participate in problem-solving groups. Rather than specialising in specific tasks, work was designed to require technical knowledge and skills in a range of tasks, while additional intellectual skills were now required to engage in problem-solving activities.

This form of production was more knowledge intensive in the sense that knowledge of the productive process was more widely distributed among the workforce than in the earlier form of mass production. However, the main body of technical knowledge remained with the corporate management, but the effective operation of the business model required that most operatives were familiar with the overall process and sufficiently committed to the business objectives of the company to exercise their discretion in ensuring that productivity was maximised. Unlike the earlier forms of production, the company's competitive advantage now depended not just on the skill of owners, managers and professionals but for the first time on the skill of regular employees.

Once the superior efficiency of the new production system had been demonstrated, and was visible in the success of the Japanese companies that pioneered it, the system was adopted by competitors abroad. By the late 20th century its adoption by leading companies led to extensive delayering and decentralisation of firms in the USA (Rajan and Wulf, 2006). By the early 21st century, international comparisons found this delayering to have gone further in the USA, UK and Northern European countries than in Southern Europe and Asia, although there are considerable variations across firms (Bloom and Van Reenen, 2010b: 42). Having started in manufacturing it then spread to parts of the service sector, such as hotels, financial services and retail (Ashton and Sung, 2002) and health care.[16] The adoption by firms in the West and in the new industrial countries was facilitated by developments in automation in manufacturing, such as advanced manufacturing technology, including robotics, and especially ICT, with tools such as enterprise resource planning (ERP), which permitted not just the dissemination of business information but also the simultaneous monitoring of performance throughout the organisation (Bloom et al., 2009a). In terms of the demand for skills these new TRs meant that employers were now requiring higher skill levels from their operatives, thereby raising skill levels.[17]

This change in the TRs led to a shift in the demands on national education systems. The technical skills required for operative workers to function effectively in this type of workplace meant that the majority of employees had to have a high level of general education. Of course the demand for technical knowledge for engineers and scientists remained, but the growth in demands on the education system was for more workers educated to a higher level in more general skills that enabled them to learn rapidly on the job.

Services

Technical relations in the service sector

Historically, the major gains in productivity have come from changes in TRs that have taken place in the manufacturing sector. Indeed, until the latter part of the 20th century it was thought that this could lead to economic stagnation as the labour displaced from the productive manufacturing sector was re-employed in the service sector where productivity growth was slow or non-existent (Baumol, 1967). All this changed in the 1980s and 1990s when substantial changes in productivity took place in the telecommunications industry, financial services (where productivity was on a par with higher-performing sectors in manufacturing) as well as in wholesale, retail, transport and storage (Wolfi, 2003), as employers developed new business strategies that enabled them to exploit the opportunities created by changing markets and new technology.[18] Like manufacturing, initially the business strategies were to drive costs down and sell cheaper, using a product market strategy based on Tayloristic mass production principles and task-focused skills. Only recently have we seen the emergence of more personalised delivery of mass produced services.

Technical relations in mass service delivery

The stimulus for the change in TRs in the service sector came once again from changes in the market that provided opportunities for new business strategies. Following the recovery after the Second World War we witnessed a substantial increase in discretionary income. The amount of income required to fulfil basic needs of food, clothing and shelter reduced as a proportion of total income, thereby releasing a greater proportion of family income to be spent on the consumption of goods and personal services, what Daniel Bell (1999) refers to as the 'consumer ladder'. For example, in 1900 expenditure on food accounted for 28 per cent of consumer spending in the UK, but by 1980 this fell to 17 per cent. Over the same period spending on consumer durables and travel and communications doubled to 10 per cent and 12 per cent, respectively, while between 1971 and 2004 spending on recreation and culture increased nearly seven-fold (BIS, 2010: 15). Moreover, with increased income at their disposal consumers became more demanding (Zee and Brandes, 2007), either in terms of requiring receipt of the product in a shorter period of time, or having it supplied in a particular way or delivered in such a way as to reflect or enhance their identity. This provided the basis for the further development of marketing as a specialised professional activity.

In the retail sector one of the main responses from business to these changes was the introduction of a new strategy in the form of supermarkets providing the opportunity for employers using bureaucratic, command and control systems of authority to organise the mass marketing of retail goods, achieving economies of scale and using new technologies to reduce labour and distribution costs. This allowed them to deliver a greater range of choice, in a more convenient manner, in a shorter period of time and at lower costs. In a process similar to that pioneered by the early mass producers in manufacturing, companies such as Wal-Mart were able to utilise a strategy of investing in larger stores to drive down unit costs but then using a combination of efficiency saving in the supply chain and distribution together with the flexible use of labour to further increase productivity and reduce costs.

The major productivity gains attributed to Wal-Mart were the combination of giant stores to create economies of scale, together with the establishment of its satellite own-communications network to link head office with the stores and suppliers. Whereas knowledge-intensive production companies use IT to create solutions, companies using mature mass production techniques and differentiated production use IT as a means of organising the production process. In the case of Wal-Mart, the company used ICT to integrate its business and its suppliers, to improve management processes and reduce labour costs. It was one of the first to use electronic scanners, to develop the universal product code (UPC) and utilise its own satellite system enabling it to speed up communications and automate an increasing number of processes (see Postrel, 2002). The same management techniques of mass production also enabled the company to fine-tune its use of labour, routinise tasks, juggle worker schedules and make more efficient use of part-time employees. This enabled it to drive down labour costs by hiring a large proportion of part-time employees from an ample supply of students, retirees and working spouses (Madrick, 2004).

A similar 'revolution' in the production of fast food services was pioneered by McDonald's in the food industry, standardising the product and delivering it in a shorter period of time. Here the business strategy was based on ensuring the effective control of suppliers, making extensive use of a franchise system and the utilisation of techniques of mass production and applying Tayloristic techniques to food production. As one commentator describes it:

> Perhaps the most impressive aspect of the restaurant was the efficiency with which the McDonald's workers did their jobs. Mac and Dick McDonald had taken great care in setting up their kitchen. Each worker's steps had been carefully choreographed, like an assembly line, to ensure maximum efficiency. The savings in preparation time, and the resulting increase in volume, allowed the McDonald's to lower the price of a hamburger from 30 cents to 15 cents. (Funding Universe, no date)

The principles of mass production are also being increasingly used in the hotel industry. There the business strategy is to maximise the throughput of people into and out of rooms at the lowest cost. This is increasingly reflected in the design of new hotels, as care is used to minimise the amount and ease of cleaning, of ensuring that the location of work stations minimises the check-in and check-out times and so on. Taylorist mass production techniques enabled managers to break down tasks, identifying the separate components of the tasks involved in cleaning rooms, the standards to be reached and providing a tighter control over the time taken to undertake each one (Lloyd et al., 2008).

In financial services, the growth in demand for services for banking and insurance following the rise in incomes encouraged the big financial services companies to utilise developments in ICT to introduce techniques of mass production to reduce costs, reduce the time taken for transactions and so meet the needs of a mass market. As we saw with manufacturing, there are new market opportunities for those businesses that can reduce the cost of labour, which in this case means finding ways to standardise and rationalise such work, allowing employers to recruit cheaper labour.

In banking it led to the replacement of the traditional bank managers and tellers by mechanised processes. TRs were transformed, as any transactions that could be seen as routine were standardised through the use of computer code and thereby automated; decisions previously made by bank clerks were now made through sophisticated programmes. Automated teller machines (ATMs) replaced bank tellers and interaction with the customer was controlled through call centres by computer programmes or directly through the Internet with computer-based banking.

The process spawned an explosion in the use of call centres to handle service sector transactions, with workplaces designed to minimise cost and ensure effective supervision, and operatives having their interactions with consumers scripted for them and their behaviour monitored through the use of the new technology. This reduced the time taken for transactions to be completed and also the cost. So close were these TRs to those of the old manufacturing systems that some of the consultancy companies with expertise in financial services that were instrumental in helping introduce them referred to them as 'factories for finance' (Springett, 2013).

However, this process is no longer just limited to lower-level knowledge work. The increasing capacity of computers married to the World Wide Web is permitting companies to rationalise and standardise a range of work previously undertaken by professionals, ranging from project management and decision making by bank managers to problem solving in the financial services. In other words, the process of deskilling is occurring at the higher levels of the labour market, but again in the context of a general upskilling of the labour force.

Across the service sector, once one company ('first movers' as they are sometimes known) had been able to improve performance through the application of these techniques, then competitors had to follow or lose market share. What this meant was that in huge swathes of the service sector work was transformed through the introduction of techniques of mass production, each tailored to the specific demands of sector. The result of the expansion of the service sector was the growth of large bureaucratic command and control organisations with specialised functional departments and this in turn created an increase in knowledge workers in this sector: the accountants, personnel managers, marketing managers, technical services managers and so on.

Like manufacturing, in mass service delivery, knowledge of the process of production is monopolised by these managers and professionals creating new skills such as those of buyers, R&D staff, computer technicians and so on. Their knowledge is then used to control the activities of lower-skilled workers who possess little or no knowledge of the overall process. Like the manufacturing industry in its mass production phase, the crucial skills required were those of management and professional and technical staff. It was here that high skill levels are important, as this group are essential to ensuring the competitive advantage of the company.

For the majority of employees, at the bottom of the hierarchy, their activities are highly specific, requiring little training, with their behaviour closely monitored through the technology as in retail or in the case of hotels through supervisors. For example, operatives such as check-out staff are only required to have basic skills to enable them to perform routine tasks and interact with the customer, and much of this is scripted for them. Again, in a similar process of change to that which occurred in manufacturing, many of the new jobs that were created were deskilled. In retail, the grocer's assistant who traditionally had to know how to store and present the various products from butter to green groceries, gave way to the checkout assistant who just scans the product and delivers change. In terms of the TRs, all that was required was a basic level of literacy, numeracy, IT skills and the new service skills.

What is different from the manufacturing sector is the new skills that are specific to service sector work: the soft skills of customer service, the requirement that the person dealing directly with the customer should at all time be smiling, pleasant and helpful. In place of manual dexterity the new low-skilled service workers require emotional dexterity to deliver a uniform response to the pressures that increasingly demanding consumers placed on them. Servants and salespeople have always had emotional demands placed on them (Wright Mills, 1956). What was new in the second half of the 20th century was the widespread growth of mass production in the service sector that demanded these skills from an expanding section of the predominantly female labour force (Grugulis, 2007).

In the social partnership countries (both the Germanic and Nordic) where those entering the labour market were trained through forms of apprenticeship which incorporated both academic and work-based training, the 'new skills' could be incorporated into the work-based learning component. In the Anglo-Saxon countries such as the UK the academic curriculum of the schools and its traditional form of certification had no such facility through which to incorporate the 'new skills'. Consequently for large groups of workers in the retail, hotel, restaurant and personal care sectors there were no qualifications; the educational system had nothing to offer. As a result there was pressure to introduce new qualifications that would be of relevance for this group, but significantly these were to be delivered outside the educational system through the new competence frameworks that we deal with in the next chapter.

Technical relations in mature service delivery

A business strategy using mass production methods to reduce the cost of delivering a service or to increase the speed at which it can be delivered is not the only strategy employers adopted. In the service sector as in the manufacturing sector, in more recent years some companies sought to achieve a competitive advantage through delivering a more differentiated product. They used a business strategy aimed at providing a more customised service that delivered a more satisfactory personal experience both for the buyer and the employee. This is a strategy that is more prevalent in the Nordic countries where the wage determination system reduces the likelihood of a cost reduction strategy on the part of employers (Westergaard-Nielson, 2008).

We can illustrate this form of organising the production process with reference to some of the companies from our research files. Flight Centre aims to combine the cost advantages of a large travel service company with the ability to deliver a personalised service to their clients anywhere in the world (Sung and Ashton, 2005). This is aimed at generating high levels of customer satisfaction and return business. In the UK, Timpson, a family business specialising in shoe repair, key cutting, engraving and watch repair, has succeeded in creating very high levels of customer satisfaction to such an extent that it does not have to advertise, instead growing the business through personal recommendation (Sung and Ashton, 2005). In the hotel industry, the Speedwell Hotel in Scotland has succeed in differentiating itself from its competitors and securing a niche market in catering for offshore oil workers, but in many respects it looks like any other 3- or 4-star hotel (Sung et al., 2008). The rooms are similar and facilities comparable, but what again differentiates it is the higher level of customised service it provides for its guests, virtually guaranteeing high levels of room occupancy. In the fast food restaurant industry, Kakavelakis (2008) reports the case of a large chain specialising in fast food that was able to differentiate its product from the likes of McDonald's, T.G.I. Friday's and similar fast food restaurants through the level of personal attention that it supplies to customers, generating a high level of return business and reducing staff turnover.

Like manufacturing, delivering personalised service means that knowledge of the productive system has to be distributed throughout the organisation in order that employees can exercise discretion. Unlike manufacturing, this change in TRs associated with mature service delivery may not involve a major redesign of the workplace as some of our case study companies indicate. This means that in the service sector TRs do not necessarily play the same role in facilitating the competitive advantage of the company as they do in the manufacturing sector. In the travel industry the same basic technology is available to all operators. The high street offices of Flight Centre look very like those of any other travel company offering a standard service. Those responsible for selling the product sit at desks with their own computer and telephone in front of which are seats for the customer. In Timpsons, the key cutting, engraving and shoe repair technology is the same as competitors' and the layout of Timpson's shops look very much like their competitors'. In hotels there are differences in the quality of the accommodation between hotels but within a grading band the quality is fairly consistent, and in the fast food business the technology of cooking is the same whether the company is delivering a standardised or personalised level of service. What enables these companies to differentiate their service is the quality of the service and personal attention that they deliver which is primarily determined by the IRs we discuss in the next chapter.

There is now a substantial body of evidence to illustrate how in service sector the same technology can be used to deliver both a standardised or a personalised service. In her work on American call-centres, Batt (2000: 550) found that where the value of employee and customer interaction was low, interactions were tightly controlled and technology was used to monitor employees. At the other extreme where the interactions were of high value and relied on employee discretion, then technology was used as more of an enabler. At the low end, operators dealt with an average of 465 customers per day, while at the high end the average was 32. In the UK, Grimshaw et al. (2002: 200) report the case of the firm Total Customer Solutions (TCS) providing call centre services, using similar technologies but working for different clients, delivering a very different quality of service to their respective customers as specified in the contract with the client. In the researcher's own words:

> Not only was the job task tightly designed according to the particular business contract with a client firm, but also differences in the business strategies of client firms directly shaped other factors such as employment contract, payment systems and opportunities for skill development. For example, two client firms (the mobile phone and truck rental companies) actually incorporated

certain terms and conditions of employment into the business contracts with TCS, requiring, for example, that all customer service representatives were employed on permanent contracts. The reason was that these firms placed value on the quality of services provision and believed this was dependent upon the provision of continuous and stable employment. But other client firms were more concerned with value for money, requiring intensive monitoring of work quantity; in these circumstances, TCS employed a large proportion of temporary agency workers. (Grinshaw et al., 2002: 200)

Here the major difference between companies competing through the use of mass production techniques and those competing through a strategy of differentiated production, but using the same technology, is the employment contract imposed by the business strategy of the company buying call centre services. Like manufacturing, the crucial skills are those of management but increasingly, unlike mass service delivery, in delivering a personalised service the skill levels of workers also become more important.

However, unlike the mature mass production firms in manufacturing, the business strategy of mature service delivery does not have a direct implication for the technical skills of employees. Managers and professionals still require higher levels of education and professional qualifications as a basis for the problem-solving and communications skills necessary for the effective performance of their jobs. But for the operatives, the sales and administrative staff delivering a differentiated service, there is little demand for anything other than a reasonable secondary education; this is because, as we shall see in the next chapter, the competitive advantage delivered by these firms depends on the skills and commitment developed in the workplace through the IRs. Overall the growth of mass service delivery and mature service delivery does not make major new demands on the education system. It is the IRs that create the demands on the training system that we discuss in the next chapter.

Technical relations in knowledge-intensive production

The stimulus for this latest phase in the development of the productive system came from the USA, in particular Silicon Valley, the home of the high-tech industry where major advances in ICT were made, creating new markets for computers and later with the establishment of the Internet for global communication. These technological innovations then spread from the ICT industry to other sectors, having now made a significant impact across the global economy.

As many authors have pointed out, the spread of ICT is making the distinction between the manufacturing and service sector increasingly anachronistic, especially at the high end of manufacturing (Haskel et al., 2011; Goodridge et al., 2012). As Daniel Bell pointed out some time ago, the growth of scientific knowledge and the development of computing and Internet technologies since the last decade of the 20th century has laid the foundations for the exploitation of knowledge for business purposes across all sectors (Bell, 1999). One other consequence is that it is now becoming increasingly recognised that investment and growth is being driven by knowledge-based capital (KBC), with some companies now investing more in KBC than in tangibles. For example, in 2009 the physical assets of Google were estimated at only 5 per cent of the company's worth (OECD, 2012c: 2). In the UK, research by National Endowment for Science, Technology and the Arts (NESTA) found that 'investment in knowledge, which is categorized as intangible assets, is now greater than investment in tangible assets, at around, in 2008, £141 billion and £104 billion respectively' (Haskel et al., 2011: 44).

While ICT is at the heart of KBC, it does enable it to spill over from the high-tech industries to other sectors. As we have noted, the spread of ICT has been important in the dissemination of modern business practices throughout and between sectors. Thus, the OECD recognises three types of KBC: computerised information (software and databases); innovative property (patents, designs, trademarks); and economic competencies (brand equity, networks joining people and institutions and organisational know-how that increases operational efficiency) (OECD, 2012c). We therefore split this discussion of knowledge-intensive production into two sections. The first deals with the TRs in the ICT industry, the producers of the technology. The second deals with the impact that advances in ICT have had in increasing the level of knowledge-intensive production on the TRs in other sectors, the users of that technology.

Technical relations in the producers of ICT

Developments in ICT have created a whole new market in delivering radical improvements in communications and data management. One widespread business strategy that is common in the ICT sector is to use knowledge of the new technologies to provide customised solutions to clients' communication and data management problems, whether that is other businesses directly or to customers through Google or social media.

The result has been the growth of specialist knowledge-intensive firms (epitomised by the IT sector but not exclusive to them), which sell the application of the knowledge embedded in their organisations for the resolution of customer problems. In this exchange, the knowledge producer is not selling their knowledge but rather its application in a specific context. It is used in a variety of contexts, from consulting, co-engineering, remote testing and quality control, to the delivery of dedicated technical designs (Antonelli, 1999: 253). Remote access to these services via the Internet gives these firms a global scope and consequently they tend to be more embedded in international rather than national markets.

The new technology has a different impact on TRs in knowledge-intensive industries from those we have seen in manufacturing. There, once the investment is made in a new plant the TRs they embody are relatively fixed in terms of how they can be used, at least in the short term. An adequate return on capital invested in, say, a new car production line can take years to achieve. In the new ICT industry the technology is more flexible, providing management with greater discretion in the short run over how it can be used. As in the delivery of services, the same computer-based technology can be used to organise work through autonomous, multi-skilled teams or through highly specialised individual tasks. For example, in one of our UK case studies, Data Connection, producing specialised solutions for other IT companies such as Marconi and British Telecom, work was organised around a series of teams with each team limited to no more than five members working in a collaborative manner, because the senior management believed that five colleagues was the maximum any one team leader could teach at a time (Sung and Ashton, 2005).

In another case study, this time in Singapore, in a company producing and maintaining computer programmes for use in managing business information, work was organised in terms of a strict division of labour with each employee working individually with narrowly defined tasks and responsible to a higher-level manager (Ashton et al., 2014). Here, although the work still retains a strong intellectual input, the scope for individual creativity is more limited. Barrett (2005) reports similar case studies in Australia. Which form of work organisation managers adopt depends on the competitive strategy of the firm. However, throughout this sector the flexibility of the technology allows for a more effective integration of IRs and TRs, with IRs playing a more powerful role in how the division of labour is organised. It is the business strategy that determines how the technology is used. For example, Doorewaard and Meihuizen's (2000) study of Dutch and German management consultancies found that firms oriented towards efficiency offered standard solutions to problems, while those oriented towards expertise offered client-specific solutions.

Where the business strategy is focused on research development or delivering one-off customised solutions for marketing and ICT

problems, firms tend to use the technology to create relatively autonomous teams, each dedicated to different aspects of problem solving. Here
their competitive strategy is heavily dependent on the collective skills of
the various teams, as the skills of all the staff are crucial. The reputation
of the company in the market is dependent on the output of each team
in providing unique solutions. Consequently, the knowledge required
to deliver the product is relatively equally distributed throughout the
organisation. Each individual employee and each team is dependent on
the others performing their tasks efficiently. Relationships within the
organisation are characterised by high levels of interdependence, and
power differentials within the organisation are minimised, with knowledge shared throughout the organisation. Although the IT is used as a
tool, the basis of their product is in the ideas and intellectual powers of
their employees.[19] Here the individual employees, as members of teams,
provide the source of the company's competitive advantage, far more so
than in forms of mature mass production.

As we have seen, in earlier forms of production, knowledge of the
production process was largely controlled by the entrepreneur and later
by corporate management and professionals. Only in the mature mass
production phase do we witness some firms sharing knowledge of the
production process with operatives. However, in the infocomm and creative sectors we have a new phenomenon, namely the greater reliance of
entrepreneurs and senior managers on the knowledge and skills of their
employees to deliver their product or service. This type of knowledge-
intensive firm does not therefore have the same type of divisions among
staff that are found in other forms of production with their separation of
manual and non-manual labour. Although separate groups of managers
may still exist within the organisation, where knowledge production is
collaborative and its application is done collectively, status differentials
are minimised.

Where the business strategy is focused on delivering the maintenance and modification of standard computer programmes designed
to improve business processes (e.g. 'off-the-shelf' solutions), there
tends to be more emphasis on hierarchy and specialised individual
tasks controlled from the centre. Here, the individual employees,
while making an important contribution to the final product (as any
mistakes they make can be expensive to repair), do not play such a
crucial part in determining the company's competitive advantage. It
is the management and R&D staff whose skills are crucial. The reputation of these companies in the market is far more dependent on
the quality of R&D in developing the original programme. In these
companies power differentials tend to be similar to those in forms
of mature mass production, with stronger status distinctions between
different levels of staff.

The use of ICT to change technical relations in other sectors

Outside the ICT producer sector of the economy, developments in ICT have had two other major consequences for productive systems. First, they have increased the knowledge content or knowledge intensity of other forms of production. For example, the developments in ICT are integral to the R&D activities of companies in high-end engineering, including car manufacturing and aerospace, permeating all aspects of company activities from computer-controlled production to R&D and maintenance. In the case of IBM, this resulted in the company moving away from the manufacture of hardware to offering business solutions.

In both traditional manufacturing and retailing, ICT developments have radically transformed the production process through automation in manufacturing and data management in distribution and services. The greater knowledge intensity required in moving from systems of mass production to mature mass production has therefore changed TRs. The knowledge required to achieve this has been identified by the OECD as economic competences, but more accurately it has facilitated the organisational restructuring of businesses, delivering higher levels of efficiency in the operation of many companies across the full range of sectors.

Research by Brynjolfsson and Hitt (2003) and Brynjolfsson and Saunders (2010), among others, has revealed how IT has facilitated the re-engineering of business processes (processes that we describe in more detail in Chapter 5). The new technology has been used to share information more readily throughout the organisation, to decentralise decision making, to link performance, pay and promotions in a more effective manner, to eradicate non-value-added activities, and to facilitate greater investment in training and development. However, to exploit the new technology effectively requires the employees to acquire new skills in using it and to identify areas where it can be used effectively and to design new practices through which the full potential of the technology can be exploited, what is sometimes referred to as 'organisational capital'. These organisational changes, the creation of this organisational capital, sometimes take as long as four to seven years before the impact on performance is fully felt.

The second major consequence of developments in ICT has been in the ability it provides for firms to modularise production and locate the various components in countries across the globe while maintaining control over the process from the centre (Berger, 2006). Again, this is a development that applies just as much to the financial services sector as manufacturing, with the routine activities of banks, insurance companies and others being located in call centres across the globe (Brown et al., 2011). It has provided MNCs, or more accurately TNCs, with the ability to break down the production system into component parts or modules, whether in R&D or in the production of computers and phones, and locate the production of each module in countries which generate the greatest competitive advantage.[20]

The impact of this has been dramatic as it means that the production process is no longer contained within national boundaries but is now integrated on a global basis. It means that R&D can be conducted by virtual teams around the globe, so that as work stops on a project in Asia in the evening it can be picked up by teams in Europe, and when they end their working day it can be taken up by teams in the Americas. Physical components of a product can be made wherever costs are lowest and transported to be assembled in a different location. It means that the loci of skill formation is no longer in the institutional arrangements of the nation state, as in the case of national apprenticeship systems, but is now under the control of the TNC. Providing there is a supply of educated labour, TNCs can now locate their production anywhere in the world. They now provide the skills not necessarily constrained by the national training system (Ashton et al., 2010). The consequences of this for national policies are discussed in Chapter 6.

The demands such organisations make on the national education and training systems are substantial. Before employees can operate at all in these firms they require a high level of general, and in some instances scientific education, with demonstrated competence in high-level problem solving. IT firms do not necessarily always target IT graduates, but they do require that, through their educational experience, potential employees will produce evidence of high-level analytical skills and the ability to deploy them. It is the politicians' perception of these demands for educated labour that has led to increasing proportions of each cohort entering higher education. Thus, further investment in higher education and skills is frequently justified by reference to the growth of the knowledge economy. Yet in spite of all the rhetoric, companies that make extensive use of knowledge-intensive production still account for only a small amount of total employment.[21]

Implications

What we have sought to show here is the ways in which the level of skill demand in the economy is determined by the TRs of companies, which in turn are shaped by their product market and business strategies. What is evident from this brief historical survey is that major changes in the demand for different skill levels come from major changes in the market opportunities and technologies of production, not from government action on the supply side. This is not to discount government action in delivering appropriate skill levels, as the experience of the Asian Tigers has demonstrated. However, at a national level, the major influence in helping shape business strategies in response to such new opportunities has been the wider institutional arrangements that influence the supply of skills. In the Anglo-Saxon countries these have been minimal, leaving employers with a greater range of choices in responding to market forces. In the Germanic model the existence of a strong comprehensive system of apprenticeship training has, together with other factors, tended to push employers into adopting a business strategy based on advanced high-spec manufacturing. Similarly, the existence of strong collective bargaining and trust relations between employers and workers in Denmark has pushed employers towards a strategy of mature mass production, competing on quality rather than price. In different ways, these have both impacted on TRs within their respective countries and thereby shaped the demand for different skill levels.

A second point, one that we are more fully aware of, is that over time as new business strategies and their associated TRs have changed, the shift has been in the direction of a demand for a higher level of skill.[22] This in part explains the greater skills utilisation observed over the last two decades as identified by tools such as the UK Skills Survey. However, it also demonstrates how these same business strategies are responsible for the process of deskilling, through narrower job scope and job autonomy. Moreover, this process of deskilling is not just something that affects the lower skills, as it is also affecting professional and technical work.

Third, we would highlight the fact that within any one economy diverse TRs mean that there are very different demands placed on the educational system at any one point in time. We still have many companies that utilise the TRs of Taylorist mass production and these co-exist with others that use more advanced forms of mature mass production and knowledge-intensive production. As we have seen, these differences in the skill levels they generate are reflected in the sector differences in the qualifications required for the job. The task of skills policy is to balance these demands while recognising that there are other political demands on the educational system that have little to do with the TRs of contemporary firms.

Finally, we would stress the fact that until recently business strategies have been shaped by national institutional conditions, and indeed these continue to be important. However, the growth of MNCs and TNCs is adding a new dimension to our understanding of the determinants of skill levels. Having loosened themselves to some extent from the constraints of national institutions, international companies have a greater degree of internal control over the skill formation process as different components of the production process are located in different countries. The implications of this for policy are discussed in Chapter 6.

Notes

1 At the level of the firm Findlay and Warhurst (2012) make a similar argument but also point out that we need to distinguish between 'the better use of existing skills' by employers when they want the job done better and 'the use of better skills' when they change a job to demand higher skills.

2 Mason suggest that the relationship between the supply of skills and the product market strategy is co-determined, which if we were to include the competitive strategy we would agree with, but at a societal level if we are focusing on the relationships between different business strategies and their associated productive systems, we see the primary direction of 'causality' as being from the business strategy to the skill level.

3 This is not to argue that the characteristics of national education systems can be fully explained by changes in skill demand. Clearly the political systems and the interests they represent also act as a powerful influence in shaping national education and training systems.

4 Countries such Singapore and Taiwan and South Korea were able to use government-funded businesses and other political levers to encourage the establishment of different types of higher value-added industries.

5 There is considerable debate about the origins of the factory system but the important point here is that Arkwright's first mill combined water-power with mechanised production.

6 Given these conditions it is not surprising that labour turnover was high, often in excess of 40 per cent with relatively few staying in these factories for any length of time (Fitton, 1989).

7 In 1818 Manchester mill owners' figures supplied to the House of Lords Committee indicated that out of over 7,000 names supplied only 4.2 per cent were aged over 40.

8 These were estimated quoted by Robert Dale, a fellow manufacturer, quoted in Aspin (2003:13).

9 For the source of these estimates see: www.wiley.com/legacy/products/subject/business/forbes/ford.html (accessed 14 August 2014).

10 In terms of the increasing size of companies, the UK lagged behind the USA. It was not until the late 1970s in the UK that the size of the workforce at Imperial Chemical Industries reached 143,000 employees (Hannah, 1983: 146).

11 This process of change led to the creation of a large literature in the 1960s and 1970s about the experience of factory and assembly line workers in the USA and UK (see Chinoy, 1955; Blauner, 1964; Goldthorpe et al., 1969; Blackburn and Mann, 1979).

12 This correspondence between the output of the secondary education system and the demands of jobs was explored by Ashton and Field (1976) in the UK and Bowles and Gintis (1976) in the USA.

13 Kohn and Schooler were among the first to demonstrate the detrimental impact of insecure, unskilled jobs on intellectual development.

14 This is only the case where these techniques are fully implemented, as we shall see in Chapter 5.

15 This was information derived from an internal memo circulated to Ford's management in 1980 entitled 'After Japan'.

16 Westergaard-Neilson (2008: 219) cites the use of lean principles in hospitals in Denmark.

17 See Caroli and Van Reenen (2001); Bartel et al. (2007) and Bloom et al., (2009b).

18 This has led some to argue that we are currently witnessing the 'servicestisation' of parts of manufacturing industry as companies such as Rolls Royce derive more and more of their revenue from monitoring and servicing their engines as opposed to their manufacture (Neely, 2008).

19 We distinguish knowledge intensity of the TRs from knowledge workers, or 'symbolic activists' to use Reich's term, on the basis that knowledge workers are those whose work involves the manipulation of symbols, including as it does many workers such as administrators and clerical workers, whereas we are using the term 'knowledge intensive' production to refer to systems of production that are based on the creative use of knowledge by employees.

20 This process extends bonds of interdependence between employees, not just within national boundaries but across them, part of what Elias (1978) refers to as the 'bonds or chains of interdependence' and what Adler (2004) refers to as the 'socialization of production'.

21 Estimates vary; see Haskel et al. (2011).

22 For an excellent account of this process, see Green (2006).

4

INTERPERSONAL RELATIONS AND SKILL UTILISATION

Whilst the majority of businesses do invest in their people's skills, there is significant scope for improvement. Around 40 per cent of businesses don't invest at all in any one year. There are substantial variations between different sectors and size of businesses, and levels of investment are uneven in their reach, excluding key parts of the workforce.

UK Commission for Employment and Skills (2012)

Across the OECD countries, employer provided or sponsored training is the single most important source of post-compulsory education and training for the working age population. Relative to this governments play a modest role in financing post compulsory education and training.

B. Hansson (2008)[1]

Overview

As we have seen in Chapter 1, it is a firm's competitive strategy that shapes IRs and the ways in which the company uses the skills of employees. Again, these competitive strategies are historically determined so we need to explore how the competitive strategy shapes the use of skills in each of these different types of production systems. In the early forms of productive system TRs were used to deskill work for the majority of employees, while the managers and professional workers were the only group whose skills the companies actively

developed. This is because it was their skills that were used to operate the command and control systems and develop the products on
which the company's competitive strategy depended. With later forms
of productive system the competitive strategies of the firm came to
rely more on the quality of the products and services they delivered,
which meant using the skills of larger and larger sections of the labour
force, especially as these competitive strategies and associated changes
in IRs spread to firms in the service sector.

One of the most significant changes in IRs in the last half century
has been the change from the command and control systems of management and authority that characterised the early forms of mass
production to the use of more participative forms of management associated with the use of modern HPWPs or HIPs management practices.
The use of command and control systems of management found in the
traditional mass production companies rested primarily on the use of
sanctions to control employee behaviour, whereas firms using mature
mass and knowledge-intensive management relied more on securing
the consent of their employees to control their own behaviour. This
represents a fundamental shift in the IRs, which involved companies
not only making more use of the skills of the labour force but also
changing the type of skills that are used in the workplace. These new
types of skills such as problem solving, communication and teamworking skills are usually referred to as 'competences' by employers.
They make different, broader demands on the capabilities of the labour
force and require much more active forms of management than was the
case with more task-based skills associated with command and control
forms of authority and management. As a result of the spread of these
new forms of management and the increasing demand for higher levels
of quality service skills in the service sector, issues of skill utilisation
and lifelong learning have become much more prominent in contemporary societies.

Introduction

As we have seen in the Introduction to the book, the policy concern with
the employers' use of skills is a recent phenomenon. In the Anglo-Saxon
countries how employers used labour was seen as outside the province
of politicians, apart from legislation concerning the use of child labour.
So long as skills were seen as an individual attribute for which employers and individuals made an 'investment' and then as a stock, the only
way the government could intervene was through the concept of market failure aimed at enhancing the stock. As the first quote illustrates,

governments still tend to see employer investment as failing to produce the 'optimal' level of investment. It was not until the rise of knowledge-intensive production and increased international competition with new models of IRs, introduced by the Japanese and others, that skill utilisation became a public policy issue. Even then it was seen as a 'demand side' issue about which there is little the government can do, as the second quote illustrates. Given the assumptions of existing public policy the only way it could be tackled was through voluntary measures, for example advocacy and sometimes financial incentives. As this analysis of IRs will demonstrate, this misses the point that skill utilisation is driven by the business model, not the aspirations of politicians or individual businessmen or women.

In the same way that the PMS of firms drives the TRs, which explains the level of skill required to function in the productive system, so the competitive strategy drives the IRs, which explains how employers use the skills of their employees. We illustrate this through another brief examination of how and why these relationships change over time.

Manufacturing

Interpersonal relations in early industrial production

In the early days of the Industrial Revolution when there were huge new opportunities for those who could mechanise production, the main emphasis was understandably on securing a competitive advantage through producing large quantities at lower cost. In many firms, IRs were geared to controlling the behaviour of employees and ensuring that they performed simple tasks that required little if any training. Indeed, for the most innovative firms in the textile industry their business strategy was successful precisely because they minimised the use of employee skills.

We use the cotton industry in the UK to illustrate how these relationships shaped the ways in which entrepreneurs honed the skills of employees. Under the domestic system work was often performed in the home, within the context of family relationships. In the new cotton factories work was conducted within the context of very different relationships very separate from those of the family. There, the owner/manager or their representative had almost complete authority over the process of production and had a powerful impact on shaping interactions in the workplace. They controlled the hours of work, the conditions under which work was done and the ways in which overseers or supervisors related to operatives.

Initially, as they were relatively small establishments, these relationships were personal, with the law providing owners considerable discretion over how they treated their employees. Given the threat of poverty and unemployment employers could rely on the threat of dismissal to ensure the motivation of their labour force. There were few limits to the arbitrary character of authority, and physical punishment of children was common. Most of the emphasis was on a system of punishments for the infringement of factory rules involving suspension or dismissal for damage to the works and failure to perform their jobs effectively (Fitton, 1989: 204–206). This was an early form of command and control with some factories systematising their rules of conduct and the punishments for infringing them: fear was a powerful motivator, and the beating of child workers was common (Pollard, 1968: 218).

Because they were operating a system of command and control there was little emphasis on the interpersonal skills in the workplace. Such a system was well suited to mobilising workers in delivering industrial output that was of specified standards and within a predictable time-frame. Sanctions such as fines and dismissal were powerful enough to ensure that the worker performed the minimal tasks they were expected to undertake, so the employers had little incentive to concern themselves with other aspects of their relationships. Rewards were largely confined to the payment for work done, with early forms of piecework being prominent. Typically employers paid their employees weekly through a piece-work system, apart from learners and extra hands and some of the more experienced spinners who paid their piercers from their own income (Fitton, 1989: 165).

Under systems where skills are task-focused it makes sense to tie the reward for behaviour directly to the amount the individual workers produce. These jobs could be learnt in a very short period of time, such that in many cases young children could readily acquire them, with their limited range of task skills being learnt from other workers. Compared with the craftsmen and the workers in the domestic system, the most distinctive feature of the factory system was the lack of job autonomy. From the employer's perspective, what was crucial was not the general abilities of the workers but their behavioural characteristics. What employers looked for in recruits were characteristics such as their dependability to turn up for work regularly, work long hours under strict discipline and accept orders unquestioningly. Of course, workers were involved in personal relationships with fellow workers but the IRs within the workplace, and the support required for their maintenance, such as training, were minimal or non-existent. Their focus was entirely on their limited tasks.[2]

The situation was different for the managers, for like the owners they were the repository of knowledge about the production process. This new group, such as those in the cotton spinning mills, had to be literate and educated and represent the interests of the employers/owners in the workplace. As a group they were more central to the business strategy of the owners. These early managers were typically trained through practical experience in the firm (Pollard, 1968: 147). They had conditions of service that tied them to their employer and differentiated them from the workers. In the case of many managers in the UK they had familial ties to the owner as, given the state of the legal system, that was one of the only ways owners could be sure of their loyalty. What the owners feared was that their managers would leave, taking their knowledge of the production process with them to set up on their own either within the UK or abroad where the patent laws could not be enforced.

As we emphasised in Chapter 2, there were other forms of productive system. In the production of steam engines, the system of batch rather than mass production operated, in which the owners still relied on the skills of craftsmen. Here IRs were more significant because workers had a greater input into the production of the final product and so, although their skills were limited to dealing with specific aspects of the overall production process, they were nevertheless important for the company's business strategy.

While this focus on task efficiency (where employers used mass production) provided employers with the opportunity to make massive gains in productivity and profitability, workers were not always passive participants in this process. Through their use of IRs, some workers were able to control access to specific sets of positions within the hierarchy of work organisation and use that to enforce a definition of their activities as skilled, even though this may not be justified by the technical content of their work role. For example, Turner (1962) documents the case of the strippers-and-grinders in the cotton industry. Their job was to service carding machines and by 1850 further improvement in technology meant that many of their tasks (e.g. supervisory and machine tending functions) had been removed, such that their position differed little from general labourers. However, by organising themselves and exploiting every minor technical change in carding and controlling access to their positions they managed to secure the status of skilled workers. By the 1920s, they had some of the highest wage rates in the industry (Turner, 1962: 163–165). In the later literature, authors such as Penn (1984), Steiger (1993) and Cockburn (1983) have all identified groups such as printers, plumbers and others who have been able to secure a definition of their work as skilled, even when the technical context of that work has been stripped of its practical skills. Thus, at the task-focused end of the IRs, the introduction of the factory system has facilitated the gradual appearance of a new concept of skills, one that was intimately determined by social factors at work (Form, 1987).

Interpersonal relations in Taylorist mass production

The next major change in IRs came with the rise of the modern corporation in the USA in response to the emergent mass market.

Given the phenomenal growth in the size of firms, new forms of authority and ways of organising staff had to be developed, as the old personalised forms of command and control that existed in the early phase of mass production were no longer sufficient to control such large numbers of employees. The consequence of this was the bureaucratisation of relationships and a move to the right on the IRs dimension, but only for management.

In these organisations personalised relationships governed by custom and rule of thumb could no longer be relied upon to enable those at the top to control the activities of such large numbers of subordinates. The only source of experience these societies had in controlling large numbers was in their armed forces, and it is not surprising that in Europe especially this form of command and control was extensively relied on to provide a model of management. In the USA, where this military tradition was less prominent, the search for 'principles' of management was more prominent (Drucker, 1946, 1954).[3]

As we saw in Chapter 3, the consequence was the bureaucratisation of organisations. This involved the establishment of clear hierarchies of authority, the documentation of the responsibilities attached to each job, the skills required to perform them and the establishment of fixed terms and conditions which spelt out the rewards to be offered to those that held the position. IRs became formalised. It meant that management's range of authority was increasingly specified, removing the arbitrary character of authority that delineated the enterprise in the early stages of factory production. It did not eradicate the power imbalance between managers and workers, or eradicate the managerial prerogative, but it made management's authority relatively more accountable as the behaviour of all employees became governed by written rules, procedures and regulations. These then had to be transferred to new employees requiring training to be delivered once the recruits entered the firm, but for this new group of white-collar workers, on-the-job training also became a necessity.

The other major change this introduced into IRs was to increase the centrality of management skills to competitive success.[4] In the early phase of mass production, the success of the business strategy depended largely on the abilities of the entrepreneur. During this second phase this changed; in such organisations, management became the repository of knowledge about the production process as it became technically more complex. The work of F.W. Taylor highlighted that the unification of knowledge of the production process with the execution of tasks, which was the hallmark of the craftsman, was destroyed as first the early entrepreneur and later managers sought to control the production process. Knowledge of the production process became firmly embedded in management.

This process involved management becoming more systematic with managers and professionals having to learn more effective methods of labour recruitment, more sophisticated disciplinary techniques, more complex methods of controlling production and new accountancy techniques, all of which were now necessary for the functioning of such large bureaucratic organisations (Chandler, 1990). In addition, as loyalty to the owner/manager was replaced by loyalty to a corporation, new means had to be found of committing this new breed of manager to the organisation. This resulted in the introduction of career ladders and training programmes designed to develop these skills and commitment, with some of the underlying 'principles' being taught in the new business schools, through various business and business administration degrees. Such professionalisation of business management was also reflected in the growth of personnel and training departments, as management training (or 'development' as it came to be known) itself became a separate specialised activity.

As we have seen, it was the USA that spearheaded the growth of these corporations. There management became a specialised occupation and was itself differentiated between production, finance and accounting, purchasing, marketing and sales and later personnel, each of which now required its own specialised training and technical skills. Innovation also became a specialised activity located in R&D departments. It was the collective abilities of these groups on which the success of the companies came to depend. In his study of the modern industrial enterprise, Chandler (1990) identifies management skills in terms of the abilities of management to organise the physical facilities, factories, offices and laboratories and the skills of employees as central to the success of the corporations. As he observes:

> But only if these facilities and skills were carefully coordinated and integrated could the enterprise achieve the economies of scale and scope that were needed to compete in national and international markets and continue to grow. (1990: 594)

These capabilities he saw as consisting of lower-level management's capabilities in charge of the operating units, middle management, who had functional and product specific managerial skills and the skills necessary to guide and motivate lower-level management and, most critical of all, senior executives, responsible for middle management and for directing the organisation as a whole. It is not surprising therefore that most of the resources allocated to human development were devoted to this group. Neither is it surprising that the USA led the world with the introduction of this new type of productive system.

The other advantage of these bureaucratic structures was that they provided the basis for long-term careers in the organisation, solving the problem of motivating the personnel to conform to the organisation's goals and values. The step-by-step progression they offered provided the incentive for the continuous commitment to work and the application of discretionary effort to everyday tasks. In return staff were rewarded with higher salaries and the exercise of higher levels of authority and status.

Although they were still using bureaucratised forms of command and control, for these managers people-focused skills were becoming more important. In our strategic skills model, managers were increasingly interested in practices that would utilise skill development further to the right along the IRs dimension. In the USA, these programmes were far more developed than in the UK; as Hannah notes, 'No more than a dozen major British manufacturing companies had developed management training schemes for university graduates in the 1930s' (1983: 88). In the UK, the main means of access to management at this time was still through family relationships or the patronage of directors or senior managers. The prevailing 'class' structure in the UK was delaying the introduction of changes along the IRs dimension for management. It was this delay that played an important part in the inability of the UK to compete with American and later German and Japanese companies (Wilson and Thomson, 2006).

For manual workers and clerical workers, their skills were not seen as important and there was less such movement along to the right of the IRs dimensions. The mechanisation of clerical work stemming from the introduction of the typewriter meant that these skills were more efficiently acquired through formal off-the-job courses, but often these were provided through the education system at the employees' expense (Lowe, 1987: 77), although the procedures and practices of the organisation had to be learnt on the job.

For manual workers, the content of the training, where it took place, was dominated by the TRs, as training was still limited to the acquisition of the manual dexterity required to perform a limited number of tasks.[5] For this, employers only required the same behavioural characteristics as they had under earlier forms of mass production, namely the ability to turn up for work regularly, accept industrial discipline and manual dexterity. For many workers, however, there still remained no formal training, skills were learnt on the job, often in the first day. Certainly for these workers there was no attempt to commit them to the organisation, other than through the wage they paid, while on the worker's part their commitment was through what became known as their 'instrumental orientation to work' (Goldthorpe et al., 1968); for them work was just a means of making a living. This did not mean that workers were totally detached from the workplace, as the classic Hawthorne experiments revealed the importance of informal relations. Other work by Roy (1952) and others in the 1940s provided an insight into how workers manipulated the attempts by management to control their behaviour through the piecework system to create their own system of control over the work tasks. Workers were rarely passive recipients of management's directives.

Where workers did have a more direct impact on the IRs dimension was through their unions and collective action. In the USA, the UK and other Western societies, union collective action and political action had removed the possibility of managers using threats and coercion in their relations with the labour force. In addition, the unions had succeeded in achieving the right to bargain over pay, further limiting management's discretion. In the UK, the informal organisation of shop stewards in some industries gave workers' representatives influence over the movement of labour between different (skill) categories. Also, the power of craft unions prevented the emergence of internal labour markets in manufacturing organisations, such as those developed in the USA and France, by maintaining the exclusiveness of the craft trades and preventing access to skilled work via promotion from within the plant. In the Germanic countries, however, the unions had more power through the dual system in shaping the content of the learning process within the workplace. The Meister system of trained supervisors resulted in the development of higher levels of skill formation and utilisation within the workplace.

At this phase in the development of the productive forces, IRs were clearly differentiated from TRs as determinants of skills. However, in the Anglo-Saxon countries it was only the IRs of management that were a central concern to companies, as it was here that the knowledge of the wider market and of the production process was located, and it was this that was seen to determine the overall success of the companies. The shift to the right along the IRs dimension was only taking place for the senior members of the organisation. In the Germanic countries, the establishment of the dual system ensured that the skilled workers were also included.

Interpersonal relations in mature mass production

While the skills of managers and other professional and technical staff were of crucial importance to the business strategy of companies with a mass production strategy, it was not until the next phase in the development of the productive forces – that of mature mass production – that we see for the first time the skills of the majority of labour force becoming important for the success of the firm as they became an integral part of management's competitive strategy. At this stage employers' claims that workers' skills were their most important asset became more than just management rhetoric.

We saw in Chapter 3 how lean production developed in Japan and the importance of management techniques such as BPR, Kaizan, JIT and TQM in this change. Taken together the result of these changes was the development of a very different system of authority within the Japanese enterprise to that found in the command and control system used in the West (Dore, 1973). Far fewer managers and supervisors were required and layers of management eradicated. Hierarchy and status divisions remained but authority was now more diffused throughout the organisation. Information about business processes and performance was disseminated to the employees. Managers became team leaders and workers were called upon to make decisions that were vital for identifying and implementing improvements in performance.

These new management practices were therefore important in reshaping IRs and creating a demand for new skills. These changes were also introduced in the context of a system of lifetime employment which meant that Japanese management were willing to invest in the training of their workers, creating a form of career progression and a sense of progression within the company, while payments systems rewarded length of service (loyalty) skill formation and individual performance, a system thoroughly explored and explained by Koike (1996). The consequence was very high levels of skill use among many Japanese male manual workers. Japanese female workers were generally excluded from this process and subject to different HR management practices, as they had no security of employment.

These measures, which strengthened the sense of identification on the part of the workers with the company, were reinforced by other measures such as the use of company houses and company help with education and welfare of family members and were cemented by the introduction of company unions. The result was the building of a strong sense of identification with the company among employees, which in turn engendered a degree of trust in relations between the male manual workers and their managers, although this by no means eradicated differences of interest between senior management and other employees.[6]

Koike and Inoki (1990) refer to the skills of male employees as having both 'depth' and 'breadth'. Skills in depth came from the fact that workers were trained to understand the production system and the manner in which it worked and crucially developed these skills over time as they accumulated experience. Skills in breadth come from the policy of moving workers around a range of tasks so that they understood the workings of the department in which were located and the various tasks within it (1990: 10–15). These workers were actively involved through their work teams in problem solving, improving work systems and ways of working and in effect participating in decision making and problem solving. When fully trained they could therefore spot potential problems and had the authority to stop the assembly line, and if necessary, to resolve them.

These practices then transferred to the West and the rest of the world as companies sought to respond to Japanese competition. In the West they became known as 'high-performance work practices' (HPWPs) or systems because of the improvements in performance they promised. In the academic world, although the concept is widely used it is accepted as a 'fuzzy' concept (Boxall, 2012: 171; Payne and Lloyd, 2004), with some preferring the more neutral concept of high-involvement practices (HIPs) (Boxall and Macky, 2009; Wood and de Menzes, 2011).[7] Yet whatever label we attach to such management practices, to Western companies still using bureaucratised command and control systems of authority, and with a history of mutual distrust between management and worker, the Japanese approach represented a serious challenge. As we have seen, Western companies responded by introducing the techniques of TQM, QC, cellular production, Six Sigma and BPR, JIT and Kaizan, sometimes in combination but sometimes on their own as specific management initiatives.

The early academic analysis of these issues stressed that the introduction of these techniques as part of lean production required changes in the TRs, such as the introduction of cellular manufacturing and the eradication of buffer stocks, as well as in HR management practices, but the research on HPWPs was hijacked by the HR profession and tended to focus on the importance of bundles of practices and ensuring that practices were complementary (Boxall, 2012: 171). Yet for managers and other academics working outside the HR context, the focus remained on introducing HPWPs as part of a wider process of change involving change in TRs in the form of advanced manufacturing technology and later IT, where the new HR practices were used to change IRs in order to maximise the effectiveness of the new technologies (Shah and Ward, 2003; de Menezes et al., 2010; Brynjolfsson and Hitt, 2003).

The operationalisation of the new high performance HR techniques required major changes in the ways companies were managed, moving from a system of command and control to one where the employment relationship was more firmly grounded in consent, therefore creating a system of IRs in which skills become more people-focused. For example, TQM if fully implemented involves top management initiating a culture change, away from a concern with pushing through production at any cost to meet deadlines and leaving quality issues to quality inspectors, towards a situation where all employees are concerned with quality and customer satisfaction, whether that customer is another group within the organisation or a customer outside the organisation, and where meeting or exceeding customer requirements is an integral of the company's values. Operatives were now involved in the process of ensuring that goods are made right first time and in making further improvements in the production process. To this end processes were subject to measurement and objective data were used to remedy defects in the process of production and establish a culture of continuous improvement. In many respects Six Sigma is a further development of this, the aim being to reduce process variation so that virtually all the products or services meet or exceed customer expectations. This involves process improvement, process design or re-design and process management (DTI, 2004). Again, it means the involvement of employees either in the process directly or in the implementation of solutions.

The introduction of other techniques had a similar impact on traditional ways of organising the production system. For example, 'quality circles' involve employees who are doing similar work meeting regularly to analyse product quality and production problems and identify solutions. A senior worker or a supervisor usually leads the group. These groups are also used as part of schemes for continuous improvement. Employee involvement (primarily an IRs practice but also having implications for TRs) is a technique used more by Western companies and had its origins in their experience of worker participation in decision making in the 1930s (Lawler et al., 2001). This advocated a bottom-up approach to management where jobs were organised around a complete part of the production process (as in cellular manufacturing), where the employees operating in teams made the major decisions about how the work and production was organised. It meant employers making new demands for communication, multi-skilling and multi-tasking, problem solving and monitoring skills among operatives (Westergaard-Neilson, 2008: 219).

All these techniques required that management modified the old command and control system of authority. Hierarchy and status divisions were reduced and more explicit forms of status distinction removed, such as separate canteens for different grades of staff and separate conditions for holiday pay. Information about business processes and performance that was previously the province of management had to be disseminated to the employees. This threatened the status of the old managers and the operational abilities of those socialised in a command and control culture who now had to lead rather than command. Similarly, workers who had previously been told that all decisions about production were the managers' prerogative were now involved in the production process.

As we saw earlier, the devolution of authority to workers meant that layers of management and supervision could be eradicated and labour costs lowered, spelling the end to the old system of career progression. However, this also meant that new means of motivating both managers and workers had to be found. The solution was to commit both management and workers to the values and goals of the organisation as this became the basis for personal motivation. It meant recognising the part played by all employees as important to the overall performance of the company. This involved far more than just the publication of a company mission statement, it meant the transformation of both managers' and workers' behaviour and attitudes and, as we shall see in the next chapter, this was not a change that could be achieved overnight. Managers had to be seen by their employees to buy into their own values, to 'walk the talk'; workers had to be convinced that they could trust their managers, to commit themselves to the company's values and acquire new skills and behaviours.[8] It is not surprising, therefore, that these transformations tended to be more successful when implemented by Japanese rather than Western managements (Doeringer et al., 2002).[9]

These new management practices therefore represented a major change in the employees' skills of those that operated with them. TQM, Six Sigma and quality circles required that employees develop skills in identifying quality problems in their day-to-day activities while seeking continuous improvement in their own work. Systems of employee involvement and cellular manufacturing required that employees take responsibility for the organisation of their own work and output. All these required that they have the intellectual tools to make sense of, and utilise, business information, and have the decision making capability and authority to implement solutions together with the team-working skills to operate effectively as a unit. Managers could no longer sit back and tell workers what to do, they now had to develop leadership skills, act as role models, learn to inspire better performance and support the development of employees.

What was also evident was that the full benefit of these practices on performance outcomes was only realised when workers utilised their intellectual powers and skills to identify areas where improvement could be made and then implemented the change. It was the exercise of the workers' discretionary effort that was helping companies achieve a competitive advantage in the market through continuous improvements in the product or service they produced. That effort only came through the sense of commitment to the organisation and its values, a commitment which in turn is built on a sense of mutual trust. It was based on the belief that, in exchange for the exercise of the extra discretionary effort, the employee would participate in any performance gains that the company achieved (Sparham and Sung, 2008; Boxall, 2013). It was this sense of trust and mutual gains that was missing from a number of attempts to implement these practices in response to the intensification of international competition that took place in the late 20th and early 21st century and led to many failures in implementation, a situation we discuss further in the next chapter.

One of the outward manifestations of this shift to the people-focused end of the IRs dimension was the development of new ways to link the management of personnel to the business strategy. In organisational terms this came in the form of a shift in focus of management, from treating staff as units in an administrative process to treating staff as a major human resource. This was reflected in the change of name of the appropriate management function from staffing or personnel administration, characteristic of previous forms of mass production when 'hands' were administered, to HR management where employees were regarded as assets that required developing. A competitive strategy that demanded the greater involvement of the employees meant that new ways had to be found of eliciting this involvement, of supporting all employees (managers and workers alike) in the development of their skills and of rewarding them for their contribution. New techniques for structuring these and linking them to the business objectives of the company had to be introduced. These were the techniques associated with the emergence of HR management and strategic HR management.

The qualities employers wanted from recruits also changed. Companies no longer wanted unskilled or semi-skilled labourers who could turn up regularly, accept the discipline of the factory and perform a limited range of tasks. They now wanted literate employees, who were capable of learning and developing new skills. Worker attitudes became important as companies demanded evidence of a willingness among recruits to commit themselves to company goals and values. To identify these attributes required a more elaborate recruitment process, often utilising techniques such as psychometric tests during the selection process.

The development of competence

In order to develop the new skills of team-working, decision making, communication, multi-skilling and problem solving, as well as supporting the identification of employees with the values of the organisation, new ways of supporting learning had to be devised. Less use was made of formal classroom training, and on-the-job training and workplace learning became more important. This was structured through the use of competences which enabled the company to identify the skills, abilities, attitudes and behaviours required to perform effectively in the workplace. The use of competences was itself a recognition on the part of companies that learning at work was crucial for all the workforce covered by them. They were the means by which the company ensured that employees had not only the practical skills required for the execution of tasks but also the behaviour and mental attributes that would ensure effective operation within the team and their commitment to the organisation. Crucially, competences ensured that skill formation at all levels in the organisation was tied to the objectives of the organisation. They are the source of what many refer to as the company's 'core capabilities' (see the discussion in Chapter 1), which in many mature mass production companies were now an important part of their competitive advantage.[10]

The effective use of competencies also required that they became the basis on which individual employees were evaluated and rewarded. While competency frameworks are often developed as a result of a fairly rigorous process of interviews within companies, they inevitably contain not just elements of the technical demands of the job but also crucial aspects of the culture of the organisation and the values the company promotes. These often contain competences such as 'a concern for quality' or 'a customer focus', which signify elements of the company values and as such they are crucial in shaping interaction within the organisation and ensuring that they become embedded in the culture. They are all about shaping behaviour. In this respect these competencies represent a huge extension of the range of behaviour that mature mass production and more knowledge-intensive companies seek to control on the part of their employees.[11] Of course some companies are better at identifying and using competences than others. For some companies with a weak culture it may be a superficial exercise, but for others it is a crucial part of building their competitive strategy.

To achieve these objectives, learning and performance levels had to be identified through regular appraisals. These were used to highlight the areas where further learning was required, where training may be used to help and where the individual employee was expected to focus their own efforts in the learning process. Often these were supplemented by personal development plans to specify precisely where that effort was required and where the company may be able to provide support and to identify the progress made over time.

As production in these companies was more knowledge-intensive, managers had to devise systems that would convey business information to most or all employees. These took the form of team briefings and regular departmental meetings, with extensive use being made in more recent years of the intranet. In addition, attempts were made to solicit feedback from employees through suggestions schemes, although the primary means of achieving this was through work teams and special project teams associated with the use of TQM and continuous improvement and annual surveys. For workers, training was no longer seen as a short, one-off exercise conducted on entry to the organisation during which employees were instructed in the limited number of tasks, but rather as part of a continuous learning process which the company and the line managers were expected to support. It was recognised that such learning required not only periods of formal instruction (especially for technical and theoretical issues), but also a great deal of guided or semi-structured on-the-job learning through which skills in team-working, problem solving and decision making were acquired (Green et al., 2001). Support was delivered through practices such as coaching and mentoring, which provided tuition in the workplace. This in turn meant ensuring that managers and supervisors had the requisite skills to support the learning process. In these companies the workplace now becomes an important locale for learning.

Payment systems also had to change. For managers, whose career ladders had been eradicated or condensed, increments that marked their progression were no longer appropriate. Now payment systems had to reflect all aspects of their performance, both task oriented and behavioural, and so various types of performance-related pay were developed. For workers, these took numerous forms, some rewarding individual performance, some company performance, others team performance or various combinations of these. Commitment to the success of the company was rewarded through bonuses and profit sharing schemes. For workers piece rates were now inappropriate, although performance-related pay was not as extensively used as it was for managers. In the UK in 2011, 24 per cent of non-managerial employees had their pay partly determined by performance appraisal (WERS, 2013). For those companies that adopted these changes all this recognised the importance of mutual gains, namely the employee delivering improved performance and the company or employer recognising this through a share in the productivity gains.

Once developed within companies, these competences enable the management to take control of a much greater part of the skill formation process while shaping a broader spectrum of the employees' behaviour. They were now no longer dependent on external training providers to deliver the skills and attitudes necessary for effective performance. This freed employers from reliance on national systems of training provision. They now controlled the delivery of technical skills and attributes and these could now be finely tuned to those required by the company, and resources and time would not be 'wasted' on employees learning skills that were not directly relevant to the production process. This in turn meant that the time taken to achieve effective performance could be reduced, enabling companies to reduce the cost of 'training' and the time taken to establish new operations. While these changes were important for national-based companies, they were of even more significance for

MNCs precisely because they had more options as to where they located production. Together these attributes of company competences meant that MNCs were now largely in control of skill formation and could reproduce the skills necessary to achieve their competitive advantage in any geographical location on the globe providing that a basic educational infrastructure was in place (Ashton et al., 2010).

This shift towards the people-focused end of the IRs dimension did not necessarily embrace all the employees. As we have seen, even in Japan, from the outset, female and casual employees were excluded. In the other companies in many countries these new high-performance management practices were only partially applied or fully applied only to management and other core staff, which meant excluding casual and unskilled employees. These are issues that will be discussed in the next chapter when we explore the implications of the partial introduction of HPWPs.

Service sector

Interpersonal relations in mass service delivery

As the application of the principles of mass production to the service sector took place long after they were developed in the manufacturing sector, employers could utilise the management system that had originally been pioneered there. With the advent of mass service delivery we therefore witnessed the same shift to the right along the IRs when it came to managers. Within the context of traditional command and control systems, employers used the same bureaucratic hierarchies to provide the means for controlling the commitment of managers to the organisation and used the same professional technical skills that were used in the manufacturing sector. Indeed, many of these are still in use today. However, because these changes came later, ICT played a more prominent part in their introduction.

In most service sector companies in retail and hotels and restaurants there was less emphasis on R&D skills because the end product did not require the same level of technical input as that often required for manufactured goods such as cars or electronic goods. Nevertheless, companies such as Wal-Mart did make major innovations in the use of ICT to restructure work processes. All this meant that management played the same crucial role in coordination as they did in mass production manufacturing firms. Here also there was the same gearing of company resources to the development of management skills, including the use of appraisals, management development programmes and techniques such as shadowing and personal development plans.

For the operatives in this sector there was no such shift to the right. To the contrary, the introduction of mass service delivery capitalised on the deskilling of many service sector jobs, allowing the companies to utilise pools of unskilled female and student labour. In the case of the check-out assistants and shelf-stackers in retail establishments and the waiters and waitresses and housekeepers in hotels, their skills were minimal and task-focused and therefore few resources were devoted to developing them. Jobs could be learnt in a very short period of time, usually on the job. The main concern of employers was in recruiting staff with the old behavioural traits of reliability, ability to accept discipline and in some cases low level literacy, numeracy and IT skills. What became more important for this group of workers was the need for low-level customer service skills.[12]

As Grugulis has pointed out, 'When customers purchase the process of being served as well as (or instead of) a physical product, employees become an integral part of the sale' (2007: 92). Their emotions are controlled in accordance with the requirements of the company. This may involve displaying feelings such as enthusiasm and empathy which may on occasion be genuine, but such emotions are prescribed and failure to display them can incur sanctions. They have to be warm, friendly and helpful whenever the script that defines their behaviour demands it and no matter what the circumstances. In some instances personal appearance is also scripted, as is the conversation with the customer and their responses. Of course the precise demands differ from job to job; staff in a restaurant or serving on an airline may have their appearance prescribed while those in a call centre may not, but the interactions of the call centre staff member on the telephone may be far more tightly prescribed than that of the flight attendant – what becomes important as a 'skill' is the ability of the employee to handle these demands. However, not all service sector firms rely on these skills; in parts of retail such as supermarkets as well as in the newer budget hotels, the use of IT has allowed companies to experiment with 'serving staff through the use of machines'.[13]

Interpersonal relations in mature service delivery

When companies in the service sector sought to differentiate their service through a higher quality, more personalised delivery, this involved the same shift to the right along the IRs dimension but it did not necessarily involve the same transformation of the TRs. This illustrates what we referred to earlier as the 'relative autonomy of the different relations of production'. Companies seeking to differentiate their product have been able to use many of the management practices we discussed in connection with mature mass production in manufacturing to utilise the skills of their employees in delivering a higher level of service to customers, while maintaining more or less the same TRs as used in the delivery of mass produced services. Boxall (2003: 6) makes a similar point when he argues that in capital intensive manufacturing sectors labour costs are rarely a major cost or source of comparative advantage and therefore companies are more likely to invest in HPWS as a source of competitive advantage.[14]

One consequence of the absence of capital-intensive technology is that the ensuing transformation in skill use is not always as thorough-going as that taking place in manufacturing. In manufacturing the focus for the development of IRs is more on the product, often requiring employees to acquire more complex technical skills, whereas in the service sector the focus is on customer service, which usually means that employees have less complex technical knowledge to acquire. In Koike's terms there is less depth to their knowledge. Moreover, as in manufacturing, some of the companies adopt these management techniques more extensively than others. In his analysis of competitive strategies in the service sector Boxall (2003) identifies three major segments: mass service markets such as fast food outlets and supermarkets; differentiated markets in professional and knowledge-intensive services that we deal with in the next section; and mixed mass markets and higher value-added segments where higher value-added customers can be targeted, as in hotels (Haynes and Fryer, 1999, 2000) and care homes (Eaton, 2000; Hunter, 2000).

We illustrate this here through the use of two case studies from the mass service market where the business strategy was to create a distinctive customer experience. The first case is that of Flight Centre, a travel agency whose extensive use of HPWPs shifts the IRs dimension to the right in delivering a personalised service, although the technology is the same as that used by other travel agents. The second is that of Javi's, a pseudonym for a restaurant delivering fast food with a personalised service but using the same mass produced technology as that typified by companies such as McDonald's. In this case the use of HPWPs is less extensive and the shift to the right on the IRs dimension less pronounced.

The case of Flight Centre

Flight Centre is a global company operating in a very competitive market providing a 'one stop' package selling low-cost travel. It was established in the UK in 1995, and has grown at the rate of 20 per cent per annum. Flight Centre's competitive strategy is to provide a high level of service that not only surpasses customer expectations but has them coming back regularly to Flight Centre and to the same consultant.

As a global company it can obtain economies of scale in purchasing travel, but it also prides itself on its ability to deliver consistency of service. This it does through the use of its standard organisational system, a series of procedures called the One Best Way that is used in every outlet across the globe. These uniform procedures for handling transactions aid staff mobility and enable staff to set up their own outlets in new locations. The company places a high value on innovations as this enables them to keep their system responsive to customer needs and business opportunities. Innovation is particularly important in a market where profit margins are slim and innovations can make a big difference to the everyday business. Each year a Director's Award is given for innovation. If an innovative practice is developed in one shop, it is extensively discussed and then adopted by the rest of the company. Staff get together four or five times a year to work out as a global company which is the best practice, and then all follow that practice.

In order to involve staff in the business and secure their identification with the company and its values, each outlet is run as a separate profit centre making its own decisions about what costs are required for the everyday running. This enables them to incentivise performance at the shop and individual level. Each shop, team and individual have their own targets and each individual staff member manages their own expenditure in order to produce a profit. Staff have a basic salary and then obtain commission but they have to cover their own costs such as phone, desk, accounting costs and then take a share of the profit. Business skills, such as the ability to understand profit and loss, to take advantage of new opportunities and problem solve are central for each member of staff.

The company make extensive use of teamworking, with each shop operating as a team, with staff standing in for each other in the event of illness or absence when they look after each other's client base. When new staff are recruited the shop team has a say in the decision to appoint after the potential recruits spend a day with them. High levels of communication among all staff is encouraged through a variety of techniques. These include weekly meetings and newsletters, while the intranet is used extensively as a tool for updating business information and facilitating comparisons of performance to encourage 'internal' competition between teams. HR managers or directors attend national and global business forums in order to share good practice and information about what has worked elsewhere. In addition, regular SWOT meetings are held among six of the key UK management teams and everyone attends a national conference in the UK.

Part of the culture is the value attached to egalitarianism and this takes the form of a 'flat' hierarchy, where leadership is by example rather than position, with leaders training other staff by example rather than telling them what to do. The front-line staff, the consultants, are seen as the drivers of the business and are supported by a range of departments.

All staff wear the same uniform regardless of their function. Similarly, everyone is treated in the same way when it comes to benefits and perks of the job, regardless of their position in the company. No one has a secretary as they do their own back-office work and they all travel together in the same class. The company seeks to celebrate unity.

In order to generate and develop the skills required to operate in this environment, the company has an extensive system of learning support. For all staff a continuous programme of training and development starts from day one. A range of training and personal development is provided both in the office and in the Flight Centre UK Learning Centre, and covers a range of areas that are built up as the individual develops. To support development, monthly one-to-one sessions are given. These sessions provide continuous feedback and the opportunity for staff to air any problems or areas for development. Leadership is highly valued and there is a Leadership Development Programme provided for those identified as having potential, resulting in 90 per cent of team leaders being promoted internally.

In order to further support their staff and reinforce their identification with the company and its values, two further programmes are in operation to support well-being (Health Wise) and the development of financial acumen (Money Wise). Health Wise provides a personal health and fitness consultation, followed by 'a lifestyle assessment' and individual training plan. The Health Wise team also organise social events. Money Wise provides professional financial advice to staff, which covers matters ranging from pension schemes to advice on products such as insurance, mortgages and investments.

The success of the Flight Centre in securing the commitment of its employees is reflected in the fact that it regularly features among the top 100 in the UK *Sunday Times 100 Best Companies to Work For* surveys. However, while it continually develops its employees, it is worth remembering that driving this is a desire to stay ahead of the competitors through constant innovation in a highly competitive market where companies operate on thin margins.

The case of Javi's

Like Flight Centre, Javi's[15] is a company that seeks to differentiate its service from that offered by competitors by offering low-cost fast food but with a family friendly personalised service (Kakavelakis, 2008). To deliver this did not require staff to develop the same business problem solving, leadership and teamworking skills that were evident at Flight Centre but it did require the use of management practices that made a partial shift to the right on the IRs dimension resulting in the development and utilisation of customer service skills.

As with many fast food restaurants the company had a limited food menu, with menu preparation, food prices and décor centrally determined. The staff wore standard uniforms and even the music was centrally determined. Customers placed their order at the till and took their own cutlery, paying for the food before delivery. Staff took the food to table and took orders for sweets. Unlike many other fast food outlets, interactions with customers were not scripted.

Interpersonal relations were designed to generate a caring, family-like atmosphere in the workplace and to encourage this to inform the staffs' interaction with customers. The company had made a step towards devolving authority but the researchers described authority relations as paternalistic, with the manager taking on a surrogate parent role, dealing with the personal problems of staff, always open to chat and providing a role model as someone to learn from. The company recognised the importance of this as the managers' store performance was checked against staff welfare.[16]

The family friendly values that the staff were encouraged to adopt were reinforced by a number of practices. Recruitment tended to be through family members to ensure that staff fitted into the 'family' theme. In addition, the company encouraged staff to have family days where managers and staff got families together and socialised outside working hours. To support these the restaurant had a fun budget of £1,200 per year and a competition based on mystery shopper results. The staff then decided how to spend the money.

Training was given to ensure that staff could exercise personal discretion in handling the interaction with customers. New recruits learnt through a 'buddy' system over two weeks followed by a period of shadowing during which the skills in customer service were transmitted. Appraisals were conducted every three months. These were used to ensure adherence to standards, but there was no monitoring against detailed training and operation manuals as at McDonald's. After three months staff could be cross-trained. Half the management positions were filled from within, providing possibilities for career progression.

Although there was still a clear hierarchy, attempts were made to minimise differences. Managers had to be able to do all the jobs and jump in to help when necessary. All this encouraged an 'all in it together' attitude and a commitment to the goals of the company. It encouraged a friendly attitude among staff, supported by a system of sharing out tips on a monthly basis. The result of these practices was to create a friendly family-like atmosphere which was used to attract customers and also to compensate staff for the low wages. This produced a substantially lower turnover rate than is typical for the sector, reducing labour costs and thereby increasing performance.

These then are just some ways in which the competitive strategies of companies have led them to utilise the skills of their employees.

In the service sector, while they do not necessarily involve employees in acquiring detailed technical skills, they do involve them in acquiring knowledge of the overall business and its processes, and using the knowledge to forestall and resolve problems and to communicate effectively with other staff and customers. The two case studies also highlight the considerable variation there is in the extent to which employers do use skills even when their competitive strategy drives them to rely on employee skills.

The other point to be raised in discussing the use of HIPs or HPWPs in the service sector is that in some parts, such as retail, companies may choose to use such practices for their managers and core staff but not for their more 'marginal' part-time and seasonal staff. Boxall (2012) reports the example of a large British retail company investigated by Seibert and Zubanov (2009), who found that some full-time managers and experienced employees were managed on a 'commitment system'. This group represented approximately 20 per cent of the workforce, whereas the large group of part-time workers were managed in a 'secondary system'. These employees had less responsibility, less specialist training, fewer promotion opportunities and a flat pay structure. Boxall argues that this is not unusual in retail because of the seasonality of the business. Others such as Huselid and Becker (2011), Lepak et al. (2006) and Lepak and Snell (1999) have noted the significant differences in terms of the extent to which employers use HR practices. Again, this serves to highlight the variations in the extent to which employers in the services sector use the skills of their employees as a source of competitive advantage.

In the service sector, as in manufacturing, the other factor that influences the extent to which employers choose to follow the high-commitment, 'high road' route as opposed to the low-commitment, cost reduction 'low road' approach, is the institutional context within which the market is located. In the Nordic countries there is evidence that employers in the service sector operating in an institutional context of high levels of unemployment insurance, low wage differentials and high levels of trust between employers and workers, are more likely choose to adopt this type of 'high road' competitive strategy, based on delivering quality services rather than one based on cost reduction. Sorenson (2008) found that even in Danish call centres employers were more likely to use employee involvement, redesigned jobs, basic career structures and provision for the exercise of employee discretion as the basis for their competitive strategy. Again, this strategy is the choice of the employer, and some Danish companies do opt to compete just on price but it is a choice that is clearly influenced by the labour market context within which the companies operate.

Knowledge-intensive production

Interpersonal relations in knowledge-intensive production

During this latest phase of economic development the growth of knowledge-intensive production has created the opportunity for business leaders to utilise the skills of their employees as their competitive advantage in a way that we have never seen before. Under mature mass production, we saw for the first time that the skills of most employees had the potential to contribute to the competitive advantage of the business. Although the skills of manual workers/operatives were not developed to the same potential as those of managers, they nevertheless could make a serious contribution to the competitive advantage of the company. Under knowledge-intensive production we take a significant step further to the right along the IRs dimension in that the skills of all employees can make a major contribution to company success. Where employers choose to adopt this strategy, employees' intellectual and practical skills are developed to very high levels. It is not surprising therefore that research has shown that such firms operating in skill-intensive industries invest more in 'people management' practices (Bloom and Van Reenen, 2007). Of course, as with other types of productive system, some employers will choose not to utilise their employees' skills to the same extent in their competitive strategy. At the moment there is only a sparse literature on employee skills in these organisations so in what follows we rely largely on our case studies (Sung and Ashton, 2005; Sung et al., 2009b).

The reason why there is this potential for the greater development of employee skills in knowledge-intensive firms is that there is less reliance on the technology to deliver the competitive advantage and more on the knowledge and commitment of employees. We use three companies from our research files to illustrate the point. St Luke's, a UK-based advertising agency, provides innovative marketing for a range of national and international companies; W.L. Gore, a USA-based R&D company, provides innovative ways of utilising the Gore-tex® fabric; and Data Connection (now called Metaswitch), a UK-based firm, provides solutions to the communication problems of MNCs. In each case the companies rely almost totally on the capabilities of their staff to generate and deliver the goods or services.

Where employers do choose to use the skills of their employees as the source of their competitive advantage, the authority relations that underpin IRs are very different from earlier forms of production. The need to generate and sustain the commitment of employees to company goals and objectives, and reinforce their buy-in to company values, means that these companies often used share ownership and profit sharing schemes to provide a direct link between group performance and individual reward. This is also instrumental in generating a sense of fairness in the distribution of rewards and is the basis for the development of high levels of trust between employees at all levels. Organisational hierarchies are reduced to a minimum so that authority tends to be more consensual than bureaucratic. In St Luke's the employees have their own form of employee council through which they can challenge managerial decisions. In W.L. Gore, the company policy is to keep its operating units below 250 members in order to reduce the use of formal bureaucratic rules and regulation. There, leaders are not appointed by senior management but rather they are people who emerge with a good idea and have succeeded in persuading their colleagues to join them in its development. These are organisations that are consciously experimenting with new forms of post-bureaucratic authority.

What this means for members/employees of these organisations is that they must learn to exercise high levels of self-control. As these employees internalise the values of the company, these values are used to guide their behaviour. Where this happens there is no longer any need for formalised rules with their associated sanctions to shape behaviour. What we have is a situation that encourages collaborative and collegiate behaviour. In contrast to command and control organisations, where control is maintained through sanctions such as fines, dismissal, warnings and so on, which come into play whenever rules are broken, these new organisations rely on the employee internalising the goals of the organisation and utilising these to monitor their own behaviour. For example, in W.L. Gore, employees are expected to make decisions on where they work, which innovations should be developed and even what length of absence personal bereavement should warrant, all such decisions being made in the light of the consequences of their decisions for the other members of the organisation. This requires very high levels of emotional intelligence and communication skills.[17]

As such organisations rely primarily on the skills of all their employees for their competitive advantage the process of learning tends to take on different characteristics from that found in mature mass production. In mature mass production, learning is still viewed as requiring a separate budget for training activity, with formalised provision and clear boundaries established on what can and cannot be learnt, and what information should be supplied to different categories of employees. There, a great deal of learning still takes place through formal, off-the-job training provision, and separate provision for group participation in continuous improvement sessions, quality circles and so on. Under knowledge-intensive production the ability of staff to generate new knowledge is so crucial to business success that learning becomes all-pervasive.

The growth of these companies has given substance to the phenomenon of knowledge management. These companies have to capture their new knowledge if they are to sustain a competitive advantage in the market. Knowledge management focuses on how that knowledge is organised, combined and leveraged in order to enhance the performance of the organisation. Modern IT has further increased the importance of knowledge management as it has facilitated the dissemination and sharing of information and ideas across functions and organisations. Initially, the idea of knowledge management was something of a fad, in the same way that TQM and other practices were propagated by consultancy companies and publications such as Senge's *Fifth Discipline* (1990) as one-off solutions to problems of performance. However, where the concept of the learning organisation was misleading was in the impression it gave that all learning was important, whereas in fact it is only the learning that is central to the business objectives of the company that is crucial, and this is primarily to be found in companies in the software and professional services and the R&D in knowledge-intensive organisations.

The all-pervasive character of learning means that it is far more likely to be treated as a central component of the competitive strategy for companies with this type of productive system. Where it is, learning is so tightly integrated into operational processes that it does not make sense to have a separate training budget. It is so much a part of the everyday process of production, of everyday interactions of staff as they create new products or deliver customer solutions, that company accountants find they cannot isolate costs for it.[18] For example, part of the manager's job is to foster the process among colleagues, therefore mentoring and coaching are not seen as separate activities but part and parcel of the manager's everyday activities. In Data Connection managers are evaluated, as a central part of their performance review, on how well they develop their subordinates. Feedback on performance is a part of their everyday interactions and leadership functions. Informal interaction between members of the teams working on common problems is routine and special provision is made for sharing knowledge within the company and bringing in new knowledge from outside, both from other companies and academia.

This is not to say that the process of learning is unstructured. Indeed, given that it is so central to competitive success in the marketplace in companies such as Data Connection, it is highly structured. Central to the process is the ability to give and receive criticism and feedback, without giving offence or destroying self-esteem, and without which learning cannot take place. At Data Connection this is the only area where the company insists that all new employees attend a formal course, provided by their own staff. As for the content of the learning, this is structured around company competences. These identify both the technical knowledge required and the cultural and leadership attributes expected in the course of development. In W.L. Gore, these competences were articulated in the founder's basic principles and, while there were no officially designated managers to transmit them, each new employee nominated one member of the group to act in an advisory capacity to transmit these attributes.

In knowledge-intensive companies the competences then provide the focus around which learning takes place, and this is monitored and supported by the team managers both informally in everyday interaction and formally in evaluation sessions. At Data Connection these take the form of weekly team meetings where the team performance is discussed in the context of the budget and where problems are identified and measures to overcome them agreed. In addition to these weekly meetings there are regular review meetings. In these one-to-one meetings managers provide individuals with feedback on performance and crucially how the company will provide support for any areas where improvement can be made. These reviews can take the manager a day to prepare for and include a detailed discussion of the individual employee's progress and career objectives.

A further characteristic of these knowledge-intensive companies is the establishment and maintenance of high levels of trust between colleagues at all levels, fellow professionals, managers and company chiefs. As we have seen, trust is important in companies using mature mass production, but in knowledge-intensive companies it is vital. Without such trust, the process of collaborative learning is halted, as individuals respond to criticism by holding on to their own knowledge to protect their position. For learning to proceed there has to be an assumption that no one intentionally makes mistakes and that when individuals do, they do so because of a failure on the part of others to show them the correct way of doing things or to provide the relevant knowledge. These are some of the conditions required to create and sustain the exercise of discretionary knowledge and collaborative learning. Another obvious condition is the widespread dissemination of business knowledge so that employees make decisions in full knowledge of the companies' business situation. Business information is therefore routinely shared across the organisation and business awareness is an important part of the learning process for all employees. Such conditions can be difficult to sustain but easy to destroy, as once lost, trust is difficult to regain, and without it company leadership cannot generate the commitment and levels of innovative thinking that is necessary for business success. Together, these developments in the latest phase of the development of the productive system are moving the competitive strategies of these organisations towards the people-focused end of the IRs dimension.

There are of course some exceptions. As we mentioned earlier, not all knowledge-intensive companies rely on the collective skills of all their staff for their competitive advantage; in some areas of the financial services such as fund management, much still rests on the ability of the individual manager, while other companies will seek to make a profit from using the skills of programmers to provide codes without investing in the development of those skills. In other instances, where the company is under strong cost pressures, then that component of knowledge work which can be rationalised (e.g. the use of standardised processes that can be codified and computerised) will be undertaken by lower-skilled employees (Holmes, 2008). Even at this level, the process of deskilling is still operating.

Conclusions

The realm of skill use is where we have witnessed the major change in employers' use of skills and in the type of skills demanded by employers. This has led academics to carve out a new sub-discipline of workplace learning, while governments have responded to these changes by introducing programmes of lifelong learning. Yet the main driving force behind these changes has been the growth of organisations using business strategies requiring mature mass and knowledge-intensive production. Formal classroom-based training characteristics of industrial mass production have declined relative to the growing importance of the workplace as the source of the acquisition of the new skills, reflecting the growing use of competence frameworks to organise the new forms of learning. As we have seen from the case studies cited above, each workplace has its own set of norms and values and processes of change that constrain behaviour and which have to be learnt and accommodated for. The other driving force has been the rise of consumer demand and the need for the service industries to compete through customer service.

The other important aspect of this change is the transformation of the skills required for these new forms of production to function efficiently. There is still a tendency to conceptualise skills as personal attributes that have value in the market based on the notion of the craftsman as possessing 'real' skill. The reality of the change is that the attributes required to function effectively in the context of these new production systems are more relational in character and are shaped by the organisations to which we belong, making more demands on the emotions and our ability to handle them and our values as well as our cognitive abilities to resolve problems. At the present time we are struggling to conceptualise these, as we tend to do with all new social phenomena, but it is already abundantly clear that to retain a notion that skills are personal attributes or 'things' that can be sold in the market is to fail to see the enormity of the changes we are witnessing.

While these drivers have changed the type of skills required and the importance of the workplace as a source of learning, it is important to remember that there are still large parts of the economy that are dominated by industrial mass production organisations in both the private and public sectors, using command and control authority systems in which the lower-level worker's job requires relatively few skills, even if some are no more than basic customer service skills (Roberts, 2013).

Notes

1 Cited by Garrett et al. (2010).
2 There were some notable exceptions, such as the early Quaker entrepreneurs, as typified by Cadbury and Rowntree, while others such as Robert Owen had more secular ideals. Their values and beliefs led them to concern themselves with their workers' welfare, but these were unusual.
3 Ducker was critical of the command and control system of authority and advocated a more decentralised form of management.
4 The centrality of managements' skills to business success has more recently been recognised in the work of Huselid and Becker (2011), using the concept of differentiation to point out that the skills of some groups are more central to the success of the enterprise than others.
5 For a description of training for manual workers in a contemporary bureaucratically organised food processing company, see van der Krogt and Warmerdam (1997).
6 Japanese workers tended to be more dissatisfied with their company than English workers, but this may be due to the fact that they had broader expectations (Dore,1973: 216–218).
7 There is a considerable literature that is critical of the concept of HPWPs, with critics pointing out that there is little agreement on what constitutes core practices, that they differ between societies, that the implementation of such practices varies from firm to firm and that the link to performance has never been proved through the use of longitudinal studies (Guest, 2011). Notwithstanding these criticisms, there is an extensive body of evidence that these practices are often linked to improvements in performance (Garrett et al., 2010; Hughes, 2008).
8 There are a number of publications by managers who lead this process of change and which stress the importance of senior managers exhibiting the new behaviours through their own actions (see Wickens, 1999).
9 Not all companies adopted these practices in response to foreign competition; consultancy companies were important in spreading these practices but our research revealed some cases where employers adopted them from their own experience as just sound common sense, e.g. Timpsons (Sung and Ashton, 2005).

10 These core competences refer to the competences that provide a company with its advantage in the market. For example, Apple's core competences refer to its expertise in the design and manufacture of electronic communication devices. Competency frameworks identify the range of skills, beliefs and attributes that employees within any company are expected to acquire. These are usually arranged in a hierarchical manner within the company framework.

11 There is considerable debate in the literature about whether these competences are 'really' skill. This debate misses the point, namely that whether or not we call them skills, these are aspects of employee behaviour that companies seek to control and are important to performance (see Grugulis, 2007: 72).

12 For a discussion of the distinctive nature of service work, see Belanger and Edwards (2013).

13 Here our research has revealed instances of budget hotels in the UK using machines for check-in and the allocation of room keys as well as the more well-known use of automated check-out systems by supermarkets.

14 We would argue that because of the relative autonomy of interpersonal relations companies using labour-intensive mass production technologies can also use HPWS to generate a competitive advantage providing they can establish a market niche to support the extra costs.

15 Kakavelakis (2008) locates this case study in the context of the literature on 'best fit' HR strategy. We have not dealt with this literature because we are not concerned with identifying 'best practice', as our focus is on explaining why companies make different use of skills.

16 In our research into smaller firms we often found a comparable situation in which paternalistic relationships provide the context for the informal use of high-performance work practices (Ashton et al., 2008)

17 For a discussion of emotional intelligence in the context of work in contemporary organisations, see Hughes (2005).

18 This stems from our own research findings in discussions with companies that relied heavily on the skills of their employees for their competitive advantage in knowledge-intensive production.

5

SKILLS, PERFORMANCE AND CHANGE

There are also questions around management and leadership and how we utilise staff. Only 29% of businesses achieve higher performance working, whilst 40% of people report that their skills are under-utilised.

UK Commission for Employment and Skills, 2012

Overview

The last two chapters have demonstrated the ways in which business strategies and productive systems have changed through time, which in turn has driven changes in the demand for skills. In doing this we have tended to assume that the different types of TRs and IRs are associated with each other: for example, task-focused skills are associated with mass production, people-centred skills with knowledge production. Yet we have also noted that once established the TRs and IRs can persist when the conditions that gave rise to them have changed, or to put it another way, these relationships have a degree of relative autonomy. However, we have also stressed that employers have a choices in deciding on their business strategies. Thus if an employer manufacturing mass produced goods wishes to compete less on price and more on quality, this will mean changing the IRs within the company. This is our next task, to explore how firms can modify their TRs and IRs in response to changes in their business strategy, a process that is vital if we are to encourage companies to create jobs of higher quality and that are more demanding in their skills use.

The existing literature provides interesting insights into the barriers that prevent change, especially in the mindsets of employers, as well as the difficulties of introducing change into management practices. However, the process of change is best illustrated and understood through the use of case studies which demonstrate the profound impact that can be made on the level of skills demanded from employees as well as the ways in which employers use the skills of employees in the workplace. To achieve this objective we use case studies: one of a company whose business strategy resulted in the transformation of both TRs and IRs; and another where the change in the company's competitive strategy resulted in a change in IRs, creating new skill demands on employees and substantially increasing performance. While representing successful change, we also spend time examining the case of a company where the attempt to introduce similar new HPWPs and changes in IRs to a system of mass batch production was only partially successful. This highlights the importance of contextual factors, industrial relations, short-term business finance and low-trust relationships that are important in shaping employers' and senior managements' decision making process, barriers to change that are more difficult to tackle and which must be addressed if public policy is to be more effective. These are the issues that we tackle in this chapter.

Introduction

The quotation at the beginning of this chapter, taken from a publication of the UK Commission for Employment and Skills, implies that higher levels of skill utilisation can be achieved by employers simply making more use of HPWPs. It sounds like a straightforward solution but in reality the answer is more complex. It demands a more complete understanding of how companies change their business strategies and how such change affects TRs and IRs within the firm. Once this is accomplished, we can then examine the impact that changes in the TRs and IRs have in shaping skill formation and use within an organisation. It means that we have to step back from involvement in immediate policy issues and understand just how skills are formed and how the process of skill formation is changing. This is the focus of this chapter.

The first section starts by examining what the literature tells us about introducing change into business strategies and management practices, and how these then impact on the process of skill formation and use, for both management and employees. Here it is important to note the difference between improved skill level and use as an outcome and improved skill leading to improved performance, because improved performance may be a result of work intensification and not skill use (Ramsay et al., 2000; Guest, 2011: 4). The second section then explores the issues in greater depth through the use of case studies as we seek to identify the main factors at work in changing both the way skills are formed and how employers use them. It illustrates the problems to be tackled in implementing change at the level of the firm.

Strategic decision making among owners and senior managers

Senior management: changing the business strategy

To understand change in skill levels and utilisation we must therefore start not with individuals but with business strategy. It is senior management/owners who are the interface between the firm and the opportunities and constraints that comprise the market, and it is they who shape how the company reacts to those pressures, although not necessarily in circumstances of their making.

As leaders of companies the skills of this group are crucial as they control the power resources necessary for entry into new markets and for shaping the internal organisation of the company (Teece et al., 1997).[1] It is this group that have to be able to formulate a strategy and drive the changes necessary to pursue the new goals (West and Anderson, 1996). They need the abilities to perceive new opportunities and be willing to act. Here research presents us with a mixed picture. Some leaders do operate in the rational manner characterised by economists, taking advantage of opportunities created by global markets and changes in political regulation of markets, as happened with the deregulation that has taken place since the 1980s, to create and enter new markets. Research has also identified the leadership qualities that senior managers and consultants aspire to: for example, the ability to think outside the box, to inspire colleagues, to think systematically, to grow people through performance and so on (Kouzes and Posner, 2002; Tamkin et al., 2010).

While it is easy to see how these qualities will enable those who may possess them to seize new opportunities and inspire staff to accept change, we just do not know how widespread these 'talents' are or whether they are always effective as leadership qualities. Indeed, other research tells us that there are many business leaders whose behaviour does not match the template of economic actors rationally calculating risks and then taking action as outlined in the economic literature. Instead, it paints a picture of human beings who are apprehensive, emotionally tied to existing procedures and often unwilling to take risks and therefore refusing to take advantage of new opportunities (Storey and Salaman, 2005). This leads to the variety of competitive behaviour that we discuss in Chapter 1. Much of the research under the Miles and Snow (1978) model would agree that rationality is not an adequate explanation of competitive behaviour. What may influence 'defender' or 'prospector' behaviour is very much tied to the interaction between leadership and the environment, the culture/tradition of the organisation and the interpretation of a competitive advantage. Rationality, if applicable, is often defined in these contextual circumstances.

Researching the commercial cleaning industry, Storey and Salaman (2008) encountered firms whose directors were aware of the possibility of moving from the delivery of low value-added to higher value-added activities, of moving from simply supplying services to taking responsibility for planning and coordinating these services and expanding the range of services they delivered. This was a golden opportunity to move up the value chain and to enhance employee skills and to increase productivity and profitability, yet they failed to respond to these opportunities. Storey and Salaman remark that:

> they remained imprisoned by their historic mental models and assumptions, constrained not only by their unwillingness or inability to think in new ways about what their relationship with and propositions to clients and indeed to staff – but also limited by historic and organisational arrangements (management styles and professionalism, staff capacities, organisational systems and cultures) – which seriously limited the capacity of the organisation and its staff to deliver anything other than low-cost, low-skill, provision of conventional and limited cleaning services. (2008: 37).

It is therefore not very surprising that change comes about as a result of other pressures, such as the threat of bankruptcy or as a result of a take-over and, in the public sector, as a result of the appointment of a news CEOs in response to political pressure (Ashton and Sung, 2002; Sung et al., 2009b). One of the problems with current research is that it treats the decision making process as though it were only the province of single individuals, whereas in reality employers' decisions are constrained by other aspects of the relationships they are bound up in. For example, the threat of bankruptcy may 'force' reluctant employers to consider alternative courses of action; competitors marketing a new or upgraded product or service will place pressure on other employers to change their strategy; while political regulation of companies operating a virtual monopoly, as in the utilities, may also constrain decision making (Sung et al., 2009b). In view of this we cannot place sole reliance on attempts to change the employers' mindsets in isolation but we can explore how, in policy terms, the government can influence these broader relationships.

One other important source of constraints on employers can be the internal organisation of their own company. In some instances managers may wish to introduce an innovation but are unable or unwilling to make the changes necessary to implement it, being 'prisoners' of their own organisational structure. When studying innovation in private and public sector organisations, Storey and Salaman (2005) identified major differences in the mindsets of owners and senior managers as of crucial importance. In organisations seen as poor innovators by staff, the senior managers defined innovation in incremental terms, as a risky business that needed to be controlled within the context of formalised structures. At the other extreme were managers in organisations seen as successful innovators who saw innovation as an opportunity for improvement and a chance for all, encompassing change within flat decentralised organisational structures. It is these senior staff that have the greatest power to change both the company strategy and the TRs and IRs, yet we have relatively little knowledge of them in spite of the fact that it is their skills that are often problematic.

There has been some recognition of this in the literature, especially in the UK where management skills are often portrayed as below those of the country's major competitors (Campbell, 2013). However, we tend to have limited means by which to measure management skills. Education qualifications are the most widely used measure, although there is only indirect evidence of a link between educational levels and the ability to make the type of strategic decisions identified by Storey and Salaman. Bloom and colleagues (2011) have used management practices as a more adequate measure, identifying a series of practices that deliver high performance, and assessing management against these practices. While this is a step forward in our knowledge, there is always a danger in such comparisons that what are seen as the 'best' practices are those which perform best in a Western context. Given what we know about the impact of culture, it may be that practices developed by Asian companies may operate better in an Asian context.[2]

We do know that national cultures and institutional structures have an impact on their decision making. We have already seen how, in the UK, the value attached to 'amateurism' among the owners and senior managers of much of British industry after the Second World War was among a number of societal factors that led to a late introduction of professional management techniques of mass production (Wilson and Thomson, 2006).[3] While in the UK this retarded change, in Denmark there is evidence that the institutional structures which delivered 'flexicurity' have been instrumental in facilitating change, for example by increasing the likelihood of managers adopting HPWPs

(Westergaard-Nielson, 2008). We will follow up on the importance of the national cultural and institutional factors when we explore the policy implications in Chapter 6.

Changing management systems and practices and their impact on skills

When we shift the focus from senior managers' general abilities to tackle change and focus more narrowly on those changes that rely more on utilising the skills of employees to deliver a competitive advantage, we can identify two strands of research that have contributed to our understanding. The first we have encountered above, namely that of Bloom and his colleagues, the second concerns the use of HPWPs and HIPs that we saw in the case of some of the companies highlighted in Chapter 4. Here we are concerned with identifying how these two approaches help explain the increase in skill utilisation that has taken place and also how far they help explain the change in the type of skills demanded.

Management quality, skill intensity, work practices and productivity

What these researchers have done is to identify a range of management practices that are correlated with high levels of performance and, indirectly, skills. Bloom and Van Reenen's (2006) survey tool measures practices in three main areas:

- *Monitoring performance* – how well do companies monitor what goes on within their firm and use it for continuous improvement?

- *Use of performance targets* – whether companies set targets and take action if they are not met.

- *Human capital management and reward* – whether companies promote and reward best performance and try to keep their best employees.

They use a total of 18 measures. While many of their measures, especially in the incentive category, are similar to those used by researchers in the HPWPs tradition, these researchers do pay more attention to the TRs, namely the use of automation and IT systems for support, which are included within their monitor category.[4] What they find is that the education levels of management and non-managers (skill level) is linked to superior management practices (Bloom and Van Reenen, 2010a). They argue that the more highly educated managers are more likely to be aware of the benefits of new practices, especially lean production, while the implementation of these practices may be easier when the workforce is more knowledgeable. Our own analysis would doubt the validity of this line of causality, but it does not invalidate the link between education level and the adoption of these practices.

Other work by members of this group has explored the link between HR management practices and skills in more depth (Bloom and Van Reenen, 2010a). Bloom and Van Reenen (2007: 35) found that firms specialise more in investing in 'people management' (referring to promotion, rewards, hiring and firing) when they operate in a more skill-intensive industry. They also find that skill-intensive firms experience greater productivity growth when decentralising their system of authority. These are findings in line with our discussion of knowledge-intensive industries in Chapter 4.

This group has also done significant work on the decentralisation of authority. After highlighting the process of decentralisation, and the associated stripping out of middle management that has been underway in the USA since the 1980s (Rajan and Wulf, 2006), they examined the implications of this process for skills. What they found is that the process of decentralisation has gone further in the USA and Northern Europe than in Southern Europe and Asia. They also found that while the use of computer networks was associated with centralisation, the use of computer-based management tools for managing information, such as Enterprise Resource Planning, was associated with the decentralisation of authority. This they saw as a result of senior management being able to use such tools to monitor outcomes at the operational level and therefore feel comfortable in delegating decision making. Finally they found, not surprisingly, that decentralising leads to skill upgrading within firms (Bloom and Van Reenen, 2010a).

How HPWPs increase the demand for skills

The importance of bundles

We know that HPWPs are associated with higher skill levels among employees (Ashton and Sung, 2002) and we saw in Chapter 3 that these practices are more typically found in companies with high value-added product market strategies. Higher skill levels are also found in companies that compete in international markets (Osterman, 1991) and in knowledge-intensive sectors.[5] Although these practices first appeared in private sector organisations, they are now frequently to be found in public sector organisations (Kalleberg et al., 2006; Wood et al., 2013). They are also more frequently found in the older industrial countries than in the new industrial countries. However, there are problems when it comes to understanding how these practices are linked to an increase in the demand for skills.

First, as we have seen in Chapter 4, there is a longstanding debate in the literature about just what the management practices consist of, with some researchers such as Kalleberg et al. (2006) defining them narrowly in terms of practices that create opportunities to engage in self-directed teams and off-line problem solving committees: multi-skilling practices designed to increase organisational flexibility through cross-training and job rotation and incentives to reward performance designed to enhance commitment to the organisation and reward the exercise of discretionary effort. On the other hand, the UK Commission for Employment and Skills (Wood et al., 2013) defines the practices very broadly, focusing again on three broad areas of employee involvement, skill acquisition and motivational practices but including 22 items (see Table 5.1). This debate is important because, as we shall see, just how widely you define HPWPs has implications for the formation and use of skills.

Second, it is well established in the literature that these practices operate better in bundles, but again there is limited evidence as to how these practices are actually bundled at the level of the firm and therefore how they are linked to the process of skill formation. In the UK this bundling of practices has been explored by Wood et al. (2013). Using a large national survey of employers that identified 14 HPWPs, they found that the use of such practices varied significantly by sector; for example, while only 16.3 per cent of establishments in manufacturing used at least nine of the practices, in financial services it was 43.6 per cent and in public administration it was 54.3 per cent (2013: 15). Using time series data, Wood et al. found that some of these practices (namely providing training, having a training plan, a training budget, evaluating training, having a business plan, employee consultation and performing annual reviews) are highly correlated with each other, suggesting that they are usually interconnected and implemented together. However, while this tells us that such organisations take training seriously within the constraints of their own business strategy, it reveals little about the content of training or the type of skills being transmitted, and these practices are all compatible with traditional command and control organisations. All such practices are doing is to formalise and systematise the existing training for existing skills.[6] They tell us nothing about the type of skills that are being developed or acquired.

Table 5.1   List of High-performance Work Practices (HPWPs) as used in the UK Commission's skills surveys. Adapted from Wood et al., Table 2.1, 2013

High-Performance Work Practices		
Awards performance-related bonuses	Holds ISO 9000	Give employees information about the financial position of the establishment
Individual performance-related pay	Creates teams to work on projects	Have teams of people that solve specific problems
Flexible benefits	Business plan	Have an equal opportunities policy
Training provided		
Training plan	Employee consultation	Formal procedure for dealing with discipline and dismissals
Training budget		Methods to communicate or share information
	Training needs assessment	Employees have task discretion and variety in their work
Annual performance review		Access to flexible working
	Consult with trade unions	Steps taken to overcome a lack of proficiency amongst staff
Work shadowing		Types of on- and off-the-job training provided
	Steps taken to overcome recruitment difficulties	Staff have formal written job description
Formally assess performance after training	Identification of high potential individuals	
Investors in People accredited		

Some HPWPs are of limited use in developing skills

Used on their own, other practices designed to commit employees to the company, such as company-sponsored social activities, wages linked to company profits, participation in events designed to celebrate company values and family-friendly policies, will not necessarily enhance existing skills. In our own research we encountered establishments at the luxury end of the retail markets selling expensive jewellery and luxury goods where the individual salespeople developed personalised links with customers, making sales staff very valuable assets for the companies. Practices designed to secure employee commitment were then used to secure the loyalty of their sales force and so reduce labour turnover. The impact of such practices on skills use was only indirect as they did not increase skill levels or use but they did help the company secure a return on the investment in their skills which they had already made. These practices will only increase skill levels and use when implemented with the other bundles.

The importance of the systematic implementation of practices

The importance of the systematic implementation of bundles has been emphasised by Doeringer et al.'s (2002) study of the use of HPWPs in 48 new branch plants (start-up factories) in three industries that began operating between 1978 and 1990 in the USA. The companies were compared in terms of their use of the newest technology and high-performance management practices and their impact on job quality and productivity. The criteria that came closest to identifying the most successful from the least successful was ownership. Here the researchers found that:

> Japanese-owned transplants typically adopt clusters of high performance management policies that are designed to interact with plant location decisions, operations management practices, and supply logistics. In contrast, most domestic start-ups adopt high performance management practices less frequently and they combine them less systematically with other high performance management strategies. The results are often a piecemeal model of workplace organization that retains many features of command and control management. "This piecemeal model does not exploit the workforce's problem-solving capabilities and it neglects the attention to complementarities that give coherence to the Japanese hybrid model of management." (Doeringer et al., 2002: 209)

Of course this does not mean that there are no American start-ups that resemble the best of the Japanese or that all Japanese start-ups perform equally well. In terms of everyday management practice, what the researchers found was that the Japanese transplants recruit staff who can work in teams, control quality and solve operating problems. These qualities are then reinforced through extensive training and then used in day-to-day situations. By contrast, the domestic plants use these management practices less frequently, have less reliance on problem solving, less concern with hiring workers with teamworking skills and less commitment to identifying interactions among practices.

How HPWPs increase skill utilisation

The importance of devolving authority

What we can be more confident about is that if skills are to be deepened and organisations are to make more use of employees' skills, then authority relations may have to change and other practices introduced. By definition, some practices such as multi-skilling and multi-tasking will, if effectively implemented, generate greater skill use. These practices will increase organisational flexibility and may or may not be welcomed by workers. However, on their own these practices will not necessarily increase the depth of workers' skills unless the organisation implements other practices. To deepen worker skills requires that management devolves responsibility for decision making with regard to the workflow to self-managed problem-solving teams to provide the opportunity to enhance learning and exercise new skills (Felstead et al., 2005). It must also implement practices that will ensure the dissemination of business information to the teams that will enable them to make those decisions in the light of organisational objectives. In addition, the process of learning needs to be supported by practices such as additional off- and on-the-job training, appraisals to obtain feedback on performance, and mentoring and coaching to provide ongoing support in skill acquisition and use.

The importance of sharing information and knowledge

The introduction of teams without the responsibility for problem solving will not necessarily lead to employees developing problem-solving skills, if information and knowledge is not disseminated and if authority to shape work processes has not been devolved. If the teams just consist of a group under the control of a team leader who makes all the relevant decisions and monopolises all the relevant knowledge, then new skills cannot be developed. If authority is devolved to make decisions but workers are not provided with support for developing the necessary problem-solving skills, then skill formation may not take place. The effective development of skills therefore requires that very specific bundles of practices are implemented. Felstead et al. (2009) provide an interesting case of higher levels of learning occurring in the case of a group of health visitors in the UK. In this case authority over the work tasks of the professional staff was fragmented and this provided them with the opportunity to determine their own work processes. However, once traditional forms of authority were re-established, the group of professional nurses were unable to sustain the conditions necessary to support their expansive learning (Felstead et al., 2009: Ch. 4) This serves to remind us that in some instances these institutional supports for learning can be very fragile (Ashton, 2004).

The importance of trust and discretionary effort

Once management practices have been used to change skill levels, if these skills are to be fully used, then there is the separate question of securing the exercise of discretionary effort on the part of the worker. This means persuading the worker to go beyond the basic requirements of the job and to exercise discretion in taking every opportunity to increase performance. For workers to make this effort requires the establishment of trust and the provision of mutual gains by the management.

With regard to trust, this is important for ensuring the commitment of the employee to the organisation's values and to support the process of ongoing learning which provides the basis for the exercise of discretionary effort. Here there is evidence that at the national level some countries have stronger institutional supports than others. In Germany this is provided through the use of works councils (Bloom et al., 2009b; Bosch and Weinkopf, 2008), and in Denmark through the close union–management collaboration (Westergaard-Nielson, 2008). At the organisational level, if employees are to buy in to the values and goals of the organisation, then current research suggests that policies and practices to ensure fairness in the distribution of rewards and equity in treatment of employees need to be put in place. At the individual level, trust is important in ensuring that workers are able to make mistakes as part of the learning process without fear of retribution from their superiors (Ashton, 2004).

The importance of reward and mutual gains

With regard to mutual gains, then, it is important that workers are rewarded for the extra effort their exercise of discretion involves. There is some evidence that workers do obtain some reward in the form of increased work satisfaction from the exercise of higher level skills

(Sterling and Boxall, 2013) and that retention rates increase (Sung et al., 2008), but the sustained use of discretionary effort is likely to be linked to mutuality in the employer–employee relationship (Sparham and Sung, 2008; Boxall, 2013). This requires that employees receive part of the economic gains from the higher performance. This can take different forms. In some contexts it may be in the form of job security or institutionalised career paths, in others it may be in the form of monetary compensation through various techniques such as profit-sharing schemes, performance-related pay and bonuses. It is here that trade unions have a role to play in ensuring that employees share in productivity gains, while they may also be able to help realise those gains by persuading or assisting management in adopting efficiency enhancing changes in their management practices (Green, 2010). What is evident is that higher levels of skills and their exercise in the delivery of higher levels of performance requires that many conditions are in place. It is of no surprise therefore that such a combination of management practices can be difficult to achieve and to sustain over time.

Implementing management practices

The importance of management's buy-in

What is crucial when it comes to the use of skills as a source of competitive advantage is that the changes in these management practices aimed at developing and using employee skills should be thoroughly and carefully implemented. This involves action at a number of levels. It means that implementation should not only be supported by owners and top management but that line managers should also buy in to any change (Guest, 2011). Here the human resource management (HRM) literature suggests that senior management start by ensuring a consistent message to all staff both in terms of what is communicated and by whom. This is reflected in the lessons that ex-managers and consultants often cite in terms of the need for managers to 'walk the talk' (Wickens, 1999). In addition, managers have to be provided with the resources to ensure effective implementation (Stanton et al., 2010).[7]

Further down the hierarchy it is now clear that line managers have a crucial role to play in the implementation of policies, especially where there has been the decentralisation of authority. McGovern et al. (1997) had found the role of the front-line manager to be problematic with regard to the implementation of HR policies, as these managers could distort and undermine official policies. It is important therefore to distinguish between the policies and practice, and also highlight the importance of the employees' experience of them, in order to understand the effectiveness of the implementation. Purcell and Hutchinson (2007) found that front-line managers or team leaders played an important role in mediating the impact of HR policies on employees and that the employees' experience of their relationship with the front-line manager had an impact on their commitment to the organisation and job satisfaction. In this respect Nishii et al. (2008) point to the need for an understanding of the intentions behind management practices as this shapes the response of workers. If workers feel that managers are not sincere in their attempts to implement HPWPs, and that they are only using them as a means of enhancing short-term performance or profits, then they are going to be sceptical about conforming with them in a serious manner. In short, as Purcell and Hutchinson point out, there is an interactive and dynamic relationship between the leadership behaviour of front-line managers and the impact of HR practices, and this can have a serious impact on skill formation and use.

The work of Sterling and Boxall (2013) illustrates this point. They report the case of a company that introduced teamworking and the delegation of authority, enabling workers to make decisions about the organisation of work, and supported by training in problem-solving techniques, with the additional use of key performance indicators to monitor outcomes, many of the right ingredients to increase skill levels. What they found was that in some departments this resulted in higher levels of skill formation with a deeper understanding of the business, and personal benefits for workers from enhanced understanding and seeing improvements in performance. These are the kind of supports that are crucial to support 'expansive' learning (Fuller and Unwin, 2003).[8] In other departments the process of change encountered problems. Some of the workers lacked literacy skills and were reluctant to participate in decision making, while the front-line managers, under pressure to meet production targets, and with staff with literacy problems, were reluctant to delegate authority. In these departments the tasks remained virtually the same and so there were more limited opportunities to develop new skills, and as a result there was limited or more 'restrictive' learning among employees. Crucially, where skill formation and use had been hampered, there was no change in authority relations as the line managers had 'undermined' the policies of senior management.[9]

Worker experience of management practices

This also highlights the importance of understanding the worker experience when looking at change in the process of skill formation and use. Here there has been a significant contribution to our understanding from work in the labour process tradition. This has come about in two ways. First, through their continuing focus on the TRs and especially on the ways in which new technologies were used to introduce Taylorist mass production techniques to deskill white-collar work. For example, Taylor and Bain's (1999) initial work on call centres and the ways in which the technology was used to create 'assembly lines in the head', although the same techniques, as we have seen, have been used to organise work in very different ways (Glucksmann, 2004).

The second major contribution from this tradition has been to our understanding of the impact of HPWPs and HIPs. Here they have provided an important critique of HPWPs, with authors such as Delbridge (1998) highlighting cases where some HPWPs have been used as a means of tightening the control over workers who continued to perform highly routinised tasks and who made little in the way of suggestions for improvement or group problem solving. The company he researched had introduced many HPWPs. Workers were organised in teams but authority was not delegated to the work group, with the team leader making all the decisions about the allocation of work. Similarly, when it came to quality issues, only the team leaders were held directly responsible for quality and performance. Daily briefings of workers rarely last more than two minutes and seldom invoked feedback from workers. Even at management level some managers were withholding information from their superiors in order to meet their efficiency targets. He concludes:

> For workers at Nippon CTV the experience of work – positioned at a moving assembly line repeating endlessly the same limited cycle of standardised tasks – is very similar to that described by previous studies into assembly line. (Delbridge, 1998: 204)

It reminds us that the mere existence of HPWPs may lead to work intensification and does not automatically lead to higher levels of skill or skill use by workers.

This brings us back to the importance of business strategy. If the business strategy is not going to leverage on discretionary effort and mutual gains, HPWPs can be the tools for greater task-based performance and work intensification. From the perspective of people development, the most effective form of HPWP is one that derives performance from workers' discretionary effort. Not only does it provide the basis for higher skills utilisation but there is also some evidence that this form of HPWP provides a sustainable and longer-term enhancement of performance (Birdi et al., 2008; Bloom and Van Reenen, 2010a).

Explaining changes in the type of skills used

Studies of management practices are important in explaining how they generate a demand for different levels of skill and how new skills are acquired. They are of more limited use in explaining how *the type of skills* required in contemporary society are changing. To understand this we need to turn to the debates and research concerning the use of competencies both at the firm and the national level. At the national level, the growth of the service sector meant more employees are engaged in handling IRs to achieve their performance outcomes, creating a demand for teamworking, communication and customer service skills, albeit often at a very basic level.

At the level of the firm, changes in business strategy have been the most important driver leading to the adoption of HPWPs by firms in both the service and the manufacturing sector. When a business starts, it is natural and necessary to provide sufficient training and skills to meet the requirements of TRs. This is the basic level of skills (e.g. technical skills) with which to start a business. What is 'optional' for firms to adopt are the various positions along the IRs dimension. These represent ways in which firms can create a competitive advantage through enhanced performance. Over the last 25 years there has been a long line of management literature that has urged firms to recognise that much of the performance gap between companies is due to the different positions adopted along the IRs dimension. This started with Waterman and Peter's *In Search of Excellence* (1988), followed by Peter Senge's (1990) learning organisation, Daniel Goleman's (1996) emotional intelligence and more recently the HPWPs literature, all of which are different attempts to push companies' positions to the right-hand side of IRs. This has meant more employees working in teams to achieve their objectives, creating a further demand for communication skills and teamworking skills but also for more in-depth problem-solving skills.

With the growth in demand for these soft skills or competences, attempts to measure them on a national scale revealed the existence of underlying or generic competences. First, in the UK and later in Singapore, national surveys used to measure job skills revealed these generic competencies that characterised the labour force. In Figure 5.1 we present the Singapore generic skills index, which identifies 10 major categories, of which four (leadership, influencing, teamworking and emotional labour, referred to as EQ) are primarily concerned with skills in handling IRs at different levels. While we do not have measures of employee skills in the mid-20th century against which we can measure the emergence of these competences, these recent measures underline the significance of soft skills in the management of IRs among the current labour force.

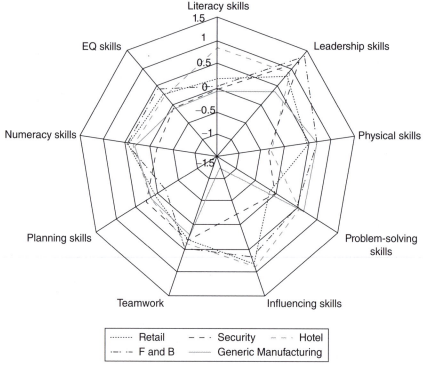

Figure 5.1   The Singapore generic skills index

Source: authors

The academic literature on competences has been dominated largely by the study of national systems (see, for example, Young and Allais, 2011). Here, as in other areas of the skills agenda, the literature illustrates the impact of cultural factors on the ways in which competences are structured. National differences reflect not just the tasks to be performed but also the cultural meanings of skill that stem from differences in national institutions. Thus while the Anglo-Saxon countries tend to focus on the competence required to execute specific tasks, the German definition encompasses the knowledge needed to perform a broader set of functions within the occupation as a whole (Green, 2013: 16; Brockmann et al., 2011; Brockmann, 2013).

At the level of the firm, companies increasingly adopted competence frameworks to structure their learning and skill formation systems. A British survey of HR staff, all members of the Chartered Institute of Personnel and Development (CIPD), revealed that by 2006, 60 per cent of organisations had competency frameworks with half of those without one planning to introduce one in the next two years (CIPD, 2007). Some had different frameworks for different groups of staff, while almost half (47 per cent) had framework(s) that covered all staff. The content of such frameworks provides an insight into the types of skills these companies were seeking to develop within their labour forces. These were: communications skills, 63 per cent; people management, 59 per cent; team skills, 58 per cent; customer service skills, 54 per cent; leadership decision-making skills, 53 per cent; problem-solving skills, 50 per cent; technical skills, 45 per cent; results-orientation attitudes, 42 per cent; and other, 9 per cent.

Such frameworks highlight the behaviours and skills that the company sees as important in achieving their long-term objectives. In view of this it is not surprising that in spite of the similarities with the generic skills cited above, 85 per cent of the organisations that used them had developed them in-house as opposed to adopting those produced by an external organisation. In discussing their implementation in the UK, the CIPD note that recent developments in competency frameworks have led to them becoming broader and more ambitious and including more technical competencies and focusing on the strengths of individual employees (CIPD, 2012).

As we mentioned earlier these frameworks, successfully implemented, enable companies to shape more precisely the skills, attitudes and behaviours of their employees in line with company objectives. Such an approach to the development of employee 'skills' stands in marked contrast to those companies using a command and control authority system and mass production technologies, for whom the skills of their manual employees were of no consequence apart from their abilities to perform routine tasks. This contrast provides a crude indication of the changes that have taken place in the types of skills that are regarded as important, and provides an important part of the explanation for the change in the type of skills used. Of course when discussing these competence systems, the same provisos apply as those discussed in connection with the use of HPWPs, namely that these frameworks are only as effective as their implementation permits. However, when implemented systematically they do represent a powerful tool in generating the demand for new types of skill while at the same time providing the means for controlling the behaviour and activities of the labour force.

The strategic skills model and the process of change

In the light of the lessons learnt from the literature and using the strategic skills model, we now explore the practical problems of implementing change in both skill levels and utilisation. What the strategic skills model highlights are a number of possible scenarios, for example within the manufacturing sector there are a number of theoretical possibilities that we are likely to encounter. First, IRs can remain stable but the firm changes its TRs, for example to move in the direction of knowledge-intensive production but still utilise a command and control system of authority and task-focused IRs. This may push up the demand for higher skill levels, as more such companies will demand graduates, but because of the command and control system of authority, it will not increase the level of skill utilisation. A second possibility is to change both the IRs in the people-focused direction and the TRs in the direction of either mature mass or knowledge-intensive production. This will both increase the demand for higher level skills and create a higher level of skill utilisation. A third possibility is that IRs may change in the people-focused direction but the TRs will remain the same. We double this range of possibilities when we add the service sector, giving us six possibilities. As there is not sufficient space to discuss all these we will take three that are important for policy purposes.

The first case is in the manufacturing sector when the company keeps TRs relatively stable but shifts along the IRs to the right, driven by the business need to improve quality. From a policy perspective this is important because it highlights the possibility of government policy encouraging companies to introduce HPWPs while not making major changes to their technology. The second case is from the service sector where radical changes are made in both the TRs and IRs. This highlights the importance of supporting changes in TRs as well as IRs if radical changes are to be introduced into skill levels and use. Both illustrate the complexities of successfully achieving change and an increase in the utilisation of employee skills.[10]

One of the problems with this type of case study approach is that many of the cases highlighted are success stories. However, many companies embark on the process of change but have only limited success, a situation that may be far more typical and yet these companies can teach us far more about the process of implementing change and the hurdles that are encountered. To explore this we use one case study where change in TRs was relatively successful but change along the IRs was more problematic. We explore the lessons this provides about the conditions necessary for effective change in skill formation.

Change along IRs while TRs relatively stable: the case of Glenmorangie

Background

The company Glenmorangie[11] traditionally produced and bottled whisky using a conventional bottling plant delivering large batches of whisky under its own brand. For the operatives the TRs were such that they demanded low levels of technical knowledge, while IRs were focused on the task skills for the operation of the machinery. The company was bought by Moët Hennessy in 2005 and introduced a new competitive strategy to the senior management. The aim was to make it one of the world's largest luxury brand companies. Moët Hennessy gave it access to their global distribution system, enabling it to get closer to the customer and to move up the value chain, from being a producer of a premium product to that of a luxury brand.

The shift involved moving out of the market for blended whiskies and concentrating on the single malt lines. Marketing was an important component of the shift up market. In 2007, the company rebranded the core portfolio and introduced new branding and packaging. However, for this branding to be effective it required substantial changes in IRs. The overall strategy paid off in that there was a growth of 26 per cent in exports, especially to Asia where a new group of aspirational consumers stimulated sales.

The new strategy required that every product was perfect in terms of its presentation to the customer, and to achieve that required significant changes within the company. For the management it meant adapting to new roles and for the operatives a shift from task-focused IRs to people-focused IRs to create a differentiated premium product. It illustrates the process of change and how what appears a relatively simple process, namely that operatives acquired higher levels of skills that were used more extensively in the production process, is in reality a difficult change to achieve.

Implementation

The TRs at the bottling plant saw change over the years. The company had invested £4 million in a more technically advanced line control system which allowed better tracking of downtime and more efficient operation of the lines. This created a demand for new technical skills among the operatives. However, the big change was in the IRs.

Marketing required that changes were made to the design of the bottles and the packaging, but the major problem the management faced was to change the culture of the plant, to achieve a transformation of the production process to eliminate defects, to achieve what the management called 'visual perfection' in the presentation of their product. However, this involved more than just attitudinal change as authority had to be devolved, as well as new competencies embedded among the workforce. Adherence to strict standards provided the basis for ensuring the maintenance of a much higher level of performance. This sounds straightforward but to achieve it required radical changes in IRs within the firm.

One of the main problems the company had to tackle was to change the attitude of staff from the old way of doing things. In the past managers and supervisors were seen to be pushing production at all costs 'to get stuff out of the door' to meet targets. This had to be stopped as it led to the acceptance of sub-standard products, high levels of wastage and subsequent problems with customer satisfaction: labels were attached incorrectly, caps were damaged and packaging was sometimes faulty. This task was made more difficult because of the cynicism of the shop floor staff, who had seen earlier attempts to improve quality fail to make significant change in lead operators' behaviour. As the literature suggests, line managers can play an important role in the hindering or helping of the change process. A lot of effort and resources were therefore put into the change process to ensure that this time it succeeded. In this, as in many other companies, training in new technical skills was the easy part in changing the skill formation process. The difficult part is changing the culture, and the attitudes that are embedded within it, on the part of both front-line managers and workers. This was tackled in a number of ways that involved introducing new management practices that were complementary to each other, the 'bundles' referred to earlier.

First, it was crucial that all staff understood the importance of visual perfection if the company was to get close to the customer. All staff including management were put through the training course "Your Role in Achieving Visual Perfection", which explained the reasons for the change. This was not so much formal training as talking people through the new approach, but it did make sure that everyone was 'talking the same language'. For the lead operators, whose commitment to the new culture was crucial, extra mentoring was put in place to make sure that they had appropriate support.

Second, the senior managers provided explicit support for those delivering the course to demonstrate the commitment of the company to the process of change. They instituted a new regime of intolerance of poor standards of production on the line and decentralised authority by provided the plant operatives with the authority to stop the line if they observed faults in the product. This significantly increased the range of discretion exercised in their jobs and enhanced the learning process. Third, information on customer requirements was fed to all staff through their monthly team briefings to enhance the knowledge base of staff. In addition, management started to work with suppliers to raise their quality standards to ensure that nothing faulty reached the line, thereby increasing their support for the operatives.

Finally, new competences were developed that would reshape the process of skill formation within the enterprise for the operatives. These new practices would effectively move the process of learning and skill use from a restricted to a more expansive learning context. To accomplish this the firm used the sand cone model shown in Figure 5.2. This emphasises the importance of having the skills in place that are necessary to deliver the basic standards, such as those required for health and safety, to ensure compliance with HM Revenue & Customs (HMRC) regulations, housekeeping requirements, legal requirements and of course those required to ensure the quality of the product. Adherence to health and safety requirements reduces accidents; if the bottles are not filled correctly that is illegal and HMRC can close the plant; if the labels are not placed correctly then losses are incurred and the customer let down. These standards are the building blocks on which company performance was built. The consequences of failure to meet these standards, both for the operator and the company, were now serious. To embed all of these standards required training and sustained commitment on behalf of both the operatives and management.

Once these standards were in place, they could ensure the reliability in business processes, the next layer in the sand cone model. For example, it enables the operator to 'get things right first time', for if you have a machine that is properly maintained and an operator that is properly trained, then you have a better chance of sustaining reliability in production and generating higher productivity. If you have reliability in these processes, this provides the basic infrastructure in order to deliver flexibility, the third layer of the sand cone model. One example of flexibility is the speed with which the production line changes over from, say a 1-litre bottle to a 70-cl bottle. This involves far more than just putting the operative on a short course, for the company must also have a system in place to ensure that the appropriate tools are at hand, and that if the operatives encounter problems, they have the knowledge to ensure that these can be quickly resolved. If you have good standards, good reliability and good flexibility, then customer service improves as you can guarantee delivering what they want when they want it – the top layer of the sand cone. This also ensures that the company does not leak money in the process of delivering quality at the lowest possible cost. Skills created in this way are crucial to achieving higher levels of customer satisfaction, productivity and profitability.

These competences provided the basis for a new four-tier system of grading which starts with the basic entry level operator with few skills, with progression to operator level for those who are competent to operate machinery, and then to technical operator who has acquired additional skills and finally the lead operator. Worker motivation increased, for as the person progressively acquires and deepens their skills they move through the grades and increase their earnings. Skill acquisition is directly rewarded and most operators have progressed through the grades. In order to support this new approach the company changed its recruitment policy, increasing its skill level demand and targeted new staff who have had experience in working with technically sophisticated machinery.

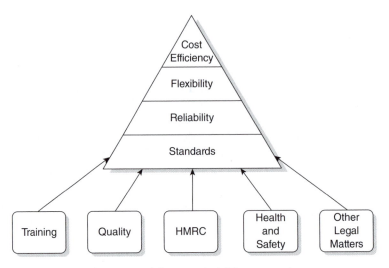

Figure 5.2   The sand cone model as used at Glenmorangie

Source: adapted from Ferdows and DeMeyers (1990)

The training is done through a combination of on- and off-the-job training, with designated trainers teaching the skills required for operating specific machines. This process of continuous training is supported by an appraisal system through which training needs are identified and objectives are set. For all staff, the completion of training courses results in the awarding of points which can be cashed in for specific items such as watches. While largely symbolic, this is meant to demonstrate the value the company attaches to learning.

For the operatives, advancement through the process of learning can also result in the achievement of national vocational qualifications. The company are moving out from their own in-house quality training to adopt the level two competencies designed by the industry to deliver the Spirits Industry Vocational Qualification. This involves taking two mandatory modules and six others chosen to match the operative's job. By getting measurable competences in place this not only provides the employee with a recognised qualification, it also sends messages to customers that all staff are well trained. Any new customers coming in can now see through the qualifications of the staff that they take quality seriously.

Managers and other staff are also involved in the process of skills training as the company seeks to improve its system of business planning and forecasting. Plans to manage the supply chain better have been activated through the implementation of the SAP Advanced Planner and Optimiser System, an IT system which monitors stock across the supply chain. For the staff this involves the mastery of new procedures and processes to take the company closer to the customer, some of which they are adopting from their French parent company. Again these new systems are meant to provide the basis for efficiency improvements throughout the organisation. However, the new systems require new skills if they are to be operated effectively; in this way 'social or organisational capital' in the organisation is increased.

The concrete result of this process of change, which took two years to complete, was improved business efficiency, increased reliability of business processes, a more flexible labour force, reduced wastage, 'visual perfection' in the delivery of their product and improved sales. In concrete terms the company saw customer complaints reduced by 12 per cent during the period 2006–7, despite an 8 per cent increase in sales volumes. When the company later relocated the bottling process to a new, more technologically advanced plant, this was built at a nearby location in order to retain the services of this skilled staff.[12]

Radical change in TRs and change in IRs: various cases

Background

Change in TRs is often seen as the most obvious way to increase productivity as the new technologies can promise radical improvements in output. Indeed, we have already seen how in earlier types of productive system this was possible, for example in the early textile and car manufacturing industries. Of course these technologies also required changes in IRs but often these are seen as non-problematic. The same has been the case with the introduction of the new IT. Initially the introduction of computers and the Internet offered the promise of huge gains in productivity, but they were often introduced as a one-off event into the existing TRs and IRs within organisations.

More than two decades ago, Osterman (1991) cited the case of General Motors spending $650 million dollars on upgrading technology in one of its plants in the 1980s without making any changes to labour practices. As a result there were no significant improvements in quality or productivity. In 2010, international consultants McKinsey were still making the same point (Brink et al., 2010). They highlighted the need for senior management to make the 'right decisions' with regard to the management practices and processes that are introduced to enable investments in new IT to be productive. They cite the case of a company that had spent more than a year implementing the software and installing the hardware for a new system, equipping all of their engineers with GPS-enabled handheld devices, and spending months training engineers and dispatchers to use these new systems. Yet the productivity gains did not materialise, response times did not improve and the number of jobs each engineer could handle in a day did not increase. This they see as typical of many attempts to use IT to increase productivity and performance. They argue that 'When IT-enablement projects in service operations go awry, it's often because these systems require processes and work practices different from those used in non-IT-enabled situations' (2010: 33).

Research has now revealed that the full benefits of the impact of investments in new technologies are only realised when complementary changes are made in business practices, changes that enhance the process of skill formation and use. These include new procedures and systems that ensure the technology is used effectively and that the staff are trained to make full use of these new technologies and have the authority to exercise discretion in exploiting the potential of the new technologies to the full. Brynjolfsson and others have shown that the major gains in productivity that came from the introduction of new IT were only realised between 4–7 years (Brynjolfsson and Hitt, 2003) years later when these complementary changes in IRs had been made. The result was that the productivity and output contributions of the same technology investments were up to five times as large (Brynjolfsson and Saunders, 2010)

American firms are far more effective than British firms in introducing these complementary business practices. Crespi et al. (2007) found that in approximately 6,000 firms in the UK, the American-owned firms operating in the UK implemented more productivity-enhancing business practices than their British-owned counterparts, and this had an impact on productivity. Similarly, Bloom and Van Reenen (2007) in a study of 8,000 establishments in the UK found that American-owned multinational establishments in the UK were more productive than British-owned counterparts, as were establishments taken over by American-owned multinationals, and that this was due to their ability to use IT more effectively. What evidence there is suggests that while investments in new technology may be a precondition for major improvements in productivity, they are not necessarily sufficient – you need to develop skills in how to use it.

Schneider National case study

In order to examine this process in more detail we use the case of an American service sector logistics company, Schneider National (Hughes and Scott Morton, 2005), to illustrate how changes in TRs, specifically new IT, were complemented by changes in IRs as the company moved from task-focused IRs and a TR that delivered a standardised service to one that delivered a differentiated service with people-focused IRs.

Implementation

Schneider National had a staff of 18,000, one of the largest transportation/logistics long-distance companies in the North America with extensive operations abroad. The change in business strategy came from pressures in the market subsequent to the 1980 deregulation of the transport industry. This intensified competition, with the result that the company needed to reduce cost per mile, improve delivery times and reliability and reduce 'deadhead trips' (empty trucks). It had been a basic trucking company – a unionised blue-collar firm, offering simple, well-delineated, undifferentiated services to its customers. With the deregulation of the industry it had to increase efficiency if it was to survive, but the deregulation also provided new business opportunities in the form of a larger market.

As a basic trucking operation providing a standardised delivery service the company had only basic information about where its trucks were. The initial response in terms of business strategy was to introduce new technology into the operation of the system to change TRs. In the late 1980s it introduced satellite communications and tracking systems into every truck. This was combined with the new (Summitt) management programme to provide sub-systems for order management, load management and carrier management. These changes created a new network that enabled them know exactly where each truck was and the location was checked every two hours. Subsequent improvements in cost and on-time delivery led to better customer service. They could now predict where a driver would be for the next load and schedule a pick-up in the immediate area, leading to better asset utilisation and fewer empty miles driven. They then applied the tracking system to trailers as well as driving units. Software captured operational processes and embedded them in the activities of the firm: for example, the Capacity and Demand Tool displays the availability of trucks in a region: colour-coded green means drivers are available and red means fewer drivers than loads and hence unavailable, but enables them to change and reschedule loads if an urgent load is required for delivery. This an instance of computerised management tools being used to provide senior management with detailed information at the local level, which then enables effective devolution of authority. However, IT does not run the system; transportation planners accept 80 per cent of the software's decisions, overriding the system in 20 per cent of cases. The company then offered on-line tools for customers to manage their transportation.

Such changes required a major transformation in IRs. The skill and knowledge required to operate the new system had to be embedded in all staff. Management tightened the selection process and identified a number of behavioural dimensions that it expected employees to conform to. For the drivers it meant that each new recruit went through six or seven hours of structured interviews in one day before they were hired. This enabled them to identify a rounded skill set and desire for continuous learning, ability with computers and compatibility with company values in their recruits. Control was no longer exercised solely through threats and punishments for rule breaking as it could now be more effectively achieved through adherence to company values.

Drivers' involvement in the company was reinforced through annual banquets for drivers and spouses. These were also used as opportunities to recognise achievements and to keep staff informed of business information. Company values were further reinforced through the CEO talking to every new driver class about the company values and goals and the need to serve the customer. All employees were expected to be innovative, responsible and enthusiastic in meeting customer expectations. To facilitate this the organisational structure was flattened and business information pushed down to driver and customer service representative levels. Staff were involved in the design and implementation of the new systems.

Work was organised on a team basis so that customer service representatives sit with regions or companies they serve. Teams comprising the customer service representative who takes orders, the transportation planner who deals with drivers and plans loads, and leaders who resolve problems, all work to ensure consistency of service. These teams have the authority to adjust the system according to any changes in customer requirements, and these changes then get relayed through to the drivers. Staff are evaluated and rewarded in terms of the level of customer service delivered.

The new system means that drivers no longer waste time in calling for instructions, while the system can accommodate the driver's family commitments, providing 'blackout days' for children's birthdays and so on and adjusting schedules accordingly. Service team leaders (STLs) are responsible for helping drivers. Routine communications are now done by technology which frees STLs to talk to drivers (up from 25 to 40 for whom they are responsible) about their health, job satisfaction, problems and so on. This helps ensure that drivers can cover enough miles to earn a good living and get home on days when they need to be there. This in turn helps create driver loyalty when driver shortage is a major constraint on growth.

Inevitably, this is a somewhat simplistic description of the change but it does capture the essence of what happened, although there still remain problems from the perspective of some drivers as the system does not always work smoothly.[13] However, for the company as a whole this represents a transformation from a basic trucking company to one that provides reliable cost-effective solutions tailored to customers' specific capacity and service needs. The results of these changes are that between 1990 and 1998 cost per mile dropped from $1 to 60 cents (in constant dollars); internal costs were down 24 per cent; there was a 25 per cent decrease in miles driven by empty trucks; late deliveries were down and cycle times accelerated. The company could afford to give guarantees with regard to delivery times and compensate customers if late. Reductions in costs paid for the new system. This has taken it into the white-collar activity of designing and managing and delivering complex logistics systems increasing its knowledge intensity. The increase in knowledge intensity is reflected in the fact that the company now sells its expertise on a consultancy basis.

Practical problems of implementing change in IRs

When discussing change in the case studies used so far we have focused on companies that have been successful in changing either the IRs or linking changes in IRs with corresponding changes in TRs. However, we have also stressed that this is not an easy process, especially when introducing change into a company that has established a stable accommodation between their TRs and IRs over a period of years. Such companies invariably have a set of mutual expectations between management and other employees that governs both performance and skill formation. In the case of Glenmorangie that was one of management expecting semi-skilled employees to pursue output targets at all costs. This was accepted by employees for whom there was no alternative. Changing these expectations and conditions is not easy. It requires substantial change in IRs. In fact many companies are only partially successful in bring about successful change.

Case study: Airframes

Background

The company under study is a British aircraft manufacturer, given the pseudonym 'Airframes' by the researchers who conducted the study (Danford et al., 2005) and from whose work this case study is taken. The establishment was a final assembly facility. Traditionally it had been organised through a paternalistic multi-layered bureaucracy, permeated by the militaristic values held by the many ex-armed forces personnel it employed, with vertical lines of command and silo-type departments – a classic command and control system of management. These departments controlled a system of low batch production, characterised by a high concentration of skilled labour, where craft workers had high levels of autonomy and where engineers were organised in their own separate R&D department. The case study illustrates the problems both management and workers face in trying to introduce HPWPs into an organisation that employed a high proportion of skilled professional and manual workers and the impact of the broader industrial relations context in shaping their response.

Implementation

In the early 2000s, the company had faced increasing international competition because of globalisation. Customers wanted more for less, which their foreign competitors were able to deliver. The size of the task confronting the company was made evident when their merger with an Italian company revealed that it was taking Airframes 16,000 hours to build an aeroplane that the Italian partner was able to build in 11,000 hours (Danford et al., 2005: 53). The response was modifications to their business strategy. The new business strategy was designed to generate substantial increases in productivity by increasing the flexibility of the production process and reducing labour costs to maintain the viability of the organisation. To achieve this they proposed to introduce major efficiencies in the design and production process, in the TRs, and these were to be complemented by changes in the IRs in the form of a more decentralised system of authority. The old hierarchical structure was to be de-layered, facilitated by the new communications technology, to create a leaner, more decentralised system based on a matrix management structure where work teams would have more authority to create a more flexible way of working. Communication was to be improved to ensure the dissemination of business information, training was to be enhanced to provide support for the necessary learning, and employees were to be encouraged to become more committed to the values of the organisation.

A major problem facing senior management was that this was an industry with a tradition of conflictual industrial relations and strong collective bargaining institutions. To achieve this change the CEO realised that they would require the support and commitment of the employees, and to this end secured a partnership deal with the unions.[14] The intention was that this would secure union commitment to at least some of the agenda and replace antagonistic union–management relations with more cooperative relations. As we have seen, building trust is essential to developing high levels of skill formation.

In terms of the TRs, production was to be through product families, each organised into product teams and led by graduate managers with strong commercial awareness, but crucially financial control remained highly centralised. The central R&D department was closed down and engineers from it were deployed across a variety of programmes.

For the skilled workers the introduction of cellular working, JIT and Kaizan and associated techniques represented major changes in division of labour. Overlaying this was the establishment of a core/periphery model, with fluctuations in production being coped with through the use of temporary staff.

An important component of change in the IRs centred around the partnership agreement with the unions. The response of the two unions involved to such partnership proposals was not uniform: the manual workers' union was sympathetic and prepared to work more closely with the management, whereas the non-manual engineers' union was suspicious as they wanted more participation in decision making. It was in this uncertain context that the company sought to make changes in four areas, namely to enhance the commitment of their employees to the company's goals, introduce teamworking, improve communication and enhance skill development.

Employee commitment

In securing employee commitment one of the main problems the company faced was the attitude of the unions. The company sought to incorporate the unions into their business agenda. It was discussed in the formal channels, through the works council and associated committees. The management was not successful in overcoming the scepticism of the non-manual unions who remained suspicious and critical of the new practices. Many of the workers felt threatened by the new system, which reduced the autonomy of the engineers and threatened the status of craft workers. The result was that for many there was a sense of loss rather than mutual gain, and for some a distrust of management.

Although the majority of employees expressed loyalty to the organisation and a willingness to work harder to help the organisation succeed, the researchers noted a growing alienation from management. This was because they felt that the traditions of engineering management and high-quality working practices had been undermined by a management intent on the cost cutting exigencies of financial control and accounting. While the majority of managers and workers agreed that they should be working as a team, overwhelming majorities of manual and non-manual workers thought this belief was not put into practice, that management was not 'walking the talk'.

Teamworking

Teamworking was introduced to help improve productivity. But there were two problems encountered here. First, the introduction of cellular working, JIT and Kaizan, and associated with this, multi-skilling, had a negative impact on skilled workers. For many of the traditionally skilled workers this meant 'a more *intensive* form of narrow task flexibility' (Danford et al., 2005: 81). These were traditionally trained skilled workers who valued their skill and some felt that they were being deskilled, leaving them resenting the introduction of these new practices. For these workers, as the authors point out, the introduction of these new practices did not represent a mutual gain. There were benefits in that these practices enabled the company to increase its performance, for example the total build hours for the aircraft fell from 16,000 to 10,000; there were also improvements in lead time and labour utilisation and downtime (2005: 81). Such benefits no doubt enabled the company to stay in business and sustain well-paid jobs, but for the traditionally skilled workers who felt that they were losing their skilled status there were also loses.

There was a similar experience for the professional engineers, as the authors conclude that 'Although there were differences of degree, for most technical workers at Airframes the overall experience of high performance work restructuring was one of diminished autonomy' (2005: 117). Some reported work intensification and increased stress levels (between 33 and 50 per cent depending on the group), although others did report increased skill levels (50–70 per cent), the two not being mutually exclusive.

Second, there were problems in implementing the devolution of decision making to the teams; this was felt acutely in the case of the engineers. Here the company used integrated project teams, but the engineers complained that they were not given the authority to make them work (2005: 116). Some of the engineers felt that they had lost authority to managers while some managers refused to listen to suggestions from other team members, illustrating low levels of trust in integrated project teams, an indication that the devolution of authority was not working.

However, the implementation of teamworking had been successful in other parts of the plant where it had encountered a positive response from workers, echoing the findings from Doeringer et al. (2002) in the USA. At Airframes, labour recruited from the armed forces – that had been socialised outside the traditions of the craft unions – were more prepared to undertake different tasks and had a more positive attitude towards teamworking and management. For example, they were willing to accept the supervisor's discretion over the allocation of overtime and ignore traditional lines of demarcation between trades, which the older skilled workers refused to countenance. For these workers there was less chance that they would experience any sense of person loss and for them mutual gains were more likely to be a reality.

Communication

Airframes used a wide range of communication tools including team briefings, intranet, surveys and meetings, but some workers never felt engaged.
Moreover, in the context of historical distrust between management and
workers these were not always used in a transparent manner. Management
was seen to be careful about the information they disseminated: for
example, they were reluctant to disclose a full order book in case workers slowed down. Workers felt they could not influence anything. As a
result, large groups felt excluded from the decision making processes. The
majority thought that managers were poor at responding to employees'
suggestions. The management seemed to be effective in getting their message across but not in involving large sections of the labour force.

Training and skill development

The company organised learning around a competency-based scheme
linked to NVQs with progression from basic skills to higher skills. By
conventional measures of off-the-job training there was a lot of training going on, three-quarters of the labour force of Airframes had one
or more days training over the past year, with between 11 per cent
of manual and 30 per cent of managers having 10 or more days. The
company also provided a learning centre which had job-related and
non-job-related courses. There were engineering skills development and
management development programmes for graduates, supervisors and
managers. Others had access to open learning.

In practice professional, administrative and managerial staff had more
training than manual workers. Also there were some barriers to taking advantage of these opportunities. Engineers had to push hard to get
access to national qualifications while line managers were reluctant to
let staff have time for training. Again, there was a problem of implementation concerning a lack of trust between management and some groups
of employees. Personal development and training needs were discussed
through formal appraisals, but as is often the case, these were not always
very effective, especially for the lower status workers.

The appraisal system worked well for graduates and managers whose
annual performance review was used to establish training needs, discuss
career paths and monitor performance. For manual workers they concentrated mostly on training needs. This suggested that the company
was only concerned about the immediate performance of their job, not
their development as individuals. Only a minority of manual workers
expressed satisfaction with the appraisal process while a small proportion felt it was primarily used to monitor performance. Indeed, there was

some dissatisfaction with the fact that appraisals were used to determine performance-related pay, a feeling that judgements here were subjective and that it was used to individualise the employment relationship. These are not the kind of experiences that are likely to stimulate learning and skill formation.

As we have seen, in spite of the problems the company encountered in introducing the new IRs, the introduction of the new TRs succeeded in increasing productivity, restoring the competitiveness of the company. As for the attempt to introduce new IRs, the story was one of partial success.

Barriers to change

The experience of Airframes in this connection highlights many of the problems encountered in companies' attempts to introduce change. First, the attempt to introduce a shift in culture away from the conflictual industrial relations of the past was never fully successful, old attitudes persisted among some employees while some of the managers did not buy into the new values, so pockets of distrust prevailed. There are examples where a shift in culture has been achieved, but this requires uniformity among senior managers in espousing the values and ensuring consistency in the implementation of practices across the organisation (Ashton and Sung, 2002).

The company had been less successful in ensuring this complementarity across practices. It had been more successful in improving communications with the workers but had not succeeded in involving them with the goals and values of the company. There was similar mixed success with training and development. While the company had done a great deal of training for managers and professional and technical staff with effective support structures, this was not the same for skilled workers, especially when it came to the support procedures such as appraisals. Again, old divisions within the workforce persisted. Finally, when it came to the crucial issue of rewards, while the company survived and continued to provide jobs, the researchers note that the workers did not receive any increase in pay for participating in this process of change.

Conclusion

We started this chapter with a quote suggesting that changing skill use was a relatively straightforward task in that all you need to do is change management practices. Yet our analysis has shown two different aspects to this challenge. One is the change in the type of skills that employees require. This involves far more than just replacing one set of technical skills with another – that is the easy part. What is more difficult is the issue of changing employees' attitudes and values in the process of creating the new 'soft' skills. That often requires new systems of authority and behaviour on the part of management and workers; the two are interdependent. When it comes to making these changes, what the strategic skills model tells us is that major change in skill level and use at the level of the firm requires changes in the TRs of production in terms of the technology, and for IRs in terms of the management of people. Neither of these are straightforward and the interaction between the two is complex.

The most powerful agent in this process of change is the owner/senior manager. Here many MNCs have an advantage in that they deliberately seek out senior managers and CEOs who have the ability or 'talent' to identify new opportunities in the market and transform both the TRs and IRs to take advantage of them and to formulate appropriate business strategy for the delivery. Yet as we have seen, it is misleading to view these individuals as all-powerful because they operate within a complex web of relationships that constrain and shape their options. In addition, many owners and managers, especially those from medium sized and smaller companies, do not possess these abilities or skills and therefore this also represents a major blockage in any attempt to generate change in skills within the economy.

Further problems were identified in the process of implementation. Changes in technology may at first sight appear to be relatively easy to introduce but unless corresponding changes are introduced into IRs, the impact on skills and performance may be negligible. Changes in authority relations often involve significant changes in the balance of power within organisations and these can take years to achieve and may be resisted by both managers and workers. It highlights the fact that the process of change can mean there are winners and losers among both managers and workers.

At the level of the individual the process involves not just more training, it involves changes in the design of jobs, in identifying learning needs, in supporting learning and supporting areas of attitudinal and behavioural change, as workers and managers acquire not just new technical skills but new skills in teamworking, communication and problem solving. For this process to be effective and new skills acquired and deployed in enhancing performance, there has to be something in it for the employees, both workers and managers, beyond just greater job satisfaction. Workers especially have to be able to see tangible benefits. It is for this reason that we have stressed the importance of mutual gains.

Yet even here, there are more issues to be considered, in particular the importance of the cultural and institutional context within which the changes are taking place. Here again we have seen how these can encourage employers to adopt changes in IRs, as in Denmark, but these institutional factors can also provide an important barriers to change, as in the case of the industrial relations context at Airframes, where senior

managers failed to convince all the unions of the benefits of collaboration. In view of all the barriers to change it is surprising that so many
companies have been successful in introducing change. As we have noted,
this is easier when the company is establishing itself on a greenfield site,
as the Japanese transplants did in the USA, and which companies such as
Nissan and Toyota have done in the UK. However, as our examples have
shown, companies can transform existing cultures and achieve success in
generating higher level skills and making greater use of employee skills
in enhancing their competitive position in the market.

Skill formation and skills utilisation in contemporary society are
complex processes, driven by markets and business strategy, in which
employers and senior managers play a crucial role in shaping that strategy and so determining the potential level and extent of skill use. Within
the company both managers and workers play equally important roles in
determining the outcomes. This is a far cry from the old notion of equat-
ing skill with formal training courses. Moreover, it is a process in which
there are winners and losers as old skills are replaced by the new. Here
again, broader institutional factors can mediate the losses.

In view of the range of issues that have to be confronted at the
national, organisational and individual level, it is not surprising that
many companies have failed to fully implement transformative change.
Neither is it surprising that many attempts by governments to transform
employers' use of employee skills have had very limited success. Yet what
this same analysis suggests is that there are numerous points at the level
of the nation, organisation and individual where change can be effected
and where hitherto it has not been effected in an effective manner. It is
these policy issues that we tackle in the next chapter.

Notes

1 The part played by agency in our understanding of the operation of
   societies is still a subject of intense theoretical debate in social science;
   see Emirbayer and Mische (1998).
2 The researchers only used management practices that were identified in
   American, British, French and German companies; see Bloom and Van
   Reenen (2006: 3).
3 Chandler (1976) cited the size of the domestic market, the application
   of new technologies and different legal constraints as the main reasons, but Wilson and Thomson (2006) argue that part of the answer
   lay in the wider values and institutions of British society including the
   short-termism of the financial institutions.
4 In this context, the research of Birdi et al. (2008) is interesting in suggesting in a longitudinal study that HR practices have more impact on
   productivity than operational and lean management approaches.

5   There have been a number of attempts to theorise these links, such as the 4A model developed by United Kingdom Commission for Employment of Skills (UKCES) and the Ability Motivation and Opportunity (AMO) model used in the HR literature. With regard to skill formation, the problem with these models is their failure to incorporate the associated changes in technical relations without which the links between the various practices are purely contingent.

6   This is effectively what much of the national standards such as IiP in the UK and People Developer in Singapore do.

7   Bowen and Ostroff (2004) have started the process of theorising this.

8   Fuller and Unwin's work on restrictive and expansive learning tells us a great deal about the process of learning and the conditions that favour it within the workplace but the focus on understanding the learning processes has tended to divert attention away from an exploration of the forces that determine which approach companies and organisations take to skill formation. Progress has been made in this direction by the Learning As Work (LAW) team with their productive systems framework, which attempts to locate learning within a broader framework that encompasses the learning process and its outcomes. This enables the researcher to identify the various factors that in different contexts influence the process but does not help identify the major drivers of the process.

9   This is not to argue that there are no opportunities for expansive learning and high levels of skill formation taking place in traditional command and control organisations, only that, as we saw earlier, this type of learning is restricted to those at the higher levels.

10   Some of these case studies are drawn from our own database and have been undertaken with our theoretical framework in mind, but others have been drawn from the wider literature and, where this is the case, knowledge of some of the dimensions of the strategic skills model is a little thin.

11   This case study is from our own files and was conducted in 2008.

12   The company moved the new HQ and bottling plant to Livingston, which is only 7 miles from the old plant at Broxburn. The Chief Executive, Paul Neep, was quoted as saying 'We wanted to locate our new bottling and office facilities close to Broxburn so we could retain our skilled workforce' (News, Scotsman.com http://news.scotsman.com/scotland/Whisky-firm-lines-up-a.4977730.jp; accessed 7 April 2014).

13   For an overview of some drivers' experience, see www.indeed.com/cmp/Schneider-National/reviews (accessed 7 April 2014).

14   'Partnerships' were a form of collaboration between managers and unions encouraged by the government as a means of introducing change into the UK business in such a way that both sides would see gains. The authors saw this as an example of why HPWPs always fail because of their inability to resolve what they see as the fundamental conflict between capital and labour.

6

A SECTORAL APPROACH TO SKILLS DEVELOPMENT AND PUBLIC SKILLS POLICY

I am playing all the right notes but not necessarily in the right order.

With apologies to comedian Eric Morecombe when explaining his poor performance at the piano to André Previn

Overview

In this chapter we return to the task of exploring the implications of the strategic skills model and the lessons we have learnt from its application for the skill policies discussed in the Introduction. The central task is to identify what the changes are that need to be made to the institutional frameworks of different countries which will ensure that they create a business environment that will change the cost–benefit calculations of employers in selected sectors such that they move their business strategy up the value chain. Here we point to the need for two components that are crucial to any successful policy, namely an industrial vision or strategy and powerful sector-based skills bodies. While the principles that we discuss are applicable to all industrial countries the presentation of them is directed at the Anglo-Saxon countries, which are in danger of adopting the low-road to industrial development if current policies persist.

Influencing skill levels and utilisation: the sectoral approach to supporting high-skilled business strategy

Perhaps our quote at the beginning of this chapter is a little tongue in cheek. But the point is serious. In today's environment where we are increasingly concerned with how skills are making an impact in the workplace, we continue to routinely design our skills policy only to boost skills supply (see the right-hand side of Figure 6.1), leaving the demand for skills to chance. There is also an irony in that we are aware of the relevant drivers for higher skills utilisation and business performance coming from the business strategy (see the left-hand side of Figure 6.1), yet, for ideological reasons, we are often half-hearted in designing skills policy to support business strategy. Indeed, while both right- and left-hand sides of Figure 0.1 are important and relevant to raising skills utilisation, we argue that the routine alignment of skills policy to the supply ideology means that we are playing the right musical notes in the wrong order.

So far in this book, we have spelled out the importance of the strategic skills model in helping us to understand why organisations use skills very differently, even though they may be in the same business. However, to support businesses to change their TR and IR positions, we would need to consider another complementary concept, namely the sectoral approach to skills development.

The sectoral approach to skills development

In this section, we are going to give the new 'sector' box on the left-hand side of Figure 6.1 a more detailed treatment. Based upon what we have learnt from various countries, we will propose a conceptual model to substantiate what we mean by a sectoral approach to skills development, one that will influence the skills strategy of employers. The model is not entirely 'conceptual' in the sense that it is remote from reality. Indeed, you may notice that some elements in the model are already in practice in some skills systems. However, the construction of current sector skills models means that we are proposing additional elements to create a different kind of dynamics needed to ensure that business strategy leads to increased skills utilisation.

The strategic skills model (SSM) we discussed in the early chapters of this book would have suggested that employers in the same sector (similar product market environment) could choose many positions in

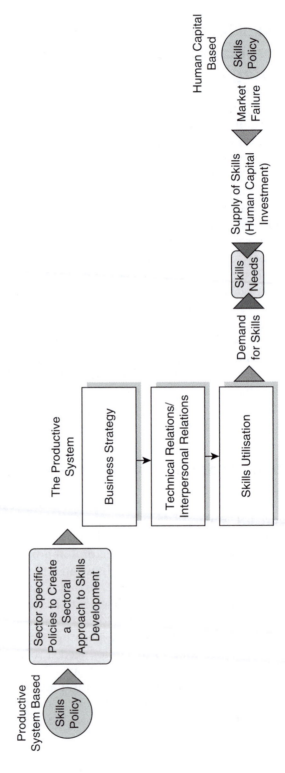

Figure 6.1 Skills policy, sectoral approach to skills development and the productive system

the business strategy space and still make a viable business within the timeframe that business owners can envisage. But these very different business strategies have different implications for skills utilisation. The problem for skills policy is how to influence business strategies to adopt TR and IR combinations that would produce a demand for higher skill levels and greater skills utilisation, usually through adopting higher value-added forms of production. This is the salient point about the SSM.

It is also important to point out that our proposed sectoral approach to skills development is not about 'telling employers what to do'. Business decisions are the domain of business owners and their managers. They carry out their cost–benefit decisions when they consider what kind of investment to make, what product markets to enter, how they use their resources and how they organise their work. However, we tend to forget that these decisions made by employers are contextual to the business (sectoral) environment within which they operate. These are calculations that are subject to a particular set of business conditions. The proposed sectoral approach to skills development is a vehicle to develop sector-based plans that will change these conditions to produce a different set of cost–benefit business calculations such that high-skills and high value-added forms of production become attractive propositions. Thus in Figure 6.2 we identify three components (layers) that form the sectoral approach to skills development,

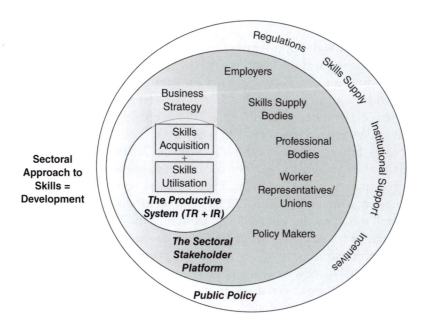

Figure 6.2   The sectoral approach to skills development

namely the productive system, the sectoral stakeholder platform and public policy.

At the centre of Figure 6.2 is the productive system. This is the business domain that belongs to the business owners and managers. Business strategy – in the form of TRs and IRs – therefore affects skills acquisition and utilisation which support the relevant productive system. What affects the calculations of businesses is the next layer, which we call the 'sectoral stakeholder platform'. This is where the sectoral approach begins.

The main purpose of the sectoral stakeholder platform is to deliver a sectoral skills strategy with the participation of the necessary stakeholders. It therefore has the following components:

1. There is a sectoral body to coordinate and to articulate a forum for an upskilling strategy that will shift the value-add position of the sector with the power to influence the business environment.

2. The sectoral body is employer-led. However, the body has multiple stakeholders, which provides a balanced view between the need to make profits and the need to move up the value chain.

3. There are representatives of the skills supply bodies, which may include public and private sector bodies as well as higher education and professional bodies, if appropriate.

4. There are also workers' representatives (or unions) and policy makers from appropriate government departments/ministries, especially those with workforce development responsibilities.

If this sectoral body sounds rather like some of the sector skills councils in some existing sectoral systems, it is because of the fact that these sectoral bodies can take on a spectrum of identities with varying degrees of strategic leadership capability. In the weakest form where the policy sphere (i.e. the outer layer of Figure 6.2) is often 'light-touched' (especially in deregulated economies) and the sectoral sphere has an ineffective employer buy-in; the sectoral bodies tend to behave like a facilitation body, with much of their function focusing on providing advice on training and qualifications provision. These sectoral bodies are incapable of taking any strategic position and have no sectoral skills strategic plans that will influence the value-added position of the sector. Examples like these can be found in the UK and Canada. At the other end of the spectrum are the strategic working groups in Singapore that focus on the role of skills, business models and processes in the context of improving productivity. They cover the key and strategic sectors in Singapore. Although they are not called sectoral bodies as such, they provide sectoral leadership and strategic plans. If these plans are accepted by the government, they influence how training funding is utilised, how qualifications (especially vocational qualifications) may be designed, and how the regulatory framework may have to be refined (e.g. minimum standards, public contracts and sometimes fiscal incentives). In between these two opposing models, there are others with varying degrees of sectoral leadership.

What we are proposing here is the type of sectoral bodies that have a much greater strategic remit and mandate than many of the existing entities. They ought to be able to promote high-skilled business models and value chain improvement. They can assess the prevailing business model that is driving the current level of value-added position. They can also examine the next business model that is most likely to provide the next higher staging post along the value chain. They will also have the power to change aspects of the regulatory environment. Together these actions will change the cost–benefit calculations made by employers in the sector in favour of adopting a higher value-added position. We are not the first to advocate the creation of stronger sector skills type bodies (McKinsey Global Institute, 2010; Lanning and Lawton, 2012; Henderson et al., 2013), but where our suggestions differs is in the proposed capability of these sector-based organisations to influence the business environment in the manner suggested above.[1]

Whilst it is impossible to transform all the businesses in the sector, the idea is to increase the proportion of companies in the sector that adopt a higher value chain position. To support this, the sector bodies will provide a wide range of analyses to identify the challenges of getting to the next value chain position. These challenges could be technical, financial, labour supply, processes, regulatory or skills-related. However, the resulting strategy takes the form of a comprehensive plan with recommended actions to bring about changes. Public policies need to consider changes in order to support these plans.

There is of course no guarantee that 'more' employers will buy into the new idea, unless the sectoral sphere is able to change the cost–benefit calculations such that it is advantageous for employers to make a different decision and to upskill. It is here that the policy sphere layer in Figure 6.2 is most important, as nearly all of the elements in the outer layer come from public policies. In the policy sphere, the most important element is to signal that skills policy is central to the wider economic development strategy, or at least to form the basis of how the economy is to be managed and improved. Thus, an economic vision statement that spells out the strategic roles of the key sectors and how skills may form a central driver within that plan is the starting point for much of the sector skills policy. Public resources (e.g. education and training, innovation incentives and fiscal incentives and financial assistance) will be the incentives to create a sectoral mandate that employers will find useful to be a part of. In many respects this economic vision is similar to the industrial strategy advocated by the Chartered Institute of Personnel and Development and the Confederation of British Industry (Mayhew and Keep, 2014) in specifying areas of the economy where the UK can compete. Where it differs is in the importance attached to leveraging skills.

When working together, the sectoral and the policy spheres form the 'institutional logics' for high-skills business strategies. In other words, it is worth employers' while to consider high value-added and high-skilled business strategies, knowing that their competitors in the same sector may well face the same incentives to do so (see discussions in Chapter 7 for the 'internationalised sectors' where competing firms do not face the same conditions). The high-skilled institutional logics allow different forms of policy implementation and design. It can be a set of institutional arrangements that formalise the position of skills as in the case of many 'corporatist' countries in Europe, or it could take the form of a series of high-level strategic committees that have a permanent role in supporting public policies and a national economic development plan, as in the case of Singapore.

This economic vision is very important as it indicates that there is a sustained resource allocation and policy support for transformational change in the sector, as defined by the sectoral skills strategy determined by institutional logics. It identifies skills as a central priority and defines how various government and related agencies should operationalise institutional logics as a part of their normal policy and operational considerations (e.g. ministries that deal with trade and development, continuing education, social support and so on). Also, because of this primacy of skills being instituted into the wider economic vision (or plan), government regulation and incentive systems have a target to follow. The resulting combinations of regulations and incentives are hugely impactful in shaping the sectoral sphere (the cost–benefit) calculations and businesses' strategic plans which ultimately lead to high-skilled productive systems (the inner core of Figure 6.2). Thus, this is how, for example, Singapore moved away from producing low value-added electronics such as computer peripherals and disk drives in the 1980s to varieties of other higher value-added and high-skilled manufacturing sub-sectors – biomedical, pharmaceutical, aircraft maintenance and turbine assembly and oil rigs manufacturing, to name a few. Some of these are now world leaders and yet they only began to emerge in the past 20 years. Notice that the government does not run any of these businesses. The effects of the regulatory and incentive regimes (the institutional logics) shape the normal cost–benefit calculations of businesses, making these decisions just like any other 'normal' commercial decisions.

The above may sound a little too 'state-led' for audiences in the West. However, the same phenomenon has also happened under so-called Western market economies. The combined effects of regulatory and incentive regimes was how the UK created the huge private sectors in energy, road-haulage, post, public transport, health and so on. The only difference is that with opposite and deregulated institutional logic, as was the case in the UK, unfettered market mechanisms may not bring high skills to the sector and instead may lead to low-cost sub-contracting and low-wage competition. So it is a different kind of transformation, in the other direction. In other cases, pseudo-monopolies were created. All the same, it illustrates that the power of the combined regulatory and incentive regimes is real. The institutional logics define the policy sphere, which in turn drives the cost–benefit environment of the sectoral sphere and therefore the options of the productive systems. There are also many similarities in the corporatist countries where sectoral behaviour and expectations, and therefore their cost–benefit calculations, are driven by the combination of regulatory and incentives regimes. Decisions are then formalised through collective agreements within the corporatist equivalent of the sectoral and policy spheres.

Whilst there are some similarities to existing models, our proposed sectoral approach also differs from them in some fundamental ways. The main difference is that our model focuses on the type of institutional logics that link skills utilisation and value-added production to business strategies, while other existing models either lack the skill-biased institutional logics or they focus more on a wide range of collective agreements that could be social, wage and learning related, as for example in Germany, Denmark and the Nordic countries. If employers are to see the value of high skills, the environment has to be right for the appropriate business decisions to be made. Skills do not stand alone within a business decision. High skills only make sense if they are the vehicles to deliver a desirable business outcome.

As evident in our discussions so far, the SSM and the sectoral approach to skills development form the central core of this book. Within this perspective, we can arrive at a series of questions that are crucial for designing skills policy.

What is the new direction of national skills policy?

The debate on whether to focus public policy on the demand or supply sides has been around for decades. So to argue that skills policy should focus on the demand for skills is not new. But what is new is to take this debate to a higher level of policy intent. Here, we argue that the new direction for skills policy is no longer just to increase the level of individual skills but also to improve the competitive position of the national economy through moving higher up the value chain. And to support that, we need high-quality and high-skilled jobs.

Given the ever increasing number of graduates and other highly educated workers entering into jobs every year, the real competition is no longer about producing more graduates. Instead, the new direction should be about creating a higher proportion of companies (and their jobs) in a given sector that operate with mature mass production or knowledge-intensive forms of production. Another necessary mindset change for skills policy is that we can no longer talk about a 'high skills equilibrium'. Upskilling is a dynamic process that is driven by a skill-based business model which determines the skills content of jobs in a continuous form.

What would a skills policy based on a strategic skills model look like?

The SSM puts business strategy at the heart of policies designed to bolster jobs and skills. This means that policies must primarily focus on the business environment to shape the decision making process within the business as depicted in Figure 6.2. It would start with the outer layer of Figure 6.2, creating a clear alignment between national goals for economic and social development and the strategy for workforce development. To some extent, the principle is similar to the approach that is advocated by the World Bank after its study of national approaches to workforce development.[2]

Government policies would be articulated in the form of a sectoral skills strategy that would be used to encourage new and existing businesses to adopt a business strategy utilising mature industrial or knowledge-intensive forms of production. These business strategies would operate on the organisation's TRs to raise the demand for skills and on the IRs to use the employees' skills as a major source of the organisation's competitive advantage.

In order for any policy measures to be effective, we can expect the content of the sectoral skills strategy to vary hugely between industries. This is because each sector is characterised by different competitive contexts. Some, such as car manufacturing and advanced engineering, are part of highly competitive global markets. Others such as hotels are firmly embedded in the national market. Some such as food processing tend to be dominated by craft and industrial mass production systems. Others such as infocomm are characterised by knowledge-intensive forms of production. Sectoral institutions are the ones that are most sensitive to the different characteristics of each industry market and the changes that are transforming them, and are therefore better positioned to drive dynamic changes within them.

How would the new model be implemented?

Effective implementation would require action at two levels. First, in the policy sphere, with policies aimed at the national level. Second and just as important, in the sector sphere, where policies would be aimed at the sector level.

Policy actions in the policy sphere

As we have seen earlier, there are a number of ways in which national institutions can help shape the decision making process of owners and senior managers. One way that has been used in Western Europe is to use institutional arrangements for worker representation and welfare to block off the low-cost route and the associated race to the bottom – the need to close off the so-called 'exit options' by employers to create a level playing field (Gautié and Schmitt, 2009). We have seen how this was a consequence of training arrangements in Germany that delivered a highly skilled labour force and encouraged employers to compete at the top end of their markets for manufactured goods, although other institutional factors such as the availability of long-term capital and legislation on works councils also pushed employers in the same direction, though not in the service sector (Bosch and Weinkopf, 2008).

In Denmark, the low-skills route was even more effectively blocked off by a combination of local agreements between employers and unions over wages and working conditions, a comprehensive system of welfare provided by the government and the high level of trust between employers and workers. Together, this encouraged employers to collaborate with their employees to introduce new technology and compete on the basis of product quality and innovation, a process that has been documented by Westergaard-Nielson (2008) in sectors where traditionally the TRs are dominated by industrial forms of mass production, such as food manufacture, call centres and parts of the hotel and retail sectors. One consequence is higher levels of job quality in Denmark in terms of employee participation in decision making and skill development (Gallie, 2011).

While it would be inaccurate to say that the push towards industry competing at the top end of the value chain was a result of a well-articulated government policy in these countries, government actions did actively encourage these consequences. Often, it was a result of the interaction of a number of institutional conditions that brought about these results, not one magic bullet. However, once the consequences of these institutional arrangements became obvious, we were in a position to learn from it and other governments can thereby use those lessons.

Another more explicit strategy is that adopted by the some Asian governments. This involves using specific sectors to target expansion in global markets. This means operating at two levels: the international level to identify those sections of the global market where the country can expect or wish to establish a comparative advantage, in either mature industrial or knowledge-intensive production in both the manufacturing or service sectors; or emergent sectors, which combines elements of both as exemplified by Rolls Royce, which derives increasing revenues not just from the manufacturing of aero engines but also from the monitoring and maintenance of them.

What is required is a clear specification of the industries to be encouraged so that resources can be targeted. Some of these will be existing industries that are already doing well in world markets and provide the basis for further expansion, others will be new or emergent industries which can also provide jobs that are relatively highly paid and skill intensive. Once identified, then there exists a number of well-known policy measures that can be used to attract capital and support the development of such sectors. These take the form of direct help to attract firms in the form of subsidies or tax breaks targeted at the appropriate industries. They also include indirect measures such as those designed to help small and medium enterprises (SMEs) access foreign markets or the value chains of TNCs to provide access to venture capital, procurement rules that help SMEs develop capability, and programmes to develop the capability of owner/managers to exploit new opportunities in the market. However, what differs from similar strategies used in a piecemeal fashion before is the need to design these measures into a sectoral approach to skills development, supporting the emergence of a viable business sector that has a position along a global value chain. Finegold (1999) describes this as the high-skilled ecosystem. Similarly, measures may be used to transform the value position of existing firms in the sector.

Another clear lesson from those countries that have succeeded in breaking into and growing a presence in high-end international markets is that measures design to attract and develop such industries must be complemented by policies designed to ensure the supply of appropriately trained labour. This also requires action at the national level. This means ensuring that higher education is producing not just a sufficient flow of graduate labour – all countries are now doing that – but that the universities are capable of delivering the next generation of industrial leaders, the 'talent' necessary to ensure that companies are led by personnel with the capabilities to identify and exploit market opportunities. It also means that the higher education system is delivering the specific technical and soft skills required by the designated industries. This in turn means that at the national level there have to be mechanisms in place to ensure that changes in the demand for skills are met by corresponding actions to ensure an adequate supply. It is no longer good enough to leave it to the market to send signals to higher education systems and for universities and colleges to be reactive and merely respond to market signals. Again, a sectoral approach to skills development, as depicted in Figure 6.2, would provide an appropriate and more accurate industry view about the level of demand and emerging skills relevant to the sector.

If you leave it to the market you lose time, as the market is slow to operate. Jobs have to be created, shortages of skills have to appear, which then lead to wage increases, and these market signals then produce a corresponding increase in supply. In the meantime production is disrupted and further investment halted. Meanwhile, your competitors abroad are racing ahead. Here the sectoral body (on behalf of the state) must take on the role of coordinating demand and supply. This was done very well by some of the Asian economies, especially in the early stages of their shift from low-value to high-value production, but it becomes more difficult when you are at the leading edge of the market and when there are no precedents as to exactly what the skills are for the next shift in the productive process. It just means that at a national level mechanisms need to be in place to monitor emergent skills and ensure their supply. An employer-led sectoral approach to skills development would play a crucial role here.

Of course there are limits to this policy, not all the industries targeted will be successfully established, but in a highly competitive global market where other countries are already targeting and supporting the development of high value-added companies and industries, if this strategy is not adopted the chances of success are seriously reduced. Unless there is such a policy there is little chance that the economy will spontaneously generate high-skilled, high-paid jobs. Indeed, the example of the UK suggests that the proportion of high-skilled, relatively well-paid jobs is likely to decline as other countries succeed in attracting the capital and/or capture a greater proportion of the leading edge markets. Meanwhile, existing companies compete on the basis of costs in a race to the bottom.

Why are actions at the sector level so crucial?

Policy action in the sector sphere: changing cost-benefit calculations of employers

Actions at the sector level are crucial because, as Figure 6.2 illustrates, this is the level at which business owners and senior managers make their decisions about business strategy. It is here that the interaction between the policy sphere and the sector sphere occurs, providing the business context that shapes such decisions and thereby affecting the cost–benefit calculations concerning the company's product market and competitive strategies and the position they adopt along TRs and IRs. It is therefore at the sector level that most of the practical policy actions need to be taken. We can illustrate this best through a series of examples.[3]

First is the food and drinks processing industry. Parts of this industry are high value-added, operating in regional and global markets where there are opportunities to move up the value chain. In Scotland public–private collaborations between government agencies and industry bodies are active in promoting the Scottish brand as a premium product, helping to open up new high value-added markets where competition is on the basis of quality, enabling employers to introduce forms of mature mass production. In Singapore, government agencies and employer organisations have been active in opening up new markets, creating opportunities for employers to capitalise on the reputation of Singaporean products in Asian markets and to enlarge their market, facilitating the introduction of automation and mature mass production. In Scotland, sector bodies help in providing advice on HPWPs and ensuring a supply of skilled workers through their links with education and training suppliers. In both countries, food manufacturers face the prospect of ensuring compliance with international standards, such as those from the International Organisation for Standardisation (ISO) and the British Retail Consortium, and here again sector bodies have opportunities to offer advice on achieving the necessary standards, which in turn places pressure on employers to enhance the skill base of their employees.

What this interaction between the two spheres does is to provide a series of opportunities and constraints for employers that shape their decisions about business strategy. They open up opportunities for companies to enter higher value-added markets through marketing their products as premium, which may then induce them to adopt HPWPs to ensure the quality of their products. They also provide the opportunity to acquire advice on how to implement these practices from sector bodies. However, if they wish to ignore these opportunities, the availability of cheap immigrant labour provides the possibility of maintaining their existing low-cost strategy. How any one employer responds depends on their own motivation and priorities and how they make these cost–benefit calculations. However, if the cheap labour option was ruled out, through either the refusal of the government to accept immigrant labour or to impose a levy on it, or through agreements between the management and unions to maintain minimum wage levels, then the balance of probability would suggest that more employers would adopt the high-skills route. It is in this way that the institutional logics influence the decisions of employers about their business strategies. However, for a more rigorous form of sectoral strategy, the sectoral body in the sectoral sphere would have a mandate or institutional remit to propose a sectoral skills strategy which is in turn to be backed by resources and regulations from the policy sphere.

In the hotel industry, there are different factors that shape the options open to employers and which affect their cost–benefit calculations. For example, in Singapore the industry is facing the twin demands of raising labour costs and raising customer expectations. There the government has, through its MICE (meetings, incentives, conferences and exhibitions) policy, sought to increase the proportion of high-spending customers to visit the island through sponsoring a range of activities such as Formula 1® racing and encouraging them to stay longer through providing more cultural amenities. This increases the market for the high value-added products/experiences delivered by luxury hotels. In Scotland, public–private collaborations between government agencies and industry bodies have promoted regions and cities as destinations for high-quality experiences and conferences, again increasing the market for employers to move their organisation up the value chain. This public branding has been aided by sector-based organisations providing grading systems for hotels that not only inform customers of the level of experience they can expect but also provide employers with knowledge of the criteria they need to meet in order to move into a higher value-added segment. To coordinate these multiple stakeholders and sometimes rather complex sets of activities, a sectoral body with an appropriate mandate would be required. The sectoral body does not just come up with a sectoral skills plan, but also the coordination of resources to deliver the sectoral strategic objectives. Here again institutional logics offer the opportunity for employers to move up the value chain while the sectoral body could provide help in advising on the introduction of HPWPs or other facilitation in order to sustain mature industrial forms of service delivery.

In the creative arts sector institutional logics are very different. Here governments have very direct levers through which to influence the business strategies of organisations, such as the power to appoint leaders in the public sector organisations. This can have a powerful impact in making the company or organisation more aware of the importance of moving along the IR dimension and enhancing skills. A second lever is the power to award funding to creative arts organisations. Here again, the government can make funding dependent on the organisation investing in the skills of all their employees and introducing variants of HPWPs relevant to the industry. In the private sector there are different factors operating, with the trades unions seeking to ensure that the large companies provide training opportunities for the many freelance workers in the industry through the operation of a voluntary levy. Here again, more powerful sector bodies could provide a lead in ensuring a sectoral skills plan is owned by industry, that funding is strategically designed, and effective supply of skills are provided. We could continue with other examples: the utility sector in the UK has its own regulations that have a powerful impact on the approach companies take to training and development; in the infocomm sector in Singapore, especially the SME segment, business strategies are powerfully influenced by procurement rules. All these are very important in shaping the institutional logics that impact on business behaviour and business strategy.

Where government action may be more difficult is in those sectors directly competing in highly competitive global markets. There competitive markets are constantly driving the introduction of more efficient management practices in the organisation of work and labour (as well as profit growth), and here knowledge in the public and local private sector may lag behind that of the global corporation. However, MNCs can also provide an opportunity for local companies. For example, in the British car industry the introduction of Japanese manufacturing techniques through the establishment of new plants by Japanese MNCs provided the stimulus for national employer organisations to distribute such techniques through the supply chain, transforming the efficiency of British car manufacturing through more efficient work processes and, in some cases, HPWPs. These are all examples of the ways in which actions in the sector sphere (and in some sectors close cooperation with the policy sphere) have changed the cost–benefit calculations of employers that inform their business strategy. With greater coordination at the sector level, these levers could become much more powerful. Again, what we would stress is that no one is telling the employer what to do, all that is being done is to change the balance of cost–benefits calculations so that more employers choose to adopt a high value-added strategy.

The other reason why action at the sector level is crucial is because it is at this level that knowledge of the distinctive features of each productive system is found. Once employers decide to shift their business strategy, the sectoral body would be one of the best sources of advice on how to change their management and working practices. Only those with a knowledge of the distinctive features of each sector will be able to provide effective help for those employers who wish to access it. For example, knowledge to help improve management practices and the skills of managers and key operatives to enhance the quality of the products would need to take account of the specific characteristics of the TRs in that industry, if it is to be fully effective. Once again, such assistance and advice would need to be coordinated to ensure that appropriate management practices were in place to maximise the social capital in the plant and so maximise the impact on productivity, but these would need to be delivered by people with intimate knowledge of the productive systems in that sector. This sort of intimate expert or insider knowledge would best be delivered through a sectoral skills body.

Governments already offer a range of programmes designed to help companies improve their productivity and skill base. These range from grants toward the cost of new technology and R&D that impact on TRs, to programmes designed to help improve IRs, such as the Investors in People in the UK and People Developer in Singapore, and benchmarking systems. The central issue with regard to many of these forms of intervention is that they only become effective when delivered in the context of the organisation's overall strategy. As we saw in earlier chapters, grants to introduce new technology without advice on the best ways to use that technology could be counterproductive because without the social capital to accompany it new technology can be wasted. Similarly, offers of programmes dedicated to upskilling semi-skilled workers are of no use to employers who are adopting a low-cost, low-skilled strategy because all they do is increase their costs. What they require are programmes to improve management skills.

Advocacy of HPWPs is pointless for organisations that see their future in the utilisation of a Taylorist industrial mass production strategy. If the company is in a knowledge-intensive sector such as high-tech engineering and depends on the skills of its staff for its competitive advantage, then interventions would need to be targeted at all the workforce as their skills are crucial to the future success of the company, not just the owners/managers. In all these instances policy actions need to be implemented in bundles to ensure that they are complimentary and will reinforce each other to produce a shift in the direction of improved business performance, higher skill levels and utilisation. In practice, these components are best driven by bodies that have the support of the employers and a thorough-going knowledge of the sector.

The final point about the model depicted in Figure 6.2 is that the points at which policy action might be directed are likely to change over time. If the company has adopted a strategy of competing through low-cost products using Taylorist industrial mass production systems, the initial focus of intervention would be the owner and management hierarchy, in terms of the need to improve their entrepreneurial and management skills. This is because, as we have seen, in this type of productive system it is their skills that are the most crucial to business success. At a later stage, if the company strategy changes and aims to move their production into a higher value-added segment of the market, using mature forms of production, at that point in time the skills of the core operative labour force become of increasing importance as a source of their competitive advantage in the market. Then different policy programmes designed to introduce HPWPs and higher levels of employee skill utilisation become crucial as companies seek to tap into the discretionary efforts of their employees in order to improve performance.

What all this points to is the need for companies and organisations to be embedded in a sector-specific institutional environment in which such help and advice is readily available. It means building sector institutions and networks where employers and organisational leaders can gain ready access to the latest developments and opportunities in their markets and where the delivery of government policies designed to help can be coordinated and tailored to their specific requirements. In some respects this then provides customised support for the individual company or organisation. This will ensure that the delivery of help is sensitive to the needs of the company at that point in time and to the market within which they are operating.

Does it involve a complete revamp of policy measures?

What we are advocating is a sectoral environment (and institutions) that creates a set of conducive conditions for high-skills investment and productive systems. It would involve change and increasing the capabilities of existing sectoral institutions, but many of the requisite government actions and policies are already in use. In this sense it means using the existing policy measures in a more coordinated manner. Governments already use tax breaks and grants to help with investment in new technology, they provide help for SMEs in accessing new technology and new markets, they provide financial help for innovations in training and R&D, they have a powerful function in regulating some markets and stimulate growth in the arts and creative industries, and so the list goes on. What is missing when it comes to skills is an approach that changes the cost–benefit calculations of employers in their product market and institutional means to ensure that policy measures operate in a complementary manner to shift the business environment in the direction of creating high-skilled, high-paid jobs. This will involve coordinating many existing policies and programmes at the sector level.

What will this strategic skills model do?

The SSM highlights the importance of building institutions at the sectoral level that integrate business policy with skills issues. This is not just a question of putting business leaders in charge of the funding of public skills programmes. As we have shown, in many cases it is the business leaders themselves who require help in exploiting new opportunities.

Rather, it is a matter of creating a business environment that changes the cost–benefit calculations that business leaders make and so moves their business strategies in the direction of higher value-added and high-skills forms of production. The sector bodies will also enable leading business leaders and thinkers in these sector bodies to help guide the long tail of poorly performing companies in that sector. Public policy measures would then be used to help create a business environment that would lead owners to change their business strategies to transform both the TRs and IRs, leading to higher levels of skill formation and utilisation.

In this context the model shows how the various levers available for policy action are interdependent and need to be implemented in bundles to maximise their impact. At the sector level it will change the business environment, making the adoption of business strategies that generate higher levels of skill utilisation an attractive option for business leaders. Employers will not just be asked to take skills more seriously, rather they will drive the high-skills agenda through their business strategies. Sector bodies will support this by highlighting the links between TRs and IRs. For example, grants to help with new technology, either for automation or ICT, that act on TRs will be linked to other actions designed to make complementary changes in IRs – such as new management practices to enable the new skills necessary for their effective implementation to be acquired. Similarly, tax breaks designed to help small- and medium-sized knowledge-intensive organisations enter new markets will be complemented by actions to ensure that owner/managers are equipped with the skills to manage growth.

Finally, such a model will make policy thinking more reality congruent, bringing it closer to the realities driving skill formation and use, delivering more effective policy results in terms of driving skill levels and use in the direction of producing better quality work and higher income levels.

What kind of impact will the new model have?

A new skills policy model that focuses on changing the nature of the productive system will have a number of impacts. In the first instance, by building a new institutional regime and appropriate regulatory environment, business strategy will be informed by a new set of cost–benefit calculations. This also means that the productive system will be incentivised to adopt a high-skilled system. As job design embraces greater skills content, this also raises the extra value jobs as to performance. This leads to a greater claim of skills on earnings.

Second, increases in skills content and value-added will enable the sector as a whole to move up the global value chain. Thus skills policy is fundamentally about shifting industry sectors via changes in the productive system.

Third, there will be workers who may be displaced because of the upskilling process. While we have discussed the need to create more jobs in new sectors, skills policy is also about shifting displaced workers to other, hopefully, more highly skilled jobs. This is the most challenging aspects of skills policy, because new jobs are often in the service sector, which tends to be low-skilled.

How will it work out in different types of society?

The main core of the approach will be the same but how it is operationalised and, to a certain extent, the outcomes of the actions will differ in accordance with the influence of existing institutional structures and cultural values. It is here that the Anglo-Saxon nations have much to do to catch up with competitors. Of the societies discussed here, the UK is amongst the least well coordinated in terms of its approach to skills policy. The German system is well coordinated at the sector level, at least on the supply side, which has been effective in closing off the low-skilled route in the manufacturing sector. Singapore has more experience in coordinating the demand and supply side and the system is steered by a strong business strategy approach at the national level. However, even there the sector approach is still limited to the supply side and the mere creation of jobs. The Singapore case still faces the difficulties of sufficient numbers of high-quality jobs which have a high skills content. Whilst new sectors such as aerospace and bio-sciences have been created in the last 20 years, the number of jobs in these sectors is relatively small, compared with the number of graduates coming onto the labour market.

What does it mean for existing politicians and policy makers?

It means challenging the thinking of existing politicians and policy makers that has delivered a fragmented approach to skills policy and replacing it with one centred on the business strategy and productive systems approach. This of course requires a huge change in the mindset of politicians and policy makers. To achieve this, conventional thinking has to be challenged. The current supply side ideology means politicians cannot see the connections between business strategy and skills very clearly. Future skills policy must no longer be about who can implement market-based policy most effectively, leading as it does to endless deregulation and a race to the bottom and short-termism. Inevitably, deskilling and 'digital Taylorism' are the only skills outcomes for the majority of the labour force. To make matters worse, continuing inequality will be reinforced driven by the fact that skills, in the form of educational qualifications, are increasingly irrelevant to the earning potential of workers, creating a level of unacceptable social costs.

Once we recognise that what drives change is business strategy, then the link between the various fragmentary policy initiatives becomes evident and measures can be introduced to coordinate them. Future skills policy is then about making skills relevant again, meaning that skills policy will have the potential to transform the productive system where skills are the primary driver for business and employees' well-being.

Notes

1 Lanning and Lawton's (2012) analysis comes close to that advocated here as they stress the importance of the institutional context in terms of factors such as employment protection legislation, minimum wages, occupational regulation, union density and corporate governance, but the focus is still on training not skill formation and it fails to establish the links between these institutional factors, business strategy and employers' cost–benefit decisions, which is central to our approach.

2 See, for example, http://go.worldbank.org/32GZWRY8Z0 (accessed 7 April 2014).

3 These examples are based on our research in Scotland (Sung et al., 2009); England (Sung et al., 2008) and Singapore (Sung et al., 2012).

7

CONCLUSION

In many ways, this book is about how business decisions are made as much as how skills matter. We argue that skills, as well as learning, are fundamentally a contextual matter, which only makes sense within the confines of business strategy. We believe that the SSM has taken us a long way down a new path in understanding how skills are related to the reality of work, business operation and competitive strategy that matters to companies' survival. In this sense, the traditional way of understanding skills – much of it being inspired by the human capital theory – is deficient. It is almost naive to believe that if more skills are available in the forms of workers' knowledge or skills, they will get utilised. Business owners and managers do not exist for the purposes of creating and utilising skills. They are there to create a business performance that is driven by a particular business model. This is where the new approach to skills policy has to focus: the question then is, 'How can we influence business strategy?'

But in order to strengthen our proposed model in this concluding chapter, we think it would be useful to stand back and ask some additional questions. For example, have we missed out anything? Are public policies solely about supporting economic or business performance, as if they had no other goals? We will therefore venture into some of those complex issues in order to evaluate the worth of our model in the skills debate.

How crucial is the supply side, if demand is the policy action leader?

Our discussion, especially in the form of Figure 6.1 might have given the impression that the supply side of skills is far less significant than one might think. In fact, both are important. Our argument is that we have never paid sufficient attention to demand-related policies, and it is time we pushed for them if we recognise the importance of business strategy. But even if we are to focus on the demand side, namely the left-hand side of Figure 6.1, we still need to have coherent supply policies in order to make the demand policy work. Indeed, aspects of the outer layer of Figure 6.2 focus on the appropriate types of supply consideration in order that demand policies will work. The sector sphere is the glue that brings the demand (the inner core) and supply (the policy sphere) sides together.

The typical issues concerning the supply side may include immigration/foreign workers policy, the pricing of workers (e.g. minimum wage), regulations (e.g. work hours and employment/contract practices) and qualifications supply. All of these provide vital and important signals to the employers. What is more crucial is the fact that the supply side considerations are part of the cost–benefit calculations that shape the decisions of the employers. One good example is the use of foreign or immigrant workers. In many countries, it has been argued that extensive use of foreign workers who are more willing to take on very low-paid jobs may have both positive and negative effects. On the positive side, foreign workers may fill the labour supply gap when job numbers are expanding rapidly. In some countries, foreign workers take up jobs – in some cases vital jobs – that the locals do not want to do (e.g. construction, healthcare, agricultural work etc.). As a result, the growth momentum is maintained. On the negative side, the willingness of foreign workers to take up very low-paid work may have a depressing effect on wages for the bottom strata of the local population. This wage-depressing effect may create very little incentive for employers to upskill, to rethink their work processes and to pay serious attention to technological investment decisions. The reason is simple: it is not worth it (a simple cost–benefit calculation). Thus the purpose of this discussion is not to debate whether migrant workers are good or bad. The point we are trying to make is that labour supply decisions are not just about numbers and qualifications. The most fundamental aspect of supply decisions is about how supply decisions affect employers' behaviour and business strategy.

Some sectors are less able to lend themselves to the sectoral approach

Our advocacy for a sectoral approach to skills development may have also given the impression that the sectoral approach to delivering the SSM is applicable with equal impact in any industrial sector. This is far from the case. We can explain the differential picture in terms of Figure 6.2. The success of the sectoral approach requires the implementation of a set of coherent policies in the outer layer of Figure 6.2 in order to create the incentives and conditions needed for a high-skilled cost–benefit business decision. But in some industrial sectors, the ability for public policies to create those necessary conditions are weak for various reasons. When this happens, the policy sphere of Figure 6.2 becomes detached, and in some cases even irrelevant. When the policy sphere fades away, there are two consequences for the sectoral sphere: it either operates according to its own agenda (plans and missions of the individual stakeholders) or it becomes reactive to political and international pressure. But more importantly, the inner core (the productive system) of employers' business strategy tends to focus on a set of calculations that are only relevant to itself. In this case, the SSM tells us that employers can choose various combinations of TRs and IRs that may still be profitable (though there may be differences in terms of the longevity of that profit and the extent of investment in the productive system and risk of managing change). Many employers take the 'low road' because the profit is more immediate and is therefore more 'certain'. It's just simple human behaviour. This is the reason why we frequently see most deregulated sectors taking on the 'low road' when it comes to skills utilisation and value-added production.

So where would we find those industry sectors where the sectoral and policy spheres are such that it is difficult to form a skill-progressive institutional logic? We provide three examples to highlight the fact that although the potential for a sectoral approach may be real, it is not equally applicable everywhere. The first concerns very large often international employers that may dominate a particular sector. Multinationals are one of these cases where national policies matter relatively little in their business strategies. But even here the picture is not entirely clear-cut. MNCs in Germany and in Singapore are well known for their strong participation in the sectoral sphere and input into the policy sphere. As we have seen in the UK, they provided the stimulus for moving the car manufacturing industry up the value chain.

The second example concerns the nature of the industry where there are limited possibilities for higher value-added production. The classic examples are corner shops and mass market for personal services. Both of these sectors are subject to high demand for 'low cost' productive systems because low prices are the basis for trade in the market. Again, there are exceptions. For example, where the country's policy sphere aims at achieving narrow wage differentials and higher skills, these sectors become far less labour intensive and prices are not cheap. This forms the institutional logics for developing these sectors, if they are to be encouraged at all. Ultimately, not only is the sectoral approach not for every sector, there is also a question of which sectors are most strategically suitable for the sectoral approach to skills development.

The third situation is where the policy sphere is not entirely in the hands of national governments. Here, the migrant workers moving from the much poorer EU states to the more affluent states in the EU are a prime example. As the options of the policy sphere are few and weak, the glue between the policy and sectoral spheres ceases to be effective, though this problem is mostly overlapping with the second point where low-cost productive systems are demanded by consumers.

Are we expecting too much from skills?

From the very first chapter of this book, you might recall that we emphasised that skills may not be the silver bullet for all desirable economic or social outcomes. The reason is that once we start including business strategies and competition in our analysis, we can see a range of situations where the role for skills is confined to a narrowly defined (e.g. technical) importance, where only the TRs dimension is important. For example, firms that achieve a breakthrough with a new product and obtain a first-mover advantage may not in the first instance pay too much attention to their position on the IRs dimension until such time as they find themselves competing on the basis of quality. Similarly, some firms may secure a competitive advantage in the market through acquisition or through innovative design or marketing that enables them to minimise the attention they pay to the skills of their labour force in general. With some products, such as organic food or high-quality beverages, the product may command a premium in the market but the processing is through industrial mass production involving low-skilled labour. Like most relationships we observe in the social sciences, there is no invariant relationship between competitive strategy and the TRs and IRs, just a higher probability that where competition is on the basis of quality or speed of delivery, the skills of most employees become more significant in the productive process.

To what extent is skills policy also part of the wider social policy?

One of the problems with skills policy is that in some societies it has been used as a means of addressing other political objectives, usually equity issues. Sometimes the objectives of training policy and equity policy coincide, as for example in Singapore in the 1980s when programmes to provide basic education and work skills for adult workers, delivered through employers, served the equity objectives of compensating for the inadequacies of the earlier education system. These programmes served to compensate for a lack of primary and secondary education, while at the same time delivering improvements in the basic skills of working adults. We do not know the extent to which this general training had an impact on job performance, but it was vital in providing signals to the inward investment provided by MNCs at the time. Therefore, in this sense, skills policy has a huge impact on job creation, but perhaps is indirectly linked to business performance and the competitive strategies of business.

In other instances, as in the UK in the 1990s and the first decade of the 21st century, the government attempted to use the NVQ system to compensate for the failure of the education system to deliver basic skills and also deliver help to employers to overcome skill shortages, but neither objective was fully achieved. The government created targets for the numbers achieving level 2 qualifications, in an attempt to tackle the equity issue, but these qualifications proved to be of little or no value in the labour market, while failing to meet the demand from employers for the level 3 qualifications that the productive system required. There are two implications here. The first is that from the perspective of the SSM, training and skills policy should address the requirements of the productive systems. Equity issues are a separate matter requiring different attention. Most businesses do not have a remit for achieving social equity. The second is that it is actually possible to achieve some of both objectives, provided that the institutional logics are set up in the first instance to do so, as in some Nordic countries. As such, it is easy to see that a deregulated economy – where the policy sphere is weak and the sectoral sphere is working on individual agendas – will be hard pressed to achieve the twin objectives of equity through skills development.

We also see the same confusion today with regard to the promotion of lifelong learning. Whilst lifelong learning must be good in the general sense for all people, the frequent selling pitch that lifelong learning can provide employability is a very misleading assertion. This link may or may not exist. If lifelong learning is fully embedded in the institutional logics of a sector, the impact of lifelong learning can be huge. Where lifelong learning is generally designed at the policy sphere level, it may not create the glue with the sectoral sphere, and therefore ultimately makes weak links with the business strategy core. It is therefore not surprising to see that lifelong learning may not pay, just like the previous example of the wrong level of NVQ provided for employers.

Another problem with lifelong learning policy is that it is often advocated as being a necessary measure for the creation of a knowledge-based economy. While this may at first sight seem plausible, on closer inspection it is clear that lifelong learning is only found in a limited part of the economy, namely in professional and managerial occupations and in those organisations using mature mass production and knowledge-intensive forms of production. This point echoes the argument before, that lifelong learning needs to be linked to the business strategy, as mediated via the relevant institutional logics. For employees in lower level, low-skilled occupations, and those in organisations using industrial mass production, lifelong learning is arguably meaningless in the context of their work environment, which may also provide few opportunities for mobility and contribute little to employability. Where employers are deliberately creating unskilled or low-skilled jobs as part of their business strategy, such jobs cannot provide the basis for lifelong learning. Here alternative provision has to be made if any form of lifelong learning is to be offered. A good example of such provision is the British Unionlearn[1] programme, where the trade unions provide alternative access to learning, often delivered alongside the workplace with the consent of employers. The government funds the programme. It highlights the importance of lifelong learning but also the need for it to be delivered outside the immediate work tasks for those employed in low-skilled work tasks if it is to be effective.

Although we mention the possibility of using a well-designed institutional logic to deliver both social and economic goals, it also places more stresses on the entire system. Therefore, there is a strong case to be made that learning designed for the support of equity considerations may be better delivered outside the work context if they are to be meaningful as part of broader education and citizenship programmes. To conflate the two runs the risk of delivering on neither agenda. In this book our concern has been to refocus the skills debate and skills policies. Equity issues are important but they need a separate treatment, which is outside our remit.

When is high-performance working not work intensification?

As well as skills policies and business strategies, this book is also about high-skills utilisation, especially through HPWPs in the IRs dimension, and how TR and IR designs may make a difference to skills utilisation. There is a very fine line between high-skills utilisation and work intensification. It is almost two sides of the same coin. However, we ought to make a distinction because work intensification is a very short-term position that is not sustainable as a long-term business strategy. The greatest challenge for HPWPs and high-skills utilisation is not that it is so rare in reality that no one can understand it – as we have seen throughout this book, there are numerous examples. The challenge lies in the incentive to adopt it. The answer is in creating the institutional logics within a sector to support and incentivise the full utilisation of HPWPs that benefits both employer and employee, so that it becomes an attractive business proposition not just for one business but for the sector as whole.

The most fundamental and qualitative difference that distinguishes HPWPs from work intensification is the existence of two achievable traits within an organisation, namely mutual gains and discretionary effort (Sparham and Sung, 2008). These are the outcomes that the different 'bundles' of work practices are designed to encourage and nurture. When a workplace brings in work practices that are capable of enticing greater skills utilisation from its employees, it is also a fact that the nature of work increases its intensity, its tempo or even its volume. The question is then, 'How do the employees feel about that?' It is not difficult to see that if these changes do not bring significant increases in both intrinsic and extrinsic job satisfaction at the same time, work intensification is a real consequence of HPWPs and high-skills utilisation.[2] Here, well-organised trades unions can play an important role in representing employee interests.

That is the reason why the full implementation of HPWPs involves other necessary notions such as rewards, self-growth, autonomy, trust, ownership and participation. Thus, 'What's in it for me?' is not such a difficult question to understand. Not only is it a question that every employee should ask, it also makes learning and skills development a meaningful tool within a mutual context, once the question is answered. So why aren't there more HPWP organisations? HPWP is mostly located in the right-hand side of the SSM, but the model also suggests that the same business could be located in the left-hand side space and still be 'profitable'. But in the left-hand side space it is a lot less involved in setting up the productive system. So there are 'exit options' which may be argued as 'equally attractive' (Jaehrling and Méhaut, 2013). The aim of the sectoral approach is to change the institutional logics (i.e. cost–benefit calculation) of these sorts of decisions. Hence, HPWPs and high-skills utilisation could lead to work intensification, and we can already observe that in those deregulated economies where the sectoral and policy spheres are more or less absent or weak, work intensification is a real phenomenon (Green, 2006).

Factors other than business strategy that impact on training and skill formation

Having stressed the importance of business strategy, we would be remiss not to acknowledge the fact that surveys often point to issues other than business strategy that drive training. Legislation in the form of health and safety regulations is a major one. This is reflected in the fact that the UK Commission's *Employer Skills Survey 2013* (UKCES, 2014: 63) reports that of the employers who trained their employees in the previous year (66 per cent of the total surveyed), 74 per cent undertook training for health and safety, including first aid. There are of course other regulatory reasons for undertaking training, such as the requirement to meet the standards of regulatory authority that imposed levies on employers as in countries such as France, as well as for individuals to obtain a licence to practice their trade. While these other drivers of training and skill formation are not seen as the main driving force in the SSM, they are fully acknowledged at the sector level. For it is here, at the interface between the sectoral and policy spheres, that such factors impinge on the location adopted by the employing organisation on the IR dimension.

Indeed, from the perspective of the SSM these 'external' factors are usually, but not exclusively, imposed by governments and play an important part in shaping the institutional logics at the sectoral level. In the food industry in most advanced industrial societies, health and safety has to be built into the operating procedures of the company because failure to comply would mean that the government could close them down. For those wishing to compete in high value-added markets provided by the major retailers, their business strategy has to be able to accommodate the regulations of other agencies such as the ISO and the British Retail Consortium, that purchasers impose on the supply chain. Compliance with such regulations means that companies have to embed learning within the workplace that can form the basis of higher levels of skills utilisation as in the case of Glenmorangie reported in Chapter 5.

In other sectors such as the energy and utility sector, which in the case of electricity and gas are dealing with dangerous products, the regulations are even more demanding for employers, providing tighter control over training and the standards required to achieve certification of staff. This directly affects the levels of skill formation among staff. At the same time the five-year time limit on licences to operate issued to companies in the UK and the controls over their pricing policies by the 'Regulator' mean that the institutional logics have discouraged companies from investing in higher levels of skill formation and introducing new management because these require a longer term payoff (Sung et al., 2009b). In the UK energy and utility sector, the institutional logics require a business strategy that focuses on the short term.

Once again we could use other sectors to illustrate the impact of these 'other' factors that influence skill formation on employers' business strategies. However, there is sufficient above to make the point that although these factors appear 'external' to the firm, and therefore are not being driven by business strategy, they are crucial in shaping the institutional logics of the sector and in influencing the business strategy of the companies that eventually does drive skill formation and use.

We began this book with the aim of highlighting the inadequacies of our current understanding of skills issues. Our premise was that we cannot develop a more effective skills policy without the development of a theory that provides a more appropriate understanding of the demand for skills. This we hope we have done in the belief that there is nothing more practical than a good theory. We have therefore sketched out what an effective sector approach would look like.

At the moment many nations continue to rely on a supply side approach to guide their skills policies. Some, like the UK, Australia and New Zealand, have flirted with a demand side approach but then fallen back to the old supply side approach, trying to compete with the flood of new graduates being produced by Brazil, Russia, India and China (the BRIC countries). In a world where their share of production in world markets will inevitably decline, their remaining high value-added industries face increasing competition from the new industrial countries making more determined efforts to access those markets. Meanwhile, economies such as the UK continue to produce more and more low-skilled, low-quality and insecure jobs while politicians speak wistfully of the need to create a knowledge economy. If these countries are to compete effectively in these higher value-added markets and create more highly skilled, highly paid jobs, then more effective policy measures are urgently needed that will enable them to compete more effectively at the top end of the market. This can be done not by reverting to old-style industrial policy and directly financing companies, but by creating a business environment that actively encourages business leaders to invest in and create enterprises that will generate high-skilled jobs. This is what a sectoral policy can deliver. Skills policies are no longer about supplying more skills, but they are all about changing business behaviour and models for high-skilled productive systems.

Notes

1   See www.unionlearn.org.uk/about-unionlearn/union-learning-fund (accessed 7 April 2014) for an outline of the programme.
2   Green (2010) argues, in a similar way, that the potential gains for workers can be lost if they do not compensate the employee with sufficiently greater autonomy.

REFERENCES

Adler, P.S. (2004) 'Skill trends under capitalism and the socialisation of production', in C. Warhurst, I. Grugulis and E. Keep (eds), *The Skills That Matter*. Basingstoke: Palgrave Macmillan. pp. 242–260.

Anderson, P. and Warhurst, C. (2012) 'Lost in translation? Skills policy and the shift to skill ecosystems', in T. Dolphin and D. Nash (eds), *Complex New World: Translating New Economic Thinking into Public Policy*. London: IPPR. pp. 109–120.

Ansoff, H.I. (1965) *Corporate Strategy: An Analytic Approach to Business Policy for Growth and Expansion*. New York: McGraw-Hill.

Antonelli, C. (1999) 'The evolution of the industrial organization of the production of knowledge', *Cambridge Journal of Economics*, 23: 243–260.

Ashton, D.N. (2004) 'The impact of organisational structure and practices on learning in the workplace', *International Journal of Training and Development*, 8(1): 43–53.

Ashton, D.N. and Field, D. (1976) *Young Workers: From School to Work*. London: Hutchinson.

Ashton, D. and Green, F. (1996) *Education, Training and the Global Economy*. Cheltenham: Edward Elgar.

Ashton, D.N. and Maguire, M.J. (1980) 'The function of academic and non-academic criteria in employers' selection strategies', *British Journal of Guidance and Counselling*, 8(2): 146–157.

Ashton, D.N. and Sung, J. (2002) *Supporting Workplace Learning for High-Performance Working*. Geneva: ILO.

Ashton, D. and Sung, J. (2006) 'How competitive strategy matters? Understanding the drivers of training, learning and performance at the firm level', SKOPE Research Paper No. 66. Oxford: Oxford and Warwick Universities.

Ashton, D., Brown, P. and Lauder, H. (2010) 'Skill webs and international human resource management: Lessons from a study of the global skill strategies of transnational companies', *International Journal of Human Resource Management*, 21(6): 838–852.

Ashton, D.N., Green, F.J., James, D. and Sung, J. (1999) *Education and Training for Development in East Asia: The Political Economy of Skill Formation in Newly Industrialised Economies*. London: Routledge.

Ashton, D., Loke, F. and Sung, J. (forthcoming 2014) 'Productivity and skills in the Infocomm sector', Research Report, Centre for Skills Performance and Productivity Research. Singapore: Institute of Adult Learning.

Ashton, D.N., Sung, J., Raddon, A. and Riordan, T. (2008) 'Challenging the myths about learning and training in small enterprises: Implications for public policy'. Employment Working Paper No. 1, 2008/1. Geneva: ILO. (Available at www.ilo.org/skills/what/pubs/lang--en/docName--WCMS_103625/index.htm, accessed 7 April 2014).

Aspin, C. (2003) *The Water-Spinners: A New Look at the Early Cotton Trade*. Helmshore: Helmshore Local History Society.

Bain, J. (1956) *Barriers to New Competition*. Cambridge, MA: Harvard University Press.

Barrett, R. (ed.) (2005) *Management, Labor Process and Software Development: Reality Bytes*. London: Routledge.

Bartel, A., Ichniowski, C. and Shaw, K. (2007) 'How does information technology really affect productivity? Plant-level comparisons of product innovation, process improvement and worker skills', *Quarterly Journal of Economics*, 122(4): 1721–1758.

Batt, R. (2000) 'Strategic segmentation in front-line services: Matching customers, employees and human resource systems', *International Journal of Human Resource Management*, 11(3): 540–561.

Baumol, W.J. (1967) 'Macroeconomics of unbalanced growth: The anatomy of an urban crisis', *American Economic Review*, 57: 415–426.

Becker, G.S. (1964) *Human Capital*. New York: National Bureau of Economic Research.

Becker, G.S. (1994) *Human Capital: A Theoretical and Empirical Analysis with Special Reference to Education*, 3rd edn. London: University of Chicago Press.

Belanger, J. and Edwards, P. (2013) 'The nature of front-line service work: Distinctive features and continuity in the employment relationship', *Work Employment and Society*, 27(3): 433–450.

Bell, D. (1999) *The Coming of Post-Industrial Society: A Venture in Social Forecasting*. New York: Basic Books.

Bendix, R. (1963) *Work and Authority in Industry*. New York: Harper.

Benyon, H. (1973) *Working for Ford*. London: Allen Lane.

Berger, S. (2006) *How We Compete: What Companies Around the World are Doing to Make it in Today's Global Economy*. New York: Doubleday.

Birdi, K., Clegg, C., Patterson, M., Robinson, A., Stride, C.B., Wall, T.D. and Wood, S.J. (2008) 'The impact of human resource and operational management practices on company productivity: A longitudinal study', *Personnel Psychology*, 61: 467–501.

BIS, Department for Business Innovation and Skills (2010) 'Economic growth', BIS Economics Paper No. 9. London: Department for Business Innovation and Skills.

Blackburn, R.M. and Mann, M. (1979) *The Working Class in the Labour Market*. London: Macmillan.

Blauner, R. (1964) *Alienation and Freedom: The Factory Worker and His Industry*. Chicago, IL: University of Chicago Press.

Bloom, N. and Van Reenen, J. (2006) 'Measuring and explaining management practices across firms and countries', Working Paper 12216. Cambridge, MA: National Bureau of Economic Research. (Available at www.nber.org/papers/w12216, accessed 7 April 2014).

Bloom, N. and Van Reenen, J. (2007) 'Measuring and explaining management practices across firms and countries', *Quarterly Journal of Economics*, 122(4): 1341–1408.

Bloom, N. and Van Reenen, J. (2010a) 'Human resource management and productivity', Centre for Economic Performance, Discussion Paper No. 982. London: London School of Economics.

Bloom, N. and Van Reenen, J. (2010b) 'Why do management practices differ across firms and countries?', Centre for Economic Performance, Occasional Paper 26. London: London School of Economics.

Bloom, N., Genakos, C., Sadun, R. and Van Reenen, J. (2009a) 'Management matters', LSE/Stanford mimeo. London: London School of Economics.

Bloom, N., Sadun, R. and Van Reenen, J. (2009b) 'The organization of firms across countries', CEP Discussion Paper No. 937: London: London School of Economics.

Bloom, N., Genakos, C., Sadun, R. and Van Reenen, J. (2011) 'Management practices across firms and countries', Centre for Economic Performance, Discussion Paper No. 1109. London: London School of Economics.

Bosch, G. and Weinkopf, C. (eds) (2008) *Low-Wage Work in Germany*. New York: Russell Sage Foundation. pp. 288–314.

Bowen, D. and Ostroff, C. (2004) 'Understanding HRM – firm performance linkages: The role of the "strength" of the HRM system', *Academy of Management Review*, 29(2): 203–221.

Bowles, S. and Gintis, H. (1976) *Schooling in Capitalist America*. New York: Basic Books.

Boxall, P. (2003) 'HR strategy and competitive advantage in the service sector', *Human Resource Management Journal*, 13(3): 5–20.

Boxall, P. (2012) 'High-performance work systems: What, why, how and for whom?', *Asia Pacific Journal of Human Resource*, 50: 169–186.

Boxall, P. (2013) 'Mutuality in the management of human resources: Assessing the quality of alignment in employment relationships', *Human Resources Management Journal*, 23(1): 3–17.

Boxall, P. and Macky, K. (2009) 'Research and theory on high-performance work systems: Progressing the high-involvement stream', *Human Resource Management Journal*, 19: 3–23.

Brink, H., Muthiah, S. and Nalk, R. (2010) 'A better way to automate service operations', *McKinsey on Business Technology*, 20(Summer): 38–44.

Brockmann, M. (2013) 'Learning cultures in retail: Apprenticeships, identity and emotional work in England and Germany', *Journal of Education and Work*, 26(4): 357–375.

Brockmann, M., Clarke, L. and Winch, C. (eds) (2011) *Knowledge, Skill and Competence in the European Labour Market*. Abingdon: Routledge.

Brown, P., Ashton, D., Lauder, H. and Tholen, G. (2008) 'Toward a high-skilled, low-waged, workforce? A review of global trends in education, employment and the labour market', SKOPE Monograph No. 10. Oxford: Cardiff and Oxford Universities.

Brown, P., Lauder, H. and Ashton, D. (2011) *The Global Auction: The Broken Promises of Education, Jobs and Income*. New York: Oxford University Press.

Brown, P., Lauder, H. and Green, A. (2002) *High Skills: Globalization, Competitiveness and Skill Formation*. Oxford: Oxford University Press.

Brynjolfsson, E. and Hitt, L. (2003) 'Computing productivity: Firm level evidence', *Review of Economics and Statistics*, 8(4): 793–808.

Brynjolfson, E. and Saunders, A. (2010) *Wired for Innovation. How Information Technology is Reshaping the Economy*. Cambridge, MA: The MIT Press.

Buchanan, J., Scott, L. Yu, S., Schutz, H. and Jakubauskas, M. (2010) 'Skills demand and utilisation: An international review of approaches to measurement and policy development', DECD Local Economic and Employee Development, Working Papers 2010/04. London: Department for Education and Child Development.

Cabinet Office (2001) 'In demand: Adult skills in the 21st century', A Performance and Innovation Unit Report. London: Cabinet Office. (Available at http://dera.ioe.ac.uk/4578/1/Finalrep.pdf, accessed 7 April 2014).

Campbell, M. (2012) 'Skills for prosperity? A review of OECD and partner country skill strategies', LLAKES Research Paper 39. London: London University, Institute of Education.

Campbell, M. (2013) 'Management matters: Key findings from the surveys', UKCES Briefing Paper. Wath-upon-Dearne: UKCES.

Campbell, R. ([1747]1969) *The London Tradesman: Being a Compendious View of All the Trades, Professions, Arts both Liberal and Mechanic, now Practifed in the Cities of London and Westminster*. Newton Abbot: David and Charles Reprints.

Caroli, E. and Van Reenen, J. (2001) 'Skill-biased organizational change', *Quarterly Journal of Economics*, 116(4): 1449–1492.

Chandler, A.D., Jr (1962) *Strategy and Structure: Chapters in the History of the American Industrial Enterprise*. Cambridge, MA: MIT Press.

Chandler, A.D. (1976) 'The development of modern management structure in the US and UK', in L. Hannah (ed.), *Management Strategy and Business Development*. London: Macmillan.

Chandler, A.D. (1977) *The Visible Hand: The Managerial Revolution in American Business*. Cambridge, MA: Harvard University Press.

Chandler, A.D. (1990) *Scale and Scope: The Dynamics of Industrial Capitalism*. Cambridge, MA: Harvard University Press.

Chinoy, E. (1955) *Automobile Workers and the American Dream*. Boston, MA: Beacon Press.

CIPD (2007) *Learning and Development: Annual Survey Report 2007*. London: Chartered Institute of Personnel and Development.

CIPD (2012) 'Competence and competency frameworks', Factsheet. London: Chartered Institute of Personnel and Development.

Cockburn, S. (1983) *Brothers: Male Dominance and Technical Change*. London: Pluto Press.

Connor, T. (2002) 'The resource-based view of strategy and its value to practising managers', *Strategic Change*, 11(6): 307–316.

Crespi, G., Criscuolo, C. and Haskel, J. (2007) 'Information technology, organizational change and productivity growth: Evidence from UK firms', Centre for Economic Performance, Discussion Paper 783. London: London School of Economics.

Danford, A., Richardson, M., Stewart, P., Tailby, S. and Upchurch, M. (2005) *Partnership and the High Performance Workplace: Work and Employment Relations in the Aerospace Industry*. Basingstoke: Palgave Macmillan.

Day, G.S. and Montgomery, D.B. (1983) 'Diagnosing the experience curve', *Journal of Marketing*, 47 (Spring): 44–58.

de Menezes, L., Wood, S. and Gelade, G. (2010) 'The integration of human resource and operation management practices and its link with performance: A longitudinal latent class study', *Journal of Operations Management*, 28(6): 455–471.

Delbridge, N. (1998) *Life On the Line in Contemporary Manufacturing: The Workplace Experience of Lean Production and the 'Japanese' Model*. Oxford: Oxford University Press.

Dench, S., Hillage, J., Reilly, P. and Kodz. J. (2000) *Employers' Skill Survey: Case studies – Food Manufacturing Sector*. Brighton: Institute of Employment Studies.

Department of Trade and Industry (DTI) (2004) 'Six sigma', Factsheet. London: DTI.

Dickerson, A. and Vignoles, A. (2007) 'The distribution and returns to qualifications in the sector skills councils', SSDA Research Report No. 21. Wath-Upon-Dearne: Sector Skills Development Agency.

Doeringer, P.B., Evans-Klock, C.A. and Terkla, D.G. (2002) *Start-up Factories: High-performance Management, Job Quality and Regional Advantage*. New York: Oxford University Press and W.E. Upjohn Institute.

Doorewaard, H. and Meihuizen, H. (2000) 'Strategic performance options in professional service organisations', *Human Resource Management Journal*, 10(2): 39–57.

Dore, R. (1973) *British Factory–Japanese Factory: The Origins of National Diversity in Industrial Relations*. London: George Allen and Unwin.

Drucker, P.F. (1946) *Concept of the Corporation*. New York: The John Day Company.

Drucker, P. (1954) *The Practice of Management*. New York: Harper & Row.

Eaton, S. (2000) 'Beyond unloving care: Linking human resource management and patient care quality in nursing homes', *International Journal of Human Resource Management*, 11(3): 591–616.

Elias, N. (1978) *What is Sociology?* London: Hutchinson.

Emirbayer, M. and Mische, A. (1998) 'What is agency?', *American Journal of Sociology*, 103(4): 962–1023.

Felstead, A., Fuller, A., Jewson, N. and Unwin, L. (2009) *Improving Working as Learning*. Abingdon: Routledge.

Felstead, A., Fuller, A., Unwin, L., Ashton, D., Butler, P. and Lee, T. (2005) 'Surveying the scene: Learning metaphors, survey design and the workplace context', *Journal of Education and Work*, 18(4): 359–383.

Felstead, A., Gallie, D., Green, F. and Hande, I. (2013) *Skills at Work in Britain: First Findings from the Skills and Employment Survey, 2012*. London: Centre for Learning and Life Chances in Knowledge Economies and Societies, Institute of Education.

Felstead, A., Gallie, D., Green, F. and Zhou, Y. (2007) *Skills at Work in Britain, 1986 to 2006*. Oxford: ESRC Centre on Skills, Knowledge and Organisational Performance.

Ferdows, K. and De Meyer, A. (1990) 'Lasting improvements in manufacturing performance: In search of a new theory', *Journal of Oprations Management*, 9(2): 168–184.

Findlay, P. and Warhurst, C. (2012) 'Skills utilisation in Scotland', Skills in Focus Paper. Glasgow: Skills Development Scotland.

Finegold, D. (1999) 'Creating self-sustaining high-skill ecosystems', *Oxford Review of Economic Policy*, 15(1): 60–81.

Finegold, D. and Soskice, D. (1988) 'The failure of British training: Analysis and prescription', *Oxford Review of Economic Policy*, 4(3): 21–53.

Fitton, R.S. (1989) *The Arkwrights: Spinners of Fortune*. Manchester: Manchester University Press.

Form, W. (1987) 'On the degradation of skills', *Annual Review of Sociology*, 13: 29–47.

Fuller, A. and Unwin, L. (2003) 'Learning as apprentices in the contemporary UK workplace: Creating and managing expansive and restrictive participation', *Journal of Education and Work*, 16(4): 407–426.

Funding Universe (no date) 'McDonald's corporation history'. South Jordan, UT: Funding Universe/Lendio. (Available at www.fundinguniverse.com/company-histories/McDonalds-Corporation-Company-History.html, accessed 7 April 2014).

Galbraith, J.K. (1967) *The New Industrial State*. Princeton, NJ: Princeton University Press.

Gallie, D. (2011) 'Production regimes, employee job control and skill development', LLAKES Research Paper 31. London: Institute of Education. (Available at www.llakes.org, accessed 7 April 2014).

Garrett, R., Campbell, M. and Mason, G. (2010) 'The value of skills: An evidence review', Evidence Report 22. London: UKES and the National Institute for Economic and Social Research. (Available at www.ukces.org.uk/publications/er22-the-value-of-skills, accessed 7 April 2014).

Gautié, J. and Schmitt, J. (2009) *Low-wage Work in a Wealthy World*. New York: Russell Sage Foundation.

Ghemawat, P. (2002) 'Competition and business strategy in historical perspective', *The Business History Review*, 76(1): 37–74.

Glucksmann, M.A. (2004) 'Call configurations: Varieties of call centre and divisions of labour', *Work, Employment and Society*, 18(4) 795–811.

Goldschmid, H.J., Mann, H.M. and Weston, J.F. (1974) *Industrial Concentration: The New Learning*. Boston, MA: Little Brown.

Goldthorpe, J., Lockwood, D., Bechhofer, F. and Platt, J. (1968) *The Affluent Worker: Industrial Attitudes and Behaviour*. Cambridge: Cambridge University Press.

Goldthorpe, J., Lockwood, D., Bechhofer, F. and Platt, J. (1969) *The Affluent Worker in the Class Structure*. Cambridge: Cambridge University Press.

Goleman, D. (1996) *Emotional Intelligence: Why It Can Matter More Than IQ*. London: Bloomsbury.

Goodridge, P., Haskel, J. and Wallis, G. (2012) 'UK innovation index: Productivity and growth in UK industries, 2012', NESTA Working Paper 12/09. London: NESTA. (Available at www.nesta.org.uk/publications/uk-innovation-index-productivity-and-growth-uk-industries, accessed 7 April 2014).

Green, F. (2006) *Demanding Work. The Paradox of Job Quality in the Affluent Economy*. Princeton, NJ: Princeton University Press.

Green, F. (2010) 'Unions and skills utilisation', Unionlearn, Research Paper 11. London: TUC.

Green, F. (2013) *Skills and Skilled Work: An Economic and Social Analysis*. Oxford: Oxford University Press.

Green, F., Ashton, D. and Felstead, A. (2001) 'Estimating the determinants of the supply of computing, problem-solving, communication, social and teamworking skills', *Oxford Economic Papers*, 53(3): 406–433.

Grimshaw, D., Cooke, F.-L., Grugulis, I. and Vincent, S. (2002) 'New technology and changing organizational forms: Implications for managerial control and skills', *New Technology, Work and Employment*, 17(3): 186–203.

Grubb, W.N. and Ryan, P. (1999) *The Roles of Evaluation for Vocational Education and Training: Plain Talk in the Field of Dreams*. Geneva: ILO.

Grugulis, I. (2007) *Skills, Training and Human Resource Development: A Critical Text*. Basingstoke: Palgrave Macmillan.

Guest, D. (2011) 'Human resource management and performance: Still searching for some answers', *Human Resource Management Journal*, 21(1): 3–13.

Hall, P.A. and Soskice, D. (2001) *Varieties of Capitalism: The Institutional Foundations of Comparative Advantage*. New York: Oxford University Press.

Hannah, L. (1983) *The Rise of the Corporate Economy*, 2nd edn. London: Methuen.

Hansson, B. (2008) 'Job-related training and benefits for individuals: A review of evidence and explanations', OECD Education Working Paper No. 19. Paris: OECD.

Haskel, J., Goodridge, P., Pesole, A., Awano, G., Franklin, M. and Kastrinaki, Z. (2011) Driving economic growth: Innovation, knowledge spending and productivity growth in the UK', NESTA Index Report. London: NESTA. (Available at www.nesta.org.uk/publications/driving-economic-growth, accessed 7 April 2014).

Haynes, P. and Fryer, G. (1999) 'Changing patterns of HRM and employment relations in New Zealand: The large hotel industry', *Asia Pacific Journal of Human Resources*, 37(2): 33–43.

Haynes, P. and Fryer, G. (2000) 'Human resources, service quality and performance: A case study', *International Journal of Contemporary Hospitality Management*, 12(4): 240–248.

Henderson, B.D. (1979) *Henderson on Corporate Strategy*. Cambridge, MA: HarperCollins College Division.

Henderson, G., Schmuecker, K. and Baker, R. (2013) 'The rationale for localising the skills system in the UK', IPPR Report North. London: IPPR.

Hinings, C.R., Hickson, D.J., Pennings, J.M. and Schneck, R.E. (1974) 'Structural conditions of intraorganisational power', *Administrative Science Quarterly*, 19(1): 22–24.

Hobsbawn, E.J. (1968) *Industry and Empire*. Harmondsworth: Penguin.

Holmes, A. (2008) *Commoditization and the Strategic Response*. Aldershot: Gower.

Hughes, J. (2005) 'Bringing emotion to work: Emotional intelligence, employee resistance and the reinvention of character', *Work Employment and Society*, 19(3): 603–625.

Hughes, J. (2008) 'The high performance work paradigm: A review and evaluation', Learning as Work Research Paper No. 16. Cardiff: Cardiff School of Social Sciences.

Hughes, A. and Scott Morton, M.S. (2005) 'ICT and productivity growth – the paradox resolved?', Centre for Business Research, Working Paper No. 316. Cambridge: University of Cambridge.

Hunter, L. (2000) 'What determines job quality in nursing homes?', *Industrial and Labor Relations Review*, 53(3): 463–481.

Huselid, M.A. and Becker, B.E. (2011) 'Bridging micro and macro domains: Workforce differentiation and strategic human resource management', *Journal of Management*, 37(3): 421–428.

Jaehrling, K. and Méhaut, P. (2013) 'Varieties of institutional avoidance: Employers' strategies in low-waged service sector occupations in France and Germany', *Socio-Economic Review*, 11: 687–710.

Kakavelakis, K. (2008) 'Family metaphors and learning processes in a restaurant chain', Learning as Work Research Paper No. 18. Cardiff: Cardiff School of Social Sciences, Cardiff University.

Kalleberg, A.L., Marden, P., Reynolds, J. and Knoke, D. (2006) 'Beyond profit? Sector differences in high-performance work practices', *Work and Occupations*, 33(3): 271–302.

Keep, E. (2009) 'The limits of the possible: Shaping the learning and skills landscape through a shared policy narrative', SKOPE Research Paper No. 86. Oxford: Oxford and Cardiff Universities.

Keep, E. (2011) 'The English skills policy narrative', in A. Hodgson, K. Spours and M. Warring (eds), *Post-Compulsory Education and Lifelong Learning Across the United Kingdom – Policy, Organisation and* Governance, pp. 18–38. London: Institute of Education.

Keep, E. (2013) 'Opening the "Black Box" – the increasing importance of a public policy focus on what happens in the workplace', Skills in Focus. Glasgow: Skills Development Scotland. (Available at www.skillsdevelopmentscotland.co.uk/media/645441/ek_presn_skillsinfocus_19thapril2013.pdf, accessed 7 April 2014).

Keep, E. and Mayhew, K. (2010) 'Moving beyond skills as a social and economic panacea', *Work Employment and Society*, 24: 565–577.

Kerr, C., Dunlop, J.T, Harbison, F. and Myers, C.A. (1960) *Industrialism and Industrial Man: The Problem of Labor and Management in Economic Growth*. Harvard: Harvard University Press.

Kohn, M.L. and Schooler, C. (1983) *Work and Personality: An Inquiry into the impact of Social Stratification*. Norwood, NJ: Ablex.

Koike, K. (1996) *The Economics of Work in Japan*. Tokyo: LTCB International Library Foundation.

Koike, K. and Inoki, I. (1990) *Skill Formation in Japan and Southeast Asia*. Tokyo: University of Tokyo Press.

Kouzes, B. and Posner, J. (2002) *The Leadership Challenge*. San Francisco, CA: Jossey Bass.

Krahn, H. (1997) 'On the persistence of human capital: Use it or lose it', *Policy Options*, 18(6): 17–21.

Lanning, T. and Lawton, K. (2012) 'No train no gain: Beyond free-market and state-led skills policy', IPPR Report. London: IPPR.

Lawler, E.E., Mohrman, S.A. and Benson, G. (2001) *Organizing for High Performance, Employee Involvement, TQM, Reengineering, and Knowledge Management in the Fortune 1000*. San Francisco, CA: Jossey-Bass.

LEITCH Review of Skills (2006) *Prosperity for all in the Global Economy – World Class Skills: Final Report*. Norwich: HMSO.

Lepak, D. and Snell, S. (1999) 'The strategic management of human capital: Determinants and implications of different relationships', *Academy of Management Review*, 24: 1–18.

Lepak, D., Liao, H., Chung, Y. and Harden, E. (2006) 'A conceptual review of human resource management systems in strategic human resource management research', *Research in Personnel and Human Resources Management*, 25: 217–271.

Liker, J.K. (2004) *The Toyota Way: 14 Management Principles from the 'World's Greatest Manufacturer'*. New York: McGraw-Hill.

Lloyd, C., Mason, G. and Meyhew, K. (2008) *Low-Wage Work in The United Kingdom*. New York: Russell Sage Foundation.

Lowe, G.S. (1987) *Women in the Administrative Revolution*. Cambridge: Polity Press.

Madrick, J. (2004) 'Business, Wal-Mart and productivity', *New York Times*, 2 September.

Mason, E.S. (1939) 'Price and production policies of large-scale enterprise', *American Economic Review*, Mar: 61–64.

Mason, G. (2004) 'Enterprise product strategies and employer demand for skills in Britain: Evidence from the employers skill survey', SKOPE Research Paper No. 50. Oxford: Oxford and Warwick Universities.

Mason, G. (2005) 'In search of high value added production: How important are skills? Investigations in the plastics processing, printing, logistics and insurance industries in the UK', Research Report No. 663. Nottingham: DfES.

Mason, G. (2011) 'Product strategies: Skills shortages and skill updating needs in England: New evidence from the National Employers Skills Survey, 2009', UKCES Evidence Report 30. Wath-upon-Dearne: UKCES.

Maurice, M., Sellier, F. and Silvestre, J. (1986) *Social Foundations of Industrial Power: A Comparison of France and Germany*. Cambridge, MA: MIT Press.

Mayhew, K. and Keep, E. (2014) 'Industrial strategy and the future of skills policy: The high road to sustainable growth', Research Insight Report. London: CIPD.

Mazzucato, M. (2013) *The Entrepreneurial State*. London: Anthem Press.

McGovern, P., Gratton, L., Hope-Hailey, V., Stiles, P. and Truss, C. (1997) 'Human resource management on the line?', *Human Resource Management Journal*, 7(4): 12–29.

McKinsey Global Institute (2010) *How to Compete and Grow: A Sector Guide to Policy*. Worldwide: McKinsey & Co.

Miles, R.E. and Snow, C.C. (1978) *Organizational Strategy, Structure, and Process*. New York: McGraw-Hill.

Neely, A.D. (2008) 'Exploring the financial consequences of the servitisation of manufacturing', *Operations Management Research*, 1(2): 103–118.

Ng, H., Ndengabaganizi, D. and Shiou, J. (2012) *Singapore: Aerospace Industry*. Singapore: US Department of Commerce. (Available at www.kallman.com/shows/singapore_airshow_2014/pdfs/Singapore-Aerospace%20Industry.pdf, accessed 7 April 2014).

Nishii, L., Lepak, D. and Schneider, B. (2008) 'Employee attributions of the "why" of HR practices: Their effects on employee attitudes and behaviours, and customer satisfaction', *Personnel Psychology*, 61(3): 503–545.

OECD (2011) 'Skills strategy'. OECD: Paris. (Available at www.oecd.org/edu/47769132.pdf, accessed 7 April 2012).

OECD (2012a) *Better Skills, Better Jobs, Better Lives: A Strategic Approach to Skills Policies*. Paris: OECD.

OECD (2012b) *Education at a Glance*. Paris: OECD.

OECD (2012c) 'New sources of growth: Knowledge-based capital driving investment and productivity in the 21st century', Interim Project Findings. Paris: OECD.

OECD (2013) *Skills Outlook 2013: First Results from the Survey of Adult Skills*. Paris: OECD.

Ohmae, K. (1982) *The Mind of the Strategist*. New York: McGraw-Hill.

Orlikowski, W.J. (1992) 'The duality of technology: Rethinking the concept of technology in organizations', *Organizational Science*, 3(3) Focused Issue: Management of Technology: 398–427.

Osterman, P. (1991) 'The impact of IT on jobs and skills', in M. Morton (ed.), *The Corporation of the 1990s: Information Technology and Organizational Transformation*. Oxford: Oxford University Press. pp. 220–243.

Osterman, P. and Shulman, B. (2011) *Good Jobs America: Making Work Better for Everyone*. New York: Russell Sage Foundation.

Payne, J. and Keep, E. (2011) 'One step forward, two steps back? Skills policy in England under the Coalition Government', SKOPE Research Paper No. 102. Cardiff: Cardiff University.

Payne, J. and Lloyd, C. (2004) 'Just another bandwagon? A critical look at the role of high-performance workplace as a vehicle for the UK high-skills project', SKOPE Research Paper 49. Cardiff: Cardiff University.

Penn, R. (1984) *Skilled Workers in the Class Structure*. Cambridge: Cambridge University Press.

Pollard, S. (1968) *The Genesis of Modern Management*. Harmondsworth: Penguin.

Porter, M.E. (1980) *Competitive Strategy: Techniques for Analyzing Industries and Competitors*. New York: The Free Press.

Postrel, V. (2002) 'Lessons in keeping business humming, courtesy of Wal-Mart U', *The New York Times*, 28 February.

Powell, W.W. and Snellman, K. (2004) 'The knowledge economy', *Annual Review of Sociology*, 30: 199–220.

Prahalad, C.K. and Hamel, G. (1990) 'The core competence of the corporation', *Harvard Business Review*, May–June.

Psacharopoulos, G. and Patrinos, H. (2002) 'Returns to investment in education: A further update', Policy Research Working Paper 2881. Washington, DC: World Bank.

Purcell, J. and Hutchinson, S. (2007) 'Front-line managers as agents in the HRM-performance causal chain: Theory, analysis and evidence', *Human Resource Management Journal*, 17: 3–20.

Rajan, R. and Wulf, J. (2006) 'The flattening firm: Evidence from panel data on the changing nature of corporate hierarchies', *Review of Economics and Statistics*, 88(4): 759–773.

Ramsay, H., Scholarios, D. and Harley, B. (2000) 'Employees and high-performance work systems: Testing inside the black box'. *British Journal of Industrial Relations*, 38(4): 501–531.

Ramstad, E. (2009) 'Promoting performance and the quality of working life simultaneously', *International Journal of Productivity and Performance*, 58(5): 423–426.

Reich, R. (1991) *The Work of Nations*. New York: Vintage.

Roberts, S. (2013) 'Gaining skills or just paying the bills? Workplace learning in low-level retail employment', *Journal of Education and Work*, 26(3): 267–290.

Rostow, W.W. (1960) *The Stages of Economic Growth: A Non-Communist Manifesto*. Cambridge: Cambridge University Press.

Roy, D. (1952) 'Quota restriction and goldbricking in a machine shop', *American Journal of Sociology*, 67: 157–169.

Schumpeter, J.A. (1942) *Capitalism, Socialism and Democracy*. London: Routledge. (Republished in 2003 as e-book, with an introduction by E. Swedberg.)

Senge, P.M. (1990) *The Fifth Discipline: The Art and Practice of the Learning Organization*. New York: Doubleday.

Shah, R. and Ward, P. (2003) 'Lean manufacturing: Context, practice bundles, and performance', *Journal of Operations Management*, 21(2): 129–149.

Siebert, W. and Zubanov, N. (2009) 'Searching for the optimal level of employee turnover: A study of a large UK retail organization', *Academy of Management Journal*, 52(2): 294–313.

Smith, A. ([1776]1970) *An Inquiry into the Nature and Causes of the Wealth of Nations*. London: Pelican Books.

Smith, A., Courvisanos, J., Tuck, J. and MacEachern, S. (2011) *Building Innovation Capacity: The Role of Human Capital Formation in Enterprises: A Review of the Literature*. Adelaide: NCVER.

Sorenson, H.O. (2008) 'Pay and job quality in Danish call centers', in N. Westergaard-Nielsen (ed.), *Low-Wage Work in Denmark*. New York: Russell Sage Foundation. pp. 258–299.

Sparham, E. and Sung, J. (2008) 'High-performance work practices: Work intensification or "win-win"', Centre for Labour Market Studies, Working Paper No. 50. Leicester: University of Leicester.

Springett, P. (2013) 'Factories for finance? Industrialization is back on the agenda in a big way this year', *Capco Institute Blog*. (Available at www.capco.com/insights/capco-blog/factories-for-finance-industrialization-is-back-on-the-agenda-in-a-big-way-this, accessed 7 April 2014).

Stanton, P., Young, S., Bartram, T. and Leggat, S. (2010) 'Singing the same song: Translating HR messages across management hierarchies in Australian hospitals', *International Journal of Human Resource Management*, 21(4): 567–581.

Steiger, T.L. (1993) 'Construction skills and skill construction', *Work Employment and Society*, 7(4): 535–560.

Sterling, A. and Boxall, P. (2013) 'Lean production, employee learning and workplace outcomes: A case analysis through the ability-motivation-opportunity framework', *Human Resource Management Journal*, 23(3): 227–240.

Stieger, R. (1984) *Skilled Workers in the Class Structure*. Cambridge: Cambridge University Press.

Stigler, G.J. (1968) *The Organization of Industry*. Chicago, IL: University of Chicago Press.

Storey, J. and Salaman, G. (2005) *Managers of Innovation: Insights into Making Innovation Happen.* Oxford: Blackwell.

Storey, J. and Salaman, G. (2008) 'Business models and their implications for skills', SKOPE Monograph No. 11. Oxford: Cardiff and Oxford Universities.

Streeck, W. (1991) 'On the institutional conditions of diversified quality production', in E. Matzner and W. Streeck (eds), *Beyond Keynsianism: The Socio-Economics of Production and Full Employment.* Cheltenham: Edward Elgar. pp. 21–61.

Sung, J. and Ashton, D. (2005) *Achieving Best Practice in Your Business: High-Performance Work Practices – Linking Strategy and Skills to Performance.* London: DTI in association with CIPD.

Sung, J., Ashton, D. and Loke, F. (2012) 'Skills and productivity in the manufacturing sector', Research Report, Centre for Skills Performance and Productivity Research. Singapore: Institute of Adult Learning.

Sung, J., Ashton, D. and Raddon, A. (2009a) 'Product market strategies and workforce skills: Summary report,' Futureskills Scotland. Edinburgh: Scottish Government. (Available at www.scotland.gov.uk/ Publications/2009/06/22085959/0, accessed 7 April 2014).

Sung, J., Ashton, D. and Raddon, A. (2009b) 'Product market strategies and workforce skills: Full report', Futureskills Scotland. Edinburgh: Scottish Government. (Available at www.scotland.gov.uk/Publications/2009/06/22085911/0, accessed 7 April 2014).

Sung, J., Raddon, A. and Ashton, D. (2008) *The Business Benefits of Training in the Food and Drink Manufacturing Industry.* Leicester: CLMS, University of Leicester and Improve Ltd.

Sung, J., Tan, T.K., Loke, F. and Cheah, D. (2013) *Skills Utilisation 2: Jobs Skills and Job Quality in Singapore.* Singapore: Institute for Adult Learning.

Tamkin, P., Pearson, G., Hirsh, W. and Constable, S. (2010) *Exceeding Expectation: The Principles of Outstanding Leadership.* London: Work Foundation.

Taylor, P. and Bain, P. (1999) 'An assembly line in the head: Work and employment relations in a call centre', *Industrial Relations Journal*, 30(2): 101–117.

Teece, D.J., Pisano, G. (1994) 'The dynamic capabilities of firms: An introduction', *Industrial and Corporate Change*, 1: 537–556.

Teece, D.J., Pisano, G. and Shuen, A. (1997) 'Dynamic capabilities and strategic management', *Strategic Management Journal*, 18(7): 509–534.

Tidd, J., Bessant, J. and Pavitt, K. (2005) *Managing Innovation: Integrating Technological, Market and Organizational Change*, 3rd edn. Chichester: Wiley.

Turner, H.A.F. (1962) *Trade Union Growth Structure and Policy: A Comparative Study of the Cotton Unions.* London: George Allen and Unwin.

UK Commission for Employment and Skills (2009) *The 2009 Report, Ambition 2020: World Class Skills and Jobs for the UK.* Wath-upon-Dearne: UKCES.

UK Commission for Employment and Skills (2012) 'More employers investing in the skills of their people'. Wath-upon-Dearne: UKCES. (Available at www.ukces.org.uk/ourwork/outcome-one?Ref=emailanddm_i=2CU,VSA4,16AVQ1,2MHX5,1, accessed 28 April 2014).

UK Commission for Employment and Skills (2014) 'Employer skills survey 2013: Results', Evidence Report 81. Wath-upon-Dearne: UKCES.

van der Krogt, F. and Warmerdam, J. (1997) 'Training in different types of organizations: Differences and dynamics in the organization of work', *The International Journal of Human Resource Management*, 8(1): 87–105.

Warhurst, C. and Findlay, P. (2012) 'More effective skills utilisation: Shifting the terrain of skills policy in Scotland', SKOPE Research Paper No. 107. Strathclyde: University of Sydney and University of Strathclyde.

Waterman, R. and Peters, T. (1982) *In Search of Excellence: Lessons from America's Best Run Companies*. Harper & Row: New York.

Wernerfelt, B. (1984) 'A resource-based view of the firm'. *Strategic Management Journal*, 5(2): 171–180.

WERS (2013) *The 2011 Workplace Employment Relations Study: First Findings*. London: Department for Business Innovation and Skills.

West, M. and Anderson, N. (1996) 'Innovation in top management teams', *Journal of Applied Psychology*, 81(6): 680–693.

Westergaard-Nielson, N. (ed.) (2008) *Low-Wage Work in Denmark*. New York: Russell Sage Foundation.

Wickens, P. (1999) *Energise Your Enterprise*. London: Macmillan.

Wilkinson, F. (1983) 'Productive systems', *Cambridge Journal of Economics*, 7: 413–429.

Wilkinson, F. (2002) 'Productive systems and the structuring role of economic and social theories', ESRC Centre for Business Research, Working Paper No. 225. Cambridge: University of Cambridge.

Willis, P. (1977) *Learning to Labour*. Farnborough: Saxon House.

Wilson, J.F. and Thomson, A. (2006) *The Making of Modern Management: British Management in Historical Perspective*. New York: Oxford University Press.

Wilson, R. and Hogarth, T. (eds) (2003) *Tackling the Low Skills Equilibrium: A Review of Issues and Some New Evidence*, Report for the Department of Trade and Industry. London: DTI.

Wolf, A., Aspin, L., Waite, E. and Ananiadou, K. (2010) 'The rise and fall of workplace basic skills programmes: Lessons for policy and practice', *Oxford Review of Education*, 36(4): 385–405.

Wolfi, A. (2003) 'Productivity growth in service industries: An assessment of recent patterns and the role of measurement', OECD Science, Technology and Industry Working Paper 2003/7. Paris: OECD.

Womack, J.P., Jones, D.T., Roos, D. and Carpenter, D.S. (1990) *The Machine That Changed the World: The Story of Lean Production – Toyota's Secret Weapon in the Global Car Wars That is Revolutionizing World Industry*. New York: Free Press.

Wood, S. and de Menezes, L. (2011) 'High involvement management, high-performance work systems and well-being', *International Journal of Human Resource Management*, 22(7): 1586–1610.

Wood, S., Burridge, M., Green, W., Nolte, S. and Rudloff, D. (2013) 'High-performance working in the employer skills surveys', Evidence Report 71. Wath-upon-Dearne: UKCES.

Woodward, J. (1958) *Management and Technology: Problems and Progress in Technology*. London: HMSO.

World Trade Organization (2014) 'The multilateral trading system – past, present and future', The WTO in Brief: Part 1. Geneva: WTO. (Available at http://www.wto.org/english/thewto_e/whatis_e/inbrief_e/inbr01_e.htm, accessed 7 April 2014).

Wright Mills, C. (1956) *White Collar: The American Middle Classes*. New York: Oxford University Press.

Young, M. and Allais, S. (2011) Special Issue: 'Implementing national qualifications frameworks across five continents', *Journal of Education and Work*, 24(5): 209–448.

Zee, F. and Brandes, F. (2007) 'Manufacturing futures for Europe – a survey of the literature', Foresight Briefing No. 137. European Foresight Monitoring Network.

INDEX